SIX SIGMA BEYOND THE FACTORY FLOOR

Six Sigma Beyond the Factory Floor

Deployment Strategies for Financial Services, Health Care, and the Rest of the Real Economy

Ronald D. Snee
Roger W. Hoerl

PEARSON PRENTICE HALL
An Imprint of PEARSON EDUCATION
Upper Saddle River, NJ • New York • London • San Francisco • Toronto
Sydney • Tokyo • Singapore • Hong Kong
Cape Town • Madrid • Paris • Milan • Munich • Amsterdam
www.ft-ph.com

Library of Congress Publication in Data: 2004109256

Publisher: Tim Moore
Executive Editor: Jim Boyd
Editorial Assistant: Richard Winkler
Marketing Manager: Martin Litkowski
International Marketing Manager: Tim Galligan
Cover Designer: Sandra Schroeder
Managing Editor: Gina Kanouse
Project Editor: Christy Hackerd
Copy Editor: Keith Cline
Senior Indexer: Cheryl Lenser
Compositor: Jake McFarland
Manufacturing Buyer: Dan Uhrig

© 2005 by Pearson Education, Inc.
Publishing as Pearson Prentice Hall
Upper Saddle River, New Jersey 07458

Prentice Hall offers excellent discounts on this book when ordered in quantity for bulk purchases or special sales. For more information, please contact U.S. Corporate and Government Sales, 1-800-382-3419, corpsales@pearsontech-group.com. For sales outside the U.S., please contact International Sales, international@pearsontechgroup.com.

Printed in the United States of America
First Printing October, 2004
ISBN 0-13-143988-X

Pearson Education LTD.
Pearson Education Australia PTY, Limited.
Pearson Education Singapore, Pte. Ltd.
Pearson Education North Asia, Ltd.
Pearson Education Canada, Ltd.
Pearson Educatión de Mexico, S.A. de C.V.
Pearson Education—Japan
Pearson Education Malaysia, Pte. Ltd.

This book is dedicated to our spouses, Marjorie and Senecca, whose support and understanding went well beyond what was reasonable to expect.

TABLE OF CONTENTS

ACKNOWLEDGMENTS

We are pleased to acknowledge the numerous individuals who provided examples, insights, suggestions, and constructive criticism in the development of this book. These include: Bill English, Jean Cherry, Lisa Douglas, Chris McKenna, John Hagen, and Bruce Tucker. The comments and suggestions made by the reviewers—Steve Bailey, Jim Buckman, Eric Mattenson, Ed Popovich, Rip Stauffer and Doug Zahn—were very helpful in improving the presentation of this material.

Portions of Chapter 8 appeared in an article published by Ron Snee in the June 2004 issue of *Harvard Management Update.*

We also express our sincere gratitude to Jim Boyd, Christine Hackerd, Keith Cline, Nina Scuderi, and other members of the Financial Times-Prentice Hall publication team for their guidance and assistance in making this book a reality.

Our sincere appreciation goes also to our spouses, Marjorie and Senecca, whose support and understanding went well beyond what was reasonable to expect.

ABOUT THE AUTHORS

Dr. Ronald D. Snee is principal in Tunnell Consulting's Performance Excellence Practice, which offers Six Sigma consulting, training, facilitation, and implementation, in addition to other process improvement approaches. Dr. Snee is a winner of the American Society for Quality's highest honor, the Shewhart Medal, and has served as a member of the Malcolm Baldrige National Quality Award Criteria Team. He designed DuPont's first company-wide continuous improvement curriculum.

Dr. Roger W. Hoerl is a long-time leader in GE's renowned Six Sigma initiative. As manager of GE's Applied Statistics Lab, he partners on R&D with GE businesses ranging from NBC and GE Capital to GE Aircraft Engines. He has implemented Six Sigma in a wide range of GE processes, ranging from corporate audit to delinquent credit card tracking. He recently won the American Society of Quality's 2002 Brumbaugh Award.

Snee and Hoerl are coauthors of *Leading Six Sigma* (Financial Times-Prentice Hall, 2003), the best-selling executive's guide to Six Sigma. They also cowrote *Statistical Thinking: Improving Business Performance* (Duxbury Thomson Learning, 2002), an innovative guide to the strategic use of data and statistics in solving business problems.

PREFACE

The body of evidence continues to grow. Companies such as GE, Motorola, Honeywell, 3M, Home Depot, J.P. Morgan Chase & Co., Johnson & Johnson, Quest Diagnostics, DuPont, American Express, Ford, and many others have been using Six Sigma to obtain large improvements in business performance that have produced millions of dollars in bottom-line savings. Six Sigma, a process-focused strategy and methodology for business improvement, is a strategic approach that we have seen work across all processes, all products, and all industries. The focus is on improving process performance that results in improved customer satisfaction and bottom-line results.

Six Sigma has been used extensively in improving manufacturing organizations, but only recently has it been used to improve processes outside of manufacturing—that is, *processes beyond the factory floor*. When we talk about using Six Sigma beyond the factory floor, we are referring to improving processes in the rest of the economy beyond manufacturing, such as financial services, e-commerce, health care, and so on. For reasons discussed below, we refer to this as the *real economy*. This real economy includes businesses that do not manufacture, such as banks and law offices, non-profits (including non-profit hospitals), as well as all the other (non-manufacturing) parts of organizations that manufacture products such as delivery, finance, and *human resources* (HR).

The real economy, therefore, consists of all businesses that do not manufacture physical products, as well as all the other functions and processes involved in manufacturing. All processes in an organization are opportunities for improvement. Therefore, by taking a holistic view, you will see that Six Sigma can be used to improve any process.

This book is the third in a series of books aimed at improving the processes and organizations used to serve our customers, a pursuit to which we have collectively dedicated more than 60 years of our careers. We first worked together at DuPont in the early 1980s. We continued our professional relationship over the years, and in 1995 we both independently began our work in Six Sigma. In our first book *Statistical Thinking: Improving Business Performance* (Duxbury/Thompson Learning 2002), we explained the concept of statistical thinking and its key elements: process, variation, and data. Our focus was how to use statistical thinking to improve business processes—those beyond the factory floor—by reducing variation. We believe that Six Sigma is the best way to deploy statistical thinking broadly.

In *Leading Six Sigma: A Step-by-Step Guide Based on Experience with GE and Other Six Sigma Companies* (Financial Times/Prentice Hall 2003), we showed how to deploy Six Sigma in an organization and how to integrate it with other improvement initiatives. We presented detailed case studies (both successful and unsuccessful), identified the key factors required for success, and presented a detailed deployment strategy.

We take the methodology one step further in this book, focusing on perhaps the most challenging use of Six Sigma: improving processes beyond the factory floor. This requires special attention because formal improvement methods have been applied less in this area, resulting in less being known about how to improve these processes. For example, there is typically less data available on real economy processes than manufacturing. We address this and other differences between manufacturing and real economy applications of Six Sigma. Understanding these differences will help you better understand what is required to improve processes beyond the factory floor. Our review of the Six Sigma literature shows that there are very few detailed case histories using the methodology beyond the factory floor at either the organizational deployment level or at the individual project level. We also see little or no discussion of the unique technical challenges associated with deploying Six Sigma in these areas. This book addresses each of these issues.

Features of This Book

This book has many unique features that can help you deploy Six Sigma beyond the factory floor. First, we take a broad holistic view of the organizational and technical issues and what can be done about them. We address perhaps the biggest stumbling block encountered by those working beyond the factory floor: the view that "we're different," and therefore "Six Sigma doesn't apply to us." Although there is some truth to this argument, we show that improvement in these areas has much more in common with improvement in other areas and show how Six Sigma can be applied within an organization with such a viewpoint.

We emphasize that moving beyond the factory floor means improving both non-manufacturing businesses (for example, finance, health care, non-profit) as well as those non-manufacturing functions that are needed to run manufacturing organizations (billing, human relations, delivery, and so on). We provide guidance on each of the three key levels of Six Sigma needed for success: deployment, project-by-project improvement, and methods and tools. We know of no other book that gives detailed guidance in all three areas, especially beyond manufacturing. This book provides case studies at both the organizational deployment level and at the individual project level and includes detailed advice for leaders at the business level and functional level.

We show how to take a proven road map for Six Sigma deployment and customize it to organizations and functions beyond the factory floor. This includes a discussion of how to deal with the unique technical issues involved as well as how to take a holistic view of the three aspects of process management (process design/redesign, process improvement, and process control) and how Six Sigma is used in each of theses areas.

How This Book Can Help You

This book will prove invaluable to those deploying Six Sigma beyond the factory floor, particularly managers responsible for deploying Six Sigma in their areas: Champions, *Master Black Belts* (MBBs), *Black Belts* (BBs) and *Green Belts* (GBs). You will get a holistic view of what deployment of Six Sigma entails, including your role and responsibilities and what to expect at various points in time. In addition, managers and Champions will receive specific advice about the following:

- Identifying your company's most promising Six Sigma opportunities and leaders

- Providing leadership, talent, and infrastructure for a successful launch

- Implementing systems, processes, and budgets for ongoing Six Sigma projects

- Measuring and maximizing the financial value of your Six Sigma initiative

MBBs will receive guidance on how to select projects and how projects can fail. MBBs, BBs, and GBs will get insight as to how to deal with unique technical problems such as non-normal data, discrete data, and the most useful tools.

What's in This Book?

This book is divided into four main parts: the case for Six Sigma beyond the factory floor, ensuring successful deployment, ensuring project success, and proper application of methods and tools. In this overall flow, we address strategic, tactical, and operational aspects of deploying Six Sigma.

Chapter 1 sets the context for the book, highlighting the growing importance of health care, financial, service, and non-manufacturing functions to our economy and the tremendous opportunity and need for improvement in these areas that we refer to as the real economy.

Chapter 2 addresses the fundamental barrier to improvement—the attitude that "we're different"—and shows that improvement efforts in diverse processes and environments have much more in common than not. We find that Six Sigma works very well beyond the factory floor.

The focus of Chapter 3 and Chapter 4 is on the management systems that must be put in place to effectively deploy Six Sigma. One of the key things that makes Six Sigma different from earlier improvement methods is the existence of an infrastructure of management systems to support deployment. One of the key reasons that previous improvement approaches, such as *total quality management* (TQM) and *statistical process control* (SPC), did not demonstrate long-term success, is that these approaches lacked an effective deployment method. This is not the case with Six Sigma.

Chapter 3 focuses on deployment and presents four deployment case studies: Bank of America, Commonwealth Healthcare Corporation (which is also a not-for-profit organization), the Motorola Finance function, and R&D at GE Global Research. Key learnings are identified for each case study individually and summarized to create an overall list.

Chapter 4 presents a Six Sigma deployment road map that has been effective in a number of companies representing a number of different environments. We also provide guidance on deploying Six Sigma in different environments (businesses and functions) as well as deployment success factors and pitfalls.

Chapter 5 and Chapter 6 focus on ensuring project success. The successful completion of projects, one after another in a steady stream, is at the heart of Six Sigma. The discussion consists of case studies from beyond the factory floor, the Six Sigma method for realizing project-by-project improvement, keys to completing successful projects, and technical considerations that are essential to successful improvement in the real economy. To the best of our knowledge, many of these issues are not discussed elsewhere in the literature.

Chapter 5 presents three project case studies in finance, legal, and batch records release (a health care, non-manufacturing function). The chapter concludes with a discussion of lessons learned.

Chapter 6 discusses project-by-project improvement, including the all-important subject of project selection and a list of ways projects can fail. We present a holistic model for improvement—including process design/redesign, process improvement, and process control—and show how to utilize the Six Sigma approaches of *design for Six Sigma* (DFSS) using the *define, measure, analyze, design, verify* (DMADV) and *define, measure, analyze, improve, control* (DMAIC) frameworks.

Chapter 7 focuses on the technical challenges unique to deploying Six Sigma beyond the factory floor. The topics include the tools used and unique aspects of the data analysis in such applications. For example, we discuss ways to address the common issues of skewed (non-normal) distributions, which often occur with cycle time metrics, and the prevalence of discrete data, which often occur with accuracy metrics.

Chapter 8 discusses some next steps you may want to consider to make Six Sigma an integral part of the way your organization does business and serves its customers and the community. The goal is to get more out of Six Sigma. You can accomplish this by making Six Sigma part of, if not your entire strategic signature (something for which your organization is known). As a result, all work in all areas of the organization will be utilizing some aspect of Six Sigma to help make them successful. When others look at your organization, they will see Six Sigma as your strategic signature.

How to Use This Book

This book is organized according to the three major levels at which organizations must adapt Six Sigma to receive its full benefits beyond the factory floor: the deployment (strategic) level—how to think through overall deployment of the initiative across the entire organization; the project (tactical) level—how to select, conduct, and close out projects in these environments; and the methods and tools (operational) level—how to properly apply the analytic techniques of Six Sigma when faced with difficulties common beyond the factory floor, such as skewed (non-normal) cycle time distributions or the prevalence of discrete data. As a result, this book is intended as a guide for those just starting their Six Sigma deployment; as a reference for those experienced Six Sigma practitioners such as Six Sigma leaders, Champions, MBBs, BBs, and GBs; and for others who are involved in the deployment of Six Sigma and want to assess the effectiveness of their Six Sigma deployment. Of course, different parts of this book will be of greater value to those fulfilling different roles.

Those working in departments such as HR, finance, and IT will also find this book useful. Companies following the lead of GE, Honeywell, DuPont, and 3M are using Six Sigma as a leadership-development tool. This book will help those in HR recognize the various leadership aspects of Six Sigma and how to integrate Six Sigma into their succession and leadership-development processes. The holistic view of Six Sigma presented here will help those in finance recognize their role in predicting and documenting project financial impact, as well as how to use financial records to identify opportunities for improvement. Those working in IT will see not only how to improve the processes they use to run their organization, but also the critical role that data play in improvement (and hence the need for effective data collection systems).

We have seen Six Sigma work well in all types of organizations. As an Allied Signal manager pointed out, "Six Sigma works if you follow the process. If it is not working, you are not following the process." We hope that you find our book helpful in your Six Sigma journey and look forward to hearing about your experiences.

Ronald D. Snee
Newark, DE

Roger W. Hoerl
Schenectady, NY

August 2004

PART I

THE CASE FOR SIX SIGMA BEYOND THE FACTORY FLOOR

1

A Holistic View of Six Sigma

"Only the over-all review of the entire business as an economic system can give real knowledge."
—Peter F. Drucker

You may have heard of Six Sigma, a process-focused strategy and methodology for business improvement. Companies such as General Electric, Honeywell, Motorola, DuPont, American Express, Ford, and many others, large and small, have been using it to improve business performance and realize millions of dollars in bottom-line savings (Honeywell 2002, Welch 2001, Young 2001). Six Sigma is a strategic approach that works across all processes, all products, and all industries. Six Sigma focuses on improving process performance to enhance customer satisfaction and bottom-line results. Motorola created the methodology in 1987, and the use of Six Sigma by others increased rapidly during the 1990s. Six Sigma remains in widespread use as of this writing.

You also may have heard how Six Sigma has been used to improve the performance of manufacturing organizations, but thought it doesn't apply to your situation. Perhaps you don't work in manufacturing. Perhaps you want to improve results in a financial services organization. If so, you must ask whether Six Sigma can be used to improve the performance of your organization, and if so, how. The answer to the first part is a resounding yes! In our experience, and that of many others, Six Sigma works in all processes, in all parts of the organization, and in all organizations, services and health care as well as manufacturing. The second part of the question (how) is answered throughout the remainder of this book.

Six Sigma "beyond the factory floor" refers to improving processes in the non-manufacturing parts of the economy (the rest of the economy beyond manufacturing, such as financial services, e-commerce, health care, and so on). For reasons discussed shortly, we refer to this as the *real economy*. This real economy includes businesses that do not manufacture, such as banks and law offices, non-profits (including non-profit hospitals), and all the other (non-manufacturing) parts of organizations that do manufacture products. For example, Figure 1.1 shows a systems map for a manufacturing company. You can see from this graph that manufacturing is only one of many processes—such as delivery, finance, and human resources—needed to operate the company. Figure 1.2 shows a systems map of a typical manufacturing facility. Here again you see that many non-manufacturing processes are needed to run the facility, such as purchasing, shipping, and maintenance.

The real economy therefore consists of all businesses that do not manufacture physical products as well as all the other functions and processes involved in manufacturing. All processes in an organization present opportunities for improvement. This is what we mean by a *holistic view of Six Sigma*—seeing the big picture and not allowing our deployment or results to be limited by preconceived notions about Six Sigma and where it applies.

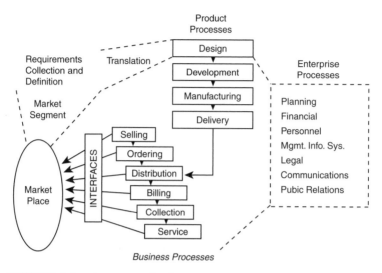

FIGURE 1.1   A corporation's core processes.

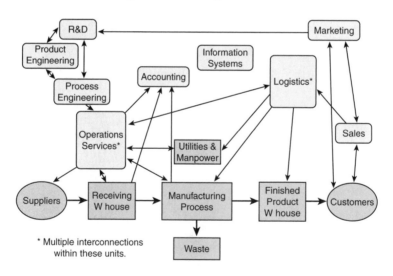

FIGURE 1.2   A manufacturing facility.

This book is organized according to the three major levels at which organizations must consider how to adapt Six Sigma to receive its full benefits beyond the factory floor:

- **The deployment (strategic) level**—How to think through overall deployment of the initiative across the entire organization.

- **The project (tactical) level**—How to select, conduct, and close out projects in these environments.

- **The methods and tools (operational) level**—How to properly apply the analytic techniques of Six Sigma when faced with difficulties common beyond the factory floor, such as skewed (non-normal) cycle time distributions, or the prevalence of discrete data.

This book is intended as a guide for those just starting their Six Sigma deployment and as a reference for experienced Six Sigma practitioners such as Six Sigma leaders, Champions, *Master Black Belts* (MBBs), *Black Belts* (BBs), *Green Belts* (GBs), and for others who are involved in the deployment of Six Sigma and want to assess the effectiveness of such. Of course, different sections of this book are likely to be of greater value to some than to others (depending on their role with Six Sigma).

In *Statistical Thinking—Improving Business Performance* (Hoerl and Snee 2002), we explained the concept of statistical thinking and its key elements—process, variation, and data. We focused on how to use statistical thinking to improve business processes—those beyond the factory floor—by reducing variation. All processes vary, and reducing variation, both between the process average and process target, and also around the process average, is a key to improving process performance. In fact, Jack Welch (Welch 2001) states that process consistency is, in many ways, more important to customers than the average level of process performance. *Statistical Thinking—Improving Business Performance* also contains detailed descriptions of the statistical thinking and Six Sigma tools, including how they apply in a business setting. These tools include basic problem-solving tools (scatter plot, histogram, run chart, Pareto chart, and so on), regression, experimental design, statistical inference, and so on. Since writing this book, Six Sigma is the best way we have found to actually deploy statistical thinking broadly.

In *Leading Six Sigma: A Step-by-Step Guide Based on Experience with GE and Other Six Sigma Companies* (Snee and Hoerl 2003), we showed how to deploy Six Sigma in an organization and how to integrate it with other improvement initiatives. We presented detailed case studies, both successful and unsuccessful, identified the key factors required for success, and presented a detailed deployment strategy. The last chapter included a set of commonly asked deployment questions; our answers to them are based on our experience deploying Six Sigma. The majority of this material was intended for those working in a manufacturing or engineering environment, although the issue of deployment in the real economy was discussed.

This book takes the methodology one step further, focusing on perhaps the most challenging use of Six Sigma: improving processes beyond the factory floor. This requires special attention because formal improvement methods have been applied less frequently here, resulting in less being known about how to improve these processes. For example, less data are typically available on real economy processes than manufacturing. Chapter 2 addresses the differences between manufacturing and real economy applications of Six Sigma more fully. Understanding these differences will help you better understand what is required to improve processes beyond the factory floor.

Those with a holistic view of Six Sigma will see the potential "big picture" impact it can offer, instead of seeing it as a narrow technical methodology used in manufacturing. They will realize that Six Sigma can and should be applied to all types of organizations, in all functions, and by all employees (or volunteers). The holistic approach also utilizes Six Sigma as a key organizational development strategy. For example, GE, 3M, DuPont, Honeywell, and several others have consciously used Six Sigma to develop their future leaders.

This first chapter discusses why Six Sigma is needed beyond the factory floor and how it can, and has, made significant impact here. The chapter then explains how Six Sigma should be viewed as part of an overall process management system. Chapter 1 concludes with a brief overview of the Six Sigma methodology and a discussion of the key roles involved.

The Impact of Six Sigma Beyond the Factory Floor

It is generally agreed that more than half the opportunity for improvement in a manufacturing company lies beyond the manufacturing function. This opportunity can be as much as 30% to 40% of sales. Improvement beyond manufacturing has been limited in the past for at least three key reasons: lack of well-defined processes, lack of process metrics and data, and lack of an appreciation for the importance of reducing variation (both internally and to the customer). The advent of Six Sigma methodology and information technology systems has changed this situation, enabling organizations of all types to focus on improvement as never before.

The need for broadening the use of Six Sigma beyond the factory floor becomes clearer when you reflect on the trends within the business world. Three key trends, closely connected to one another, are driving the world economy: migration away from manufacturing-based economies, the rapid expansion of *information technology* (IT), and increasing global competition. The economies of the United States, most of Western Europe, and many other developed countries transitioned from an agricultural base in the 1800s and early 1900s to a manufacturing base in the 1900s. This movement is known as the industrial revolution, and it brought profound economic and social changes.

With the rapid expansion of IT in the late twentieth and now early twenty-first century, the world economy has continued to evolve. For example, the occupation of computer scientist did not exist during the industrial revolution. International finance, statistics and operations research, music and entertainment, e-commerce, and consumer credit are just a few examples of professional fields whose rapid expansion has been enabled by advances in IT. The overall result of this evolution is that fewer and fewer people make their living by manufacturing something. So-called white-collar jobs, such as accounting, health care, and computer science, are replacing the traditional blue-collar jobs on the assembly line. Figure 1.3 (Bisgaard 2002) shows data on the growth of such jobs in the United States relative to drops in agriculture and manufacturing over the past century. Similar results apply to most developed countries in the world today. For the purposes of this graph, *white collar* refers to jobs involving primarily mental work (computer scientist, accountant, and so on), *blue collar* refers to primarily physical labor (construction, assembly line, and so on), and *service* refers to jobs that interact directly with customers, such as fast-food counter service, hotel receptionist, and postal delivery.

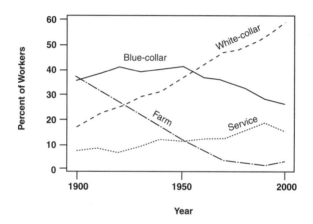

FIGURE 1.3   Occupational distribution of the
U.S. labor force.

Agricultural jobs have been decreasing steadily for more than 100 years, and blue-collar jobs began a steady decline around 1950. Clearly, the United States no longer has a manufacturing-based economy. The real economy in the United States today, as well as in most of the developed world, involves such fields as financial services, health care, e-commerce, and logistics, but less and less manufacturing, which has tended to move offshore to low-cost locations. In fact, it has been reported that manufacturing now represents less than 20% of the U.S. gross domestic product (George 2003, 3). Productivity improvements and increased use of automation continue to reduce the number of blue-collar jobs.

Some of the key players in the real economy that need to benefit from Six Sigma include the following:

- Health care
- Financial services
- Educational institutions
- E-commerce
- Government
- Retail sales
- Food service
- Logistics and transportation

Of course, the list could go on and on.

Even within manufacturing businesses, less and less of the income and profit derive from manufacturing and selling "widgets." *GE Transportation Services* (GETS), for example, is a division of GE that manufactures locomotives. In the year 2000 GE Annual Report (p. 25), GETS noted that their earnings increased that year despite lower revenues, which resulted from a softening market for locomotive sales. How did GETS increase earnings in a softening market? It was "the result of a fifth consecutive year of double-digit growth in our global services business."

By taking advantage of the latest communication and information technologies, GETS has developed value-added services, such as predicting and optimizing maintenance requirements, satellite tracking of locomotives, logistics planning, and so on. Even a "smokestack industry" such as locomotives is transitioning from selling "widgets" to selling information and value-added services. The 2001 GE Annual Report (p.5) noted that the total of contractual services agreements within GE reached the $60 billion mark (yes, $60 billion!) in 2001. These service agreements continue to grow at the time of this writing. Similarly, General Motors now makes more money from financing than they do from selling cars. The public generally thinks of GM as an automaker, but it would be more accurate to think of GM as a bank that also sells cars on the side.

These examples, the data in Figure 1.3 and system maps such as Figure 1.1, highlight the fact that even within companies that manufacture and sell things, a major portion of the people and processes critical to the organization's success lie beyond manufacturing. Part of the holistic application of Six Sigma involves taking Six Sigma to each of these areas in turn, instead of restricting Six Sigma to manufacturing. Also productivity and automation gains are reducing the cost of goods and services sold. These gains further indicate that you should look beyond manufacturing and operations for improvement opportunities.

Of course, the growth of IT has also intensified global competition, and thereby provided further impetus for real economy organizations to improve. Developing countries such as India and China are expanding the technical skills of their labor force, including in such areas as computer science and software development. With the rapid expansion of the Internet and other IT tools, developing countries have created a competitive, low-cost alternative for organizations that need skilled labor. It is now feasible for a software developer in India to work remotely for an organization located in Germany, Australia, or the United States.

In fact, *Time* magazine (Time 2003) anticipated that U.S. financial services firms would move more than 500,000 jobs to India in the next 5 years. This job-migration figure does not include migration of jobs from other developed countries, the impact of the rapidly growing Chinese economy, or the migration from industries other than financial services. This trend is reminiscent of the tremendous impact that global competition had on manufacturing industries, such as automotives and electronics, beginning in the 1970s. Clearly, improvement is just as critical to survival in the real economy today as it was to manufacturing in the latter part of the twentieth century.

This need to improve has added an additional organizational responsibility. It used to be that we had one primary task: Come to work and perform our job to serve our customers. Global competition requires of us a second task: Improve how we do our work to better serve our customers to stay ahead of the competition. Therefore, we now have two jobs: doing our work and improving how we do our work. Six Sigma provides many of the needed road maps and tools for doing this improvement work, thereby enabling us to serve our customers more effectively and efficiently.

Fortunately, many real economy organizations are "stepping up to the plate" relative to Six Sigma and reaping impressive benefits. GE has been applying Six Sigma to financial services almost since the beginning of its Six Sigma launch. A single project in credit card collections produced almost $3 million in annual benefits (Hahn et al. 2000). *Commonwealth Health Corporation* (CHC), a health-care provider based in Bowling Green, Kentucky, generated more than $800,000 in savings in the first 18 months of deployment. Chapter 3 presents CHC's case study in detail. The gains realized by American Express from Six Sigma are discussed in Young (2001). Bank of America is also deploying Six Sigma and reaping significant financial benefits ($2 billion in the first two to three years; Jones 2004).

The early implementers of Six Sigma such as Motorola and AlliedSignal began their initiative in manufacturing and moved, sometimes slowly, to applying Six Sigma across the organization. Former Motorola CEO Bob Galvin stated, "The lack of initial Six Sigma emphasis in the non-manufacturing areas was a mistake that cost Motorola at least $5 billion over a four-year period" (George 2003, 3). Note that beginning Six Sigma in manufacturing, or operations of service companies, is a good strategy because process metrics are usually well developed and significant opportunities for improvement exist there. The goal should be to move the deployment of Six Sigma as quickly as possible to the rest of the organization to maximize its benefits.

Intangible Impact

Six Sigma is increasingly recognized as an effective method for changing culture (how an organization does its work and rewards its people) as well as improving the bottom line. This is particularly important for those real economy organizations that do not have the legacy of a continual-improvement culture. As discussed in Chapter 2, our experience, and that of many others, is that few organizations outside of manufacturing have such a legacy. In the process of deploying Six Sigma, leaders enhance many systems that define the organization's culture, including developing a greater focus on improvement, changing recognition and reward systems, improving communication systems, and improving performance management systems.

Many companies are seeing Six Sigma as a way to develop leaders, build teamwork, and empower employees. Companies such as GE, DuPont, 3M, Honeywell, and American Standard have required BB and GB certification for promotion up the ranks of management. Jack Welch, then CEO of GE, stated in the 2000 Annual Report, "The generic nature of a Black Belt assignment, in addition to its rigorous process discipline and relentless customer focus, makes Six Sigma the perfect training for growing twenty-first century GE leadership." Banks, hospitals, dot.coms, and other organizations operating beyond the factory floor are beginning to see and reap these types of organizational benefits of Six Sigma.

The use of Six Sigma as a leadership development tool becomes clear when you think about what a leader does. A leader enables an organization to change the way it works, to move from one paradigm to another paradigm. Changing the way people work requires changing the process they use to do their work. Six Sigma provides the strategy, methods, and tools to improve processes. A leader skilled in the use of Six Sigma is a more effective leader, thereby making Six Sigma an effective leadership development tool. This is just as true in the real economy as it is on the factory floor.

Integration of Process Design, Process Improvement, and Process Control

Unfortunately, Six Sigma is often promoted with a great deal of hyperbole, fanfare, and outright hype. Some authors make Six Sigma sound like an organizational "snake oil" that will magically solve any issue or problem. In fact, Snee and Hoerl (2003) is the only book that we are aware of on the subject that discusses unsuccessful Six Sigma efforts. It is important for readers to understand that Six Sigma is a rigorous, disciplined improvement methodology that utilizes scientific tools and formal deployment strategies. As such Six Sigma provides leaders with a set of concepts, methods, and tools that enables them to align organizations to focus on improvement, provide road maps for change and improvement, and empower the right people to make the needed improvements. Therefore, to reap maximum long-term benefits from Six Sigma, organizations must eventually integrate it into an overall process management system utilizing the Six Sigma goals of rapid organizational change and improvement. Typically, this integration is the last phase in Six Sigma deployment (Snee and Hoerl 2003) and occurs years after launching a Six Sigma initiative. As discussed in Chapter 6, Six Sigma is not an organizational cure-all; some issues and projects are best addressed by methods other than Six Sigma.

As you think about using Six Sigma holistically as a key element of your improvement strategy, and eventually as part of your overall process management system, it is important to keep in mind the three major aspects of process management: process design/redesign, process improvement, and process control. Process design/redesign focuses on the design of new processes and the redesign (reengineering) of existing processes. Six Sigma can contribute significantly to design efforts through *design for Six Sigma* (DFSS), which can utilize the *define, measure, analyze, design, verify* (DMADV) framework. DMADV is the framework used by GE and other organizations. Other frameworks have been proposed (Creveling et al. 2003). Process improvement focuses on the improvement of existing processes without changing the fundamental design of the process. Process control focuses on keeping the process operating on target and within requirements so that the process produces products and services that satisfy customers profitably.

The key distinction between process improvement and process control is that process improvement determines how to drive the process to new levels of performance. Process control, on the other hand, identifies root causes for why the process performance has deteriorated, so that performance can be brought back to normal levels. For example, most of the routine maintenance done on cars is process control—such as doing a tune-up or oil change to maintain performance. By switching to titanium spark plugs and premium gasoline, however, an owner might be able to improve the cars' performance beyond its original capability. This would be an example of process improvement. Further improvement might require redesign of the engine.

Six Sigma uses the *define, measure, analyze, improve, control* (DMAIC) framework to improve and control existing processes. In general, the DMAI phases focus on improvement, and the C phase focuses on process control and sustaining the gains. It is interesting to note that Six Sigma considers the need for control and implements a formal control plan in each design and improvement project. Chapter 6 further discusses these aspects of Six Sigma and how they should integrate with an overall process management system.

The Essence of Six Sigma

This section provides a brief overview of Six Sigma for those with minimal background in the initiative. Table 1.1 summarizes the key elements of Six Sigma. Further detail on each of these elements is provided in Chapter 4. The approach can be broken into three key aspects: deployment of a management initiative, improvement projects, and a set of methods and tools. See Snee and Hoerl (2003) for more detail on deployment aspects of Six Sigma, and Breyfogle (2003) for more detail on the methods and tools.

TABLE 1.1   Key Aspects of Six Sigma

Deployment	Projects	Methods and Tools
Improvement	Right projects (linked to business goals)	Process thinking
Breakthrough	Project management (project reviews)	Process variation
Systematic, focused approach	Sustain the gains (new projects)	Facts, figures, data

continues

TABLE 1.1 Key Aspects of Six Sigma (*continued*)

Deployment	Projects	Methods and Tools
Right people (selected and trained)	Results (process and financial)	Define, measure, analyze, improve, control
Communication Recognition and reward	Project tracking and reporting	8 key tools (sequenced and linked)
Six Sigma initiative		Statistical tools
reviews		Statistical software
		Critical few variables

Deployment Aspects

Breakthrough Improvement. Six Sigma is about business improvement; it is not about culture change per se, although it will radically change culture. The strategy is to get the improvements, and then create the infrastructure and systems (culture) that will grow and maintain the gains. Six Sigma is not about quality—at least not in the traditional sense of the word—although it results in improved quality. It is not about training, although training is used to build the skills needed to deploy it. Viewing Six Sigma as a massive training initiative is a low-yield strategy. Six Sigma is about breakthrough business improvement, not incremental improvement. Six Sigma projects are defined to produce major improvements (30% to 60% and more) in process performance in 4 to 6 months with a significant bottom-line impact. Such changes greatly affect how business is conducted day to day. As the Six Sigma mindset permeates the organization, individuals become aware of non–value-added work, ineffective processes, and poor performance and take action to make the needed improvements.

A Systematic and Focused Approach. Not all executives are used to the discipline that such an approach requires. There are road maps and step-by-step procedures for the managerial and technical aspects of Six Sigma. These processes and systems enable the key players in the initiative, such as Champions, BBs, and GBs to move up the learning curve more quickly and keep the organization focused on rapid improvement. (These and other titles are defined in the "Roles of Six Sigma Leaders" section later in this chapter.) Six Sigma is not an art, although experience, good judgment, and creativity are certainly required.

Right People. Six Sigma is about selecting and training the right people to fill the key roles. Successful organizations select their most talented people to fill the key Six Sigma positions (Champions, MBBs, BBs, and GBs). Most companies consider these people to be their future leaders. After those selected complete their Six Sigma assignments, they move into leadership positions and utilize their Six Sigma experience to guide others in improving the organization using the same approach. In this way, the cycle of continuous improvement is ingrained into the culture of the organization, and the company is assured of having "enlightened" leaders in the future.

Communication. It is important that a communication plan be developed to support the Six Sigma initiative. In the early stages of deployment, people will be asking a number of questions: What is Six Sigma? Why is our organization using this approach? Why are we doing this now? What will the benefits be? What progress are we making? Answers to these questions and other related messages must be communicated in a clear, concise, and consistent way. The message must be repeated several times, using a variety of media to make sure that everyone is exposed to understandable information. Clear understanding of the what, why, and how of the initiative will help generate the support in the organization needed to ensure that the BB and GB projects and the Six Sigma initiative as a whole succeed.

Recognition and Reward Plan. A recognition and reward program must be created to support the Six Sigma initiative. People want to know "what's in it for me." This helps them decide whether to get involved and at what level of intensity. We know of no organization that has successfully implemented Six Sigma without a recognition and rewards program to recognize and reinforce the desired behavior. Such a program typically includes both financial and psychological rewards.

Management Reviews of the Six Sigma Initiative. It is widely recognized that regular review of initiatives is needed to ensure the success of the initiative. Accordingly, regular reviews of the Six Sigma initiative (preferably quarterly) are required to monitor progress, to ensure the initiative milestones are being met, and to identify when adjustments and major changes to the deployment plan are needed. It is unlikely that a Six Sigma initiative will succeed without regular reviews by the senior management team who is accountable for the success of the program.

Improvement Projects

Right Projects. Six Sigma is about working on the right projects: those that support the business strategy. Six Sigma projects are linked to the goals of the business and to key problems that must be solved if the organization is to be successful (for example, critical customer complaints, process downtime producing stockouts, major accounts receivables issues). As you will see in later chapters, project selection is often where the battle is won or lost. Even top talent cannot salvage a poorly selected project. BBs and GBs work on important projects during as well as after the training. The specific roles of the BBs and GBs, who lead the improvement projects and are the primary "doers" in Six Sigma, are outlined later in this chapter and discussed more fully in Chapter 4.

Working on the right projects obviously requires careful business planning and coordination. Having BBs and GBs pick their own projects is not a good strategy in our experience. It is important, however, that the goals of the BB and GB projects are realistic and achievable so that the projects will be successful and the BBs and GBs—and organization as a whole—will build confidence that Six Sigma will work "here."

Project Management and Reviews. Six Sigma is about effective project management, including project selection, planning, and management reviews. Proper planning is important to ensure success. Such planning helps to avoid "scope creep" (project size and definition slowly growing beyond what is reasonable to accomplish considering the allotted time and resources), misalignment with management, lack of resources, projects that move at glacial speed, and other common project pitfalls. Management reviews are critical to success. Projects should be reviewed weekly by Project Champions and monthly by business leaders. As noted previously, the overall Six Sigma system should be reviewed quarterly and annually. Management reviews are critical to success. The lack of management reviews significantly reduces the impact of the Six

Sigma effort. The reviews keep the BBs and managers focused on the project and emphasize the long-term commitment of management to improve the performance of the organization, ensuring it will be a long-term source of products, services, and employment.

Sustaining the Gains. As previously noted, a methodology for sustaining the gains is an integral part of the Six Sigma approach. This methodology is usually called the *control plan* and is one of the unique aspects of Six Sigma. The control plan can be viewed at both a tactical and strategic level. At the tactical level, it sustains the gains of individual projects; at the strategic level, it sustains and broadens the gains of the Six Sigma initiative overall. A key element of the strategic control plan is a system for the continual identification of new projects and the placing of those projects in the project hopper. As the BBs complete their projects, they are assigned new projects that have been taken from the hopper. It is helpful to think of the project hopper as a "project portfolio," the contents of which blend together to drive the improvement needs of the organization (Snee and Rodebaugh 2002).

Right Results. Six Sigma is about getting the right results—improvements in process performance that are linked to the bottom line. The team estimates what a project is worth, typically with the help of the finance organization, before work is initiated. After the project has been completed, the team calculates the bottom-line savings. Many organizations, such as GE, require a sign-off from the finance organization verifying the financial impact and identifying where in the income statement it will show up. In this way you will know exactly what the bottom-line impact of the project has been. Surprisingly, many previous improvement initiatives discouraged focus on the financials when identifying or evaluating projects.

Project Tracking and Reporting. To monitor the progress of the initiative, check on the achievement of milestones, and provide a corporate memory, a project tracking and reporting system is needed. The tracking system is typically a software system that contains the bottom-line financial results and the improvements to process performance metrics for each project. Such systems typically have the capability to generate management reports on financial and process performance improvements for any process, business, function, organizational level, and so forth.

Six Sigma Methods and Tools

Process Thinking. The first key method is process thinking—taking the view that all work is a process that can be studied and improved. All work in all parts of the organization, whether it is in manufacturing, new product development, finance, logistics, or procurement, is accomplished by a series of interconnected steps. When you view problems from the framework of a process with inputs, processing steps, and outputs, a common approach to improving processes and solving problems can be applied. Because Six Sigma had its roots in electronics manufacturing, there is a common misunderstanding that Six Sigma can only help in this one activity. This mistake is analogous to assuming that the Internet can only be useful in the defense industry (where it originated).

Figure 1.4 shows a schematic of a customer order process. Process variables are divided into four groups: process inputs, controlled variables, uncontrolled variables, and process outputs. Examples of these variables for the customer order process are shown in Figure 1.4. The process inputs include those things used to produce the process outputs. The controlled variables are those that run the process and, as the name implies, can be controlled ("knobs" on the process). The uncontrolled variables are those that affect the output of the process but over which there is limited control. Obviously, the inputs come from suppliers, which could be the person down the hall or another process or raw material supplier; and the outputs go to customers, either internal or external to the organization. Viewing processes this way produces the SIPOC model (*suppliers, inputs, process, outputs, customers*). In the SIPOC model, all processes, no matter the source, begin to look similar in nature, enabling common improvement strategies to be used.

Process Variation. Variation is present in all processes and every aspect of work. Unintended variation reduces process performance, decreases customer satisfaction, and negatively impacts the bottom line. Customers want a consistent product or service, one that they can count on to provide the same value all the time. Products need to work as anticipated and be delivered and serviced on time, just as financial transactions need to proceed smoothly with minimal disruptions and just as patients need to be able to count on health-care providers for consistent and quality care.

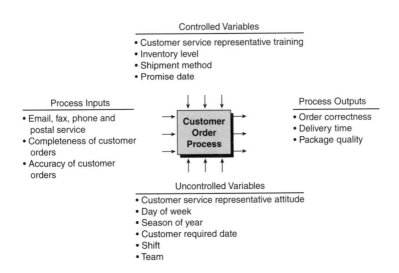

FIGURE 1.4   Schematic of a customer order process and its variables.

Six Sigma is focused on reducing the negative effects of process variation in two major ways: (1) It shifts the process average to the desired target level, and (2) it reduces the variation around the process average. This results in a process performing at the right average level with minimal variation from product to product or transaction to transaction. The need to address variation is the primary reason for including so many statistical tools in the Six Sigma toolkit. Statistics is the only science focused on identifying, measuring, and understanding variation, and therefore is a tool you can use to reduce variation.

Facts, Figures, and Data. Six Sigma is about facts, figures, and data—in other words, data-based decision making versus reliance on gut feeling and intuition. The approach requires data on all key process and input variables (see Figure 1.4). The project doesn't proceed until adequate data are available. The focus on the use of data, along with process thinking and variation, helps integrate the scientific method into the Six Sigma methodology. The integration of process thinking, understanding of variation, and data-based decision making is often referred to as *statistical thinking* (Hoerl and Snee 2002).

DMAIC Improvement Methodology. The primary improvement methodology of Six Sigma has five key phases: *define, measure, analyze, improve, and control* (DMAIC). All improvement projects touch on these phases in one way or another. (New design projects use a different process called *design for Six Sigma.*) The tools of Six Sigma are integrated into these phases. This is a strength and uniqueness of Six Sigma. All projects utilize the same improvement process, although the individual applications may be quite different. In contrast to most statistics training that throws a lot of tools on the table and lets practitioners fend for themselves, the DMAIC framework shows practitioners how to integrate and sequence the tools into an overall improvement strategy. This enables practitioners to attack virtually any problem in a systematic manner.

DMAIC is by far the most widely used road map in Six Sigma deployment. Other road maps are possible, but none are as useful in our judgment because of the effectiveness and elegant simplicity of DMAIC. We note that in the case of design for Six Sigma, DMADV or some other road map should be used. The key elements of deployment, projects, and methods and tools are still applicable.

Eight Key Tools. Six Sigma utilizes many individual tools, but the following eight tend to be most frequently applied:

- Process mapping
- Cause-and-effect matrix
- Measurement system analysis
- Capability study
- Failure modes and effects analysis (FMEA)
- Multi-vari study
- Design of experiments
- Control plans

These eight key tools are linked and sequenced in the DMAIC framework to ensure proper integration. This relatively small number of improvement tools helps the BBs and GBs move up the learning curve more quickly. They learn the order in which to use the tools and how the output of the use of one tool becomes the input for another tool. You will learn more about application of the tools beyond the factory floor in Chapter 7.

Statistical Tools. Some, but not all, of these tools are statistical tools. As noted earlier, statistical tools are required so that process variation can be dealt with effectively. Six Sigma has effectively integrated statistical tools with those from other disciplines, such as industrial engineering, quality management, operations research, mechanical and electrical design, and reliability. The result is a toolkit much broader and more powerful than available within any one discipline. Because the toolkit is diverse and flexible, and because the focus is on a limited set of core tools, BBs and GBs do not need to become professional statisticians to be successful. They are trained to use key statistical thinking and methods and data to improve processes.

User-Friendly Statistical Software. Another reason Six Sigma has been effective is the general availability of user-friendly statistical software that enables effective and broad utilization of the statistical tools. The statistical software package most widely used in Six Sigma is Minitab. JMP and other statistical software systems are also used in some Six Sigma deployments. Prior to the availability of such user-friendly software, statistical methods were often the domain of professional statisticians, who had access to, and specialized training in, proprietary statistical software. Specialists in statistical methods have an important role to play in Six Sigma, but practitioners who are not professional statisticians do the vast majority of statistical applications.

Critical Few Variables. The final key methodology of Six Sigma is its focus on the identification of the critical few input and process variables. Most processes, from performing surgery to closing the books for a global conglomerate, involve a large number of potentially important input and process variables. Studying each in-depth, and then managing them on an ongoing basis, would be time-consuming and prohibitively expensive. Fortunately, often just three to six critical process input variables drive the process output variables. Identification of these variables can lead to effective ways to optimize and control the process in a parsimonious and cost-effective way. Six Sigma finds, and then focuses attention on, these few key variables. This principle of focusing attention on a few key things is consistent with general principles of good management. The ultimate goal is to move from measuring outputs and making process adjustments (reactive) as the primary method of process control to measuring and then adjusting process inputs (proactive) to control the process and achieve the desired process performance.

Roles of Six Sigma Leaders

Six Sigma has well-defined leadership roles, and success depends on each of the roles fulfilling its unique responsibilities. Some of the key players involved in a Six Sigma initiative are shown in Figure 1.5. The lines in Figure 1.5 show the key linkages between the roles. For this discussion, we define the organization as the unit that has responsibility for identifying the improvement opportunities and chartering the Six Sigma projects. This could be a corporation, a division, a facility, or a function. The leadership team (often called the *Six Sigma Council*) leads the overall effort and has responsibility for approving the projects undertaken by the BBs. In the case of a finance function, the leadership team might be the *chief financial officer* (CFO) and selected members of his or her staff.

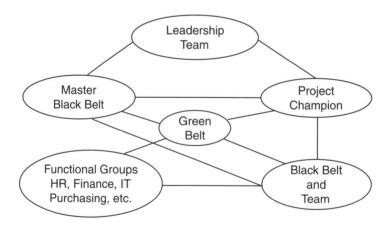

FIGURE 1.5   Roles of leaders.

Each project has a Champion who serves as its business and political leader. (Some organizations use the term *Champion* to refer to the overall leader of the Six Sigma effort.) The project Champion is typically a member of the leadership team and has the following responsibilities:

- Facilitating the selection of projects

- Drafting the initial project charters

- Selecting BBs and other resources needed to conduct the project

- Removing barriers to the successful completion of the project

- Holding short weekly progress reviews with the BBs

The BBs lead the team that does the actual work on the project. BBs are hands-on workers who are assigned to work full time on their projects and do much of the detailed work. The BB also leads the team, acts as project manager, and assigns work (for example, data collection) to the team members as appropriate. See Hoerl (2001) for a more detailed discussion of the BB role and the key skills required to perform it.

BB projects are typically defined so that they can be completed in 4 to 6 months, are focused on high-priority business issues, and are targeted to produce $175,000 to $250,000 per year to the bottom line. The team that works with the BB is typically comprised of 4 to 6 members who may spend as much as 25% of their time on the project. The amount of time spent by each team member will vary depending on the person's role. The team may also include consultants and specialists as well as suppliers and customers. BBs also act as mentors for GBs, as do MBBs.

GBs may lead a project under the direction of a Champion or MBB, or they may work on a portion of a BB project under the direction of the BB. GB projects are typically less strategic and more locally focused than are BB projects. A GB project is typically worth $50,000 to $75,000 per year to the bottom line and should be completed in 4 to 6 months. GBs do not work full time on improvement projects and typically have less-intensive training. GBs work on improvement projects in addition to their existing job responsibilities. As noted earlier, several companies have recognized the value of Six Sigma as a leadership development tool and have the objective of all members of the professional staff being at least a GB.

The MBB is the technical leader and enables the organization to integrate Six Sigma within its operations. The MBB has typically completed several BB projects and 2 to 5 weeks of training beyond the 4 weeks of BB training. The MBB helps the Champions select projects and review their progress. The MBB provides training and mentoring for BBs and, in some instances, training for GBs. The MBB is also responsible for leading mission-critical projects as needed, and sharing project learning and best practices across the organization. In essence, these resources are intended to combine technical skills beyond that of a BB with managerial and leadership skills similar to a Champion.

The functional support groups, such as human resources, finance, IT, and legal, assist the Six Sigma effort in four key ways, beyond improving their own processes through Six Sigma projects:

1. They provide specialized data as needed by BBs, GBs, and teams outside their function.

2. They provide expertise associated with their functional responsibilities.

3. They provide members for the BB and GB project teams when appropriate.

4. They help identify improvement opportunities for the organization to pursue.

Functional support groups (Enterprise Processes in Figure 1.1) are typically involved in more aspects of the organization's work than other groups, such as manufacturing. They interact across the organization, and as a result they see where improvements are needed in cross-functional processes operated by the organization. In a hospital, for example, the finance organization interacts with procurement, operations management, marketing, legal, IT, and external insurance agencies, and therefore can more easily pinpoint cross-functional issues that require attention.

There are two other types of Champions in addition to the Project Champion. As noted earlier, an organization typically names a Corporate Six Sigma Champion who reports to the president or CEO and has overall responsibility for developing the Six Sigma infrastructure. In large organizations, it is not unusual for each business and each functional unit (human resources, finance, IT, etc.) to name what they will call a Business or Functional Champion. Different organizations have used different titles for such roles, such as Quality Leader, Six Sigma Leader, and Six Sigma Champion. The role is basically the same: to oversee the implementation of Six Sigma in that unit. It is more prudent to focus on the actual role, and not get hung up on the title.

The Rest of the Story

This book is divided into four main parts: the case for Six Sigma beyond the factory floor, ensuring successful deployment, ensuring project success, and ensuring proper application of methods and tools. In this overall flow, we address strategic, tactical, and operational aspects of deploying Six Sigma. In Chapter 1, we have set the context for the book, highlighting the growing importance of health care, financial, service, and non-manufacturing functions to our economy, and the tremendous opportunity and need for improvement in these areas. We refer to these operations as the *real economy*. In Chapter 2, we address the fundamental barrier to improvement—the attitude that "we're different"—and show that, in fact, improvement efforts in diverse processes and environments have much more in common than they have differences. We find that Six Sigma works very well beyond the factory floor.

In Chapters 3 and 4, we present deployment case studies, key lessons learned from these cases, and a Six Sigma deployment road map that has been shown to be effective in a number of companies from a number of different environments. The focus of these two chapters is on the management systems that must be put in place to effectively deploy Six Sigma. One of the key things that makes Six Sigma different from earlier improvement methods is the existence of an infrastructure of management systems to support the deployment of Six Sigma. One of the key reasons that previous improvement approaches, such as *total quality management* (TQM) and *statistical process control* (SPC) were not as successful long term was that these approaches lacked an effective deployment method. This is not the case with Six Sigma.

Chapters 5 and 6 focus on ensuring project success. The successful completion of projects, one after another in a steady stream, is at the heart of Six Sigma. The discussion consists of case study presentations, the Six Sigma method for doing project-by-project improvement and keys to completing successful projects. Chapter 7 discusses technical considerations essential to successful improvement in the real economy. Many of these issues are not discussed elsewhere in the literature. The topics include the tools used and unique aspects of the data analysis in applications beyond the factory floor.

Chapter 8 discusses some next steps you may want to consider to make Six Sigma an integral part of the way your organization does business and serves its customers (and community). The goal is to get more out of Six Sigma. This can be accomplished by making Six Sigma part of, if not, your strategic signature—something for which your organization is known. As a result, all work in all areas of the organization will be using some aspect of Six Sigma to help make them successful. When others look at your organization, they will see Six Sigma as your signature.

Summary

This chapter has provided a general overview of Six Sigma—the key elements of the initiative and the key concepts, methods, and tools—and the tremendous opportunities for using Six Sigma to improve processes, functions, and organizations beyond the factory floor. An overview of the roles in Six Sigma was also provided. Now that you have a general idea of what Six Sigma is, its key uniqueness, and the roles of the players involved, you are in a position to consider the fundamental barrier to deploying Six Sigma: the common perception that "we're different," and therefore Six Sigma won't work here. As with most excuses, the belief that "we're different" does have a kernel of truth. Chapter 2 elaborates on what about the real economy really is different from manufacturing, what is really the same, and how to get beyond this issue. Process thinking and leadership are suggested as two key "antidotes" for this and other excuses.

References

Bisgaard, S. 2002. *Improving business processes with Six Sigma.* Presented at 56th Annual Quality Congress. Denver, CO (May).

Breyfogle, F.W. 2003. *Implementing Six Sigma*, second edition. New York: John Wiley and Sons.

Creveling, C. M., J. L. Slutsky, and D. Antis, Jr. 2003. *Design for Six Sigma in technology and product development.* Upper Saddle River, NJ: Prentice Hall.

George, M. L. 2003. *Lean Sigma for service.* New York: McGraw-Hill.

Hahn, G. J., N. Doganaksoy, and R. W. Hoerl. 2000. The evolution of Six Sigma. *Quality Engineering* 12 3:317-326.

Hoerl, R. W. 2001. Six Sigma Black Belts: what do they need to know? (with discussion). *Journal of Quality Technology* 33 4:391-435.

Hoerl, R. W., and R. D. Snee. 2002. *Statistical thinking: improving business performance.* Pacific Grove, CA: Duxbury Press.

Honeywell. 2002. The Honeywell edge. *Six Sigma Forum Magazine* (February) 14-17.

Jones, M. H., Jr. 2004. Six Sigma ... at a bank? *Six Sigma Forum Magazine* (February) 13-17.

Snee, R. D., and R. W. Hoerl. 2003. *Leading Six Sigma: a step-by-step guide based on experience with GE and other Six Sigma companies.* Upper Saddle River, NJ: FT Prentice Hall.

Snee, R. D., and W. F. Rodebaugh, Jr. 2002. Enhance your project selection process: every company should be able to manage its project portfolio and create an overall organizational improvement system. *Quality Progress* (September) 78-80.

Thottam, J. 2003. Where the good jobs are going. *Time* (4 August) 36–39.

Welch, J. F. 2001. *Jack: straight from the gut*. New York: Warner Business Books.

Young, J. 2001. Driving performance results at American Express. *Six Sigma Forum Magazine* (November) 19–27.

2

ADDRESSING THE FUNDAMENTAL BARRIER: "WE'RE DIFFERENT!"

"When we began our quality journey back in 2001, there were skeptics—some of them inside the company— who wondered whether we could use disciplines, methods, and tools from the factory floor and apply them at a large financial services company."
—Ken Case, CEO Bank of America

Now that we have made a case for deploying Six Sigma across all business segments and functions in Chapter 1, we want to address the major barrier that has limited deployment in many organizations. This barrier is the common perception that "we're different," a perception that often leads to the conclusion that "Six Sigma doesn't apply to us." Of course, there is a kernel of truth in the first statement; for example, bidding on municipal bonds is certainly different from manufacturing cell phones. However, our experience is that organizations typically have more in common with respect to improvement needs and methods than they have differences.

As discussed in this chapter, bidding on municipal bonds and manufacturing cell phones share some fundamental attributes. By focusing on these common attributes, while accounting for the important differences, you can successfully apply Six

Sigma to any business or function. We therefore hope to demonstrate in this chapter that the second statement ("Six Sigma doesn't apply to us") is completely incorrect, regardless of the business or function in question. Six Sigma is a generic improvement methodology that can be applied to any activity.

This chapter first covers why Six Sigma has not been deployed across the entire economy to the same degree that it has been in manufacturing. Following this, the chapter focuses on what is different, and then what is similar between *real economy* businesses and functions and manufacturing, the traditional application area of Six Sigma. Then the chapter discusses the critical role of process thinking, one of the key methods and tools aspects of Six Sigma mentioned in Chapter 1, to overcome the "we're different" barrier and deploy Six Sigma holistically. Finally, this chapter addresses the role of leadership in confronting and overcoming resistance to Six Sigma. After addressing this critical barrier in Chapter 2, the last chapter of Part I, we move on to deployment strategies in real economy businesses and functions in Part II, discuss keys to successful projects in Part III, and then tackle some of the unique technical issues that often occur in these areas in Part IV.

Why Six Sigma Hasn't Been Deployed Holistically

Our experience, and that of many other practitioners, is that despite its tremendous success, Six Sigma has not yet been deployed holistically across the entire economy, or across all functions within organizations that are deploying it. Although there are certainly counter-examples, such as Intuit, Bank of America, and the Mayo Clinic, the majority of applications have been in manufacturing and engineering. For example, a survey conducted by the journal *Quality Digest* found that the three most common areas for Six Sigma deployment were manufacturing, plant operations, and engineering (Dusharme 2003). Many organizations focus almost singularly on manufacturing, with perhaps token applications in other areas, such as finance or human resources. Some of the more-successful companies start in manufacturing and then deploy Six Sigma in other functions over time, but most of the less-successful companies never get to the other functions. Dusharme also points out that all too often smaller companies are conspicuous by their absence from the lists of companies deploying Six Sigma.

Velocci (2002) makes similar points in an article titled "Full Potential of Six Sigma Eludes Most Companies." Citing a study conducted by the technology consulting firm Pittiglio, Rabin, Todd, & McGrath, Velocci concluded that those organizations most successful in Six Sigma have typically been those with the broadest deployment. GE is perhaps the best case study for broad, holistic deployment; yet even here, Six Sigma has likely had greater impact in some areas than in others. According to Arndt (2002), for example, GE concedes that it has not made sufficient progress in applications to legal operations. Given the indisputable evidence of Six Sigma's ability to enhance customer satisfaction, deliver bottom-line savings, and drive top-line growth, such underutilization is cause for serious consideration. Why hasn't Six Sigma been more holistically deployed?

Some Potential Root Causes

As with most significant questions, there is no single correct answer. However, as we explain shortly, the various answers all lead to one common attitude, which is the fundamental barrier that needs to be addressed. One reason for the lack of holistic deployment is that the media have tended to focus their attention on large companies that are involved in manufacturing tangible goods, such as Motorola, 3M, Honeywell, DuPont, and GE. It is noteworthy that applications in GE's large financial services businesses have been largely underreported. This has created the public perception that Six Sigma is something large manufacturing companies do. It is also fair to say that many of the traditional quality and productivity improvement methodologies, such as *total quality management* (TQM), statistical process control, and Lean manufacturing, have been primarily focused on manufacturing operations. It is therefore natural that laypeople would equate improvement initiatives with manufacturing.

Real economy organizations that have looked closely at Six Sigma have often seen consultants and authors whose experience has been largely in manufacturing and engineering, not to mention books and training materials that use manufacturing terminology and examples. The non-manufacturing examples that do appear are often obviously contrived and not realistic; sometimes these were originally manufacturing examples with the names now changed to appear to be non-manufacturing examples. There are exceptions, such as the discussion of GE Capital's experiences that appears in Harry and Schroeder (2000), but these are certainly not typical. When organizations begin to ask questions such as "How does 'gauge R&R' apply to finance?" they all too often are met with either a "deer-in-the-headlights" blank gaze, or are told, "You'll have to figure that out for yourself."

We suggest that this disconnect is not due to a lack of applicability of Six Sigma to real economy applications (gauge R&R, or at least measurement systems analysis, *does* apply to finance), but is rather due to consultants, books, and training materials that lack the appropriate experience and insight that explains how. Too many consultants are only repeating what they were taught, and too many publications are only repeating what has been previously published. The result has been that Six Sigma is often portrayed as a mechanical "cookbook," where *Black Belts* (BBs) only need to blindly follow the steps listed and fill in the blank data fields in their Minitab, JMP, or Excel spreadsheets.

The emphasis of such an approach naturally reverts to the details of how to conduct each step (that is, the calculations), overlooking the bigger picture of what you are actually trying to do, and why. This type of limited approach can work when the BB's application looks just like the application in the manual, but will not work when the BB's application is radically different and creative thought is required. This is why we recommend first focusing on *what* you are trying to accomplish in each phase of Six Sigma, and *why*, prior to getting into the details of *how*. With a clear understanding of what you are trying to accomplish and why, you are in a much better position to think creatively about how to do it.

For example, if BBs clearly understand that in the Measure phase of a project, they need to verify that they can accurately and consistently measure (quantify) the key metrics of interest, so that they can segregate measurement problems from process problems; then it is much easier for them to think about how to accomplish this on a financial project. The BBs can now realize that designating a consumer as a poor credit risk, determining that an insurance claim is covered under the existing policy, or calculating a customer's balance due are all examples of measurements, measurements that are not necessarily accurate or consistent.

Certainly there are some unique challenges in applying disciplined, rigorous improvement methods such as Six Sigma in businesses such as health care or financial services, or functions such as HR or legal. Frustration over these unique challenges may play a role in the lack of holistic deployment. Such challenges often include the lack of documented work processes, poor or non-existent data-collection systems, and a scarcity of employees trained in the scientific method (that is, trained in disciplined, quantitative approaches to learning and problem solving).

Perhaps even more important than these unique technical challenges are unique conceptual or mindset challenges. One such challenge is the fact that many real economy processes produce intangible rather than tangible outputs, making it harder for people to see opportunities for improvement. For example, with the possible exception of the maternity ward, a hospital does not produce physical outputs like an automobile manufacturing plant does. Similarly, most people in businesses such as financial services or e-commerce have a difficult time seeing their work as a process. Assembly-line workers don't have this problem! In addition, organizations or functions such as these typically don't have an improvement mindset. For example, accountants generally focus on *conforming* to *generally accepted accounting practices* (GAAP), not on *improving* them. This improvement mindset was one of the elements of Six Sigma discussed in Chapter 1. We discuss these unique technical and conceptual challenges below.

In summary, some of the potential root causes are as follows:

- Media focus on manufacturing companies' experiences

- Historical focus of improvement initiatives on manufacturing

- Manufacturing orientation of many consultants, authors, and training materials

- Confusion between the mechanics of Six Sigma methods (the *how*) versus what you actually need to accomplish during each phase (the *what*), and *why* you want to do this

- Unique technical challenges of many real economy applications (discussed later in this chapter)

- Unique conceptual challenges of many real economy applications (discussed later in this chapter)

The Fundamental Barrier

The net result of all the issues and challenges discussed previously is that people in financial services, health care, e-commerce, and so on develop an attitude that Six Sigma is great *for someone else*, typically those in manufacturing. They conclude that their organization or function is different, and therefore Six Sigma doesn't apply to them. In many cases, this conclusion is just one of honest ignorance, in others it is a form of denial, and in others it is a convenient excuse to avoid change (that is, a passive form of resistance). Regardless of the underlying root cause, we believe that the attitude "we're different, Six Sigma doesn't apply to us" is *the* fundamental barrier to deployment in the real economy. Our experience suggests that this attitude has been the limiting factor in spreading Six Sigma holistically, and that all real economy organizations that have successfully deployed Six Sigma have had to deal with it.

As noted previously, the specific root cause behind this "we're different" attitude doesn't matter in terms of its effect. However, diagnosing the root cause is very important when trying to address the attitude so that you can move on. Strong leadership is needed. We realize that saying strong leadership is needed is analogous to giving the advice "buy low, sell high," but unfortunately, this is often the deciding factor between successful and unsuccessful deployments. Leaders must take the time to understand the underlying root cause and respond appropriately. We discuss the critical role of leadership in addressing this attitude, and dealing with resistance in general, later in this chapter.

We say that this attitude is the fundamental barrier to deployment in the real economy because in our experience, and that of many others, it is the predominant reason given by those who know about Six Sigma, but have decided against implementing it in these areas. This is true both at the corporate level and the level of individual functions within the organization. Interestingly, it also can become a barrier to those in the midst of implementation. For example, a primary motivation for us to write this book is the number of people who have contacted us over the past few years, either in person or by e-mail, and stated that they were trying to deploy Six Sigma in health care, finance, or some other area, but were struggling because "this is not like manufacturing." The underlying assumption, wrong as it may be, is that Six Sigma at its core is a manufacturing initiative.

As might be expected, many of these people had the bulk of their experience in manufacturing, but not all. Some had experience in their current application area, but were struggling to apply the manufacturing-oriented materials, such as books and training manuals, to their business or function. As noted above, such wounds in the Six Sigma community are primarily self-inflicted; consultants, authors, and practitioners put together manufacturing-oriented documentation, and then complain that people view Six Sigma as being a manufacturing initiative. Similarly, this can create a "self-fulfilling prophecy" among skeptical executives, in that their original experiences with typical consultants and materials reinforce their suspicion that Six Sigma is a manufacturing initiative. In reality, Six Sigma at its core is about improvement; the specific application area is not important from a technical point of view, but admittedly can be from a perception point of view.

As we show throughout the rest of this book, Six Sigma applies just as naturally in finance as in an electronics factory, and just as naturally in a hospital as a chemical plant. Some important differences must be kept in mind and accounted for, but this is true for all applications. For example, manufacturing computer circuit boards is totally different from manufacturing fibers, such as nylon. Applications in one area are not likely to translate well into the other. Similarly, someone who knows a lot about improving cell phone assembly would likely be totally lost in a paper mill. Therefore, Six Sigma training materials that focus on cell phone examples would be of little more assistance to a paper mill implementing Six Sigma than to a bank doing so. The only advantage of such materials to the paper mill would be that people there could likely relate to the concept of manufacturing a physical, tangible product, whereas people at the bank might not.

Therefore, the comment made by some real economy organizations that "we're different" is somewhat of a red herring. It is certainly true to a degree, but this is also true of everyone else who has implemented Six Sigma beyond electronics assembly, the original application area at Motorola. In no circumstances should this comment be accepted as an excuse for not deploying Six Sigma to improve the organization, and its results. A more appropriate statement would be this: "We need to figure out the best approach to deploying Six Sigma within our organization, given its uniqueness." This book is intended to help you determine such an approach.

What's Different?

As noted in the previous section, there are some unique aspects of health care, finance, e-commerce, and so on that need to be taken into account when implementing Six Sigma. This section discusses these in greater detail. We will then show how in many ways these types of application areas are just like manufacturing. In other words, there are similarities as well as differences. Our experience has been that these worlds are much more alike than different, especially when we can view applications with the appropriate lens. This is the lens of process thinking, a topic covered in more detail later in this chapter.

We have found that the key differences between real economy applications versus manufacturing segregate naturally into two major categories: conceptual differences, which are typically most relevant at the deployment and project levels; and technical differences, which are typically most relevant at the project and also methods and tools levels. The major differences that most need to be taken into account are as follows:

- **Conceptual differences**

  - ◆ Lack of tangible output or "product"

  - ◆ Lack of a process view of work

  - ◆ Lack of an improvement mindset

- **Technical differences**

  - ◆ Lack of measurement systems for data

  - ◆ Lack of standardized work processes

  - ◆ Greater human element in processes

  - ◆ Lack of "engineers"

In addition to these high-level technical differences, BBs often face more detailed technical challenges when applying the tools of Six Sigma outside traditional manufacturing areas. These include such things as the prevalence of discrete versus continuous data, or the skewed (non-normal) data distributions frequently encountered. We provide guidance on how to address these more-detailed technical challenges in Chapter 7.

Conceptual Differences

The first and most obvious difference is that in manufacturing you are, by definition, making something. In other words, you produce a tangible, physical product. This makes it easy to visualize the purpose of your Six Sigma efforts; you don't want to make defective automobiles, clothing that must be sold as "seconds," or leaky pens. How about bidding on municipal bonds, providing day care for young children, or marketing consulting services? These endeavors don't appear to produce a tangible product, so for many people it is not clear how to apply Six Sigma. As discussed below, it is also difficult to see the process used to provide these services.

In reality, these endeavors do have outputs or "products," although they may or may not be tangible. Intangible products are often referred to as *services*. For example, most parents expect their children to come home from day care safe and unharmed, clean, fed, in general properly cared for, and hopefully enriched and in good spirits. Sending children home in this condition could be considered the day-care center's primary service, or "product." Similarly, when bidding on municipal bonds, you intend to win profitable deals; that is your desired output or product. The ultimate goal of marketing is to increase sales and margins, and hopefully improve the product or service through effective marketing research. Increased sales and margins are therefore two products produced by marketing efforts.

An effective question to ask when people can't see the product or output they produce is to ask them, "What value does your work add?" Very few people will respond to this question by saying "None." Their response will lead you directly to their product or service. For example, a day-care worker might respond by saying, "I provide safe supervision and care for children"; the person who bids on municipal bonds might respond, "I ensure that we only obtain profitable deals, and that we don't leave money on the table (overbid)"; someone in marketing might say, "I create brand images for our products in customers' minds." Follow-up questions would naturally lead to identification of the key services provided or products produced in each case. So upon closer examination, this conceptual difference, after being properly identified and addressed, is not as important as one might think and can be understood and overcome.

The second major difference, lack of a process view of work, can be more difficult to overcome. In manufacturing, it is easy to see the process that is producing the product. All you have to do is follow the pipes! Most people who work in manufacturing are not confused about what process they work on (although even here people may not understand the overall system). In the three examples discussed above, however—day care, municipal bonds, and marketing—people may not know the processes in which they work, or even that they have a process. Because there are no "pipes" to follow, it is much harder to visualize the process they are working on.

Stahl et al. (2003), in an article focused on Six Sigma in health care, made a similar point when they noted, "It probably comes as no surprise to health care professionals that organizational structure can actually inhibit process thinking. Inherently, there are multiple silos across a typical facility and few examples of the big picture oversight to unify conflicting agendas and constituencies." Of course, Six Sigma improves results by improving the processes that produce the results. Therefore, if people cannot understand the process they are working on, they are unlikely to be successful in applying Six Sigma. This is why process flow diagrams (Hoerl and Snee 2002), which visually document the processes in question, are so important in these types of applications.

If people have identified the outputs or services they produce by answering our first question ("What value does your work add?"), you can usually help them identify their process by asking a simple follow-up question: "How do you produce these outputs or services?" For example, if the person in marketing says that he or she creates brand images in customers' minds, you would ask, "How do you accomplish this?" The answer—which may involve advertising campaigns, unique product designs, and so on—and perhaps some additional follow-up questions will identify the key processes that this person works in or is accountable for.

At first, this type of questioning to define the key processes can be tedious and draining. After a while, however, it begins to become second nature. With a little experience, those sincere about applying Six Sigma will begin to see every activity as a process (driving to work, taking a shower, conducting a meeting, a sales call, closing the books, and so on). From this point on, there will be no struggle to define key processes to which they could apply Six Sigma. Process thinking, the ability to view any activity as a process that can be studied and improved, is not only a key element of Six Sigma, it is *the* key to holistic deployment. We discuss this point in greater detail later in this chapter.

The third major conceptual difference is the fact that many real economy businesses and functions do not have an improvement culture or mindset. Although many counter-examples could be found, people are not generally expected to come into work thinking about how they might be able to improve their processes and results. For example, many hospital nurses are not expected, and perhaps not even legally allowed, to develop and implement improvements to standard medical procedures. As noted previously, accountants are generally held accountable for adhering to GAAP, rather than improving GAAP. Similar comments could be made of lawyers, software developers, underwriters, and many other professionals. This is not to criticize such professionals, the vast majority of whom are dedicated, honest, and hard working. Rather, we want to point out the difference in culture between *most real economy* businesses or functions versus what is needed for holistic deployment of Six Sigma.

In manufacturing, on the other hand, there is almost always constant pressure to reduce waste levels and increase productivity, at least in free-market economies. One reason for this is that manufacturing waste and production are easily seen and quantified. When major improvements are made in these organizations, further improvements are expected. Facilities unable to continue such improvement are generally shut down in favor of those that can, or in favor of newer, more efficient facilities. Improvement is not an option here; it is a matter of survival. In the United States (and many other countries), agriculture and athletics are two other examples where improvement is part of the culture. "Wait until next year" or "next season we'll be better" is the attitude. Sustained world-class performance has resulted in both instances.

U.S. steel manufacturing is one example of an industry unable to make the necessary improvements (and suffering the consequences). On a positive note, adoption of Six Sigma by Motorola in the 1980s is credited with saving their microelectronics business. Of course, real economy organizations have just as much of a need to improve to stay competitive as does manufacturing. The recent failure of many dot.coms, telecoms, and financial institutions is leading to a growing awareness of the need for continuous improvement in all business organizations.

This lack of an improvement mindset can be a deterrent to improvement initiatives such as Six Sigma. People may ask, "Why do we need to improve?" or "What's wrong with our current performance?" or they may state, "This is the way we have always done things." They may feel insulted and actively or passively resist. This attitude is often prevalent when people feel isolated from competition, such as in government jobs. Even without resistance, the lack of an improvement culture probably implies that people are not trained in basic improvement methodologies, such as the scientific method, do not typically gather data to critically evaluate their own performance, do not utilize formal problem-solving methodologies on a regular basis, and so on. As discussed in Chapter 1, such habits and skills are the foundation for Six Sigma and many other broad improvement initiatives. These basics will therefore have to be developed as Six Sigma is initially implemented, slowing the speed of deployment to some degree.

Some key modifications that organizations beyond the factory floor may need to make to be successful in deployment, and in individual projects, include the following:

- Clearly explaining the need for improvement, based on the business environment when communicating the rollout of the Six Sigma initiative

- Taking time to identify and explain the key outputs of the processes involved when launching a new project

- Incorporating a focus on process identification and evaluation in Six Sigma training material, including the use of process diagrams and flowcharts

Technical Differences

In addition to these potential conceptual differences with manufacturing, there are often some important technical differences that need to be taken into account at the project and also methods and tools levels. The first one is the frequent lack of suitable measurement systems from which to obtain data. Manufacturing organizations typically have the best measurement processes. This is primarily because they are required to keep close track of raw materials and finished goods to account for their debits and credits.

The good measurement systems have two immediate impacts that may lead to easier implementation of Six Sigma. First of all, the waste and rework in manufacturing have managerial visibility. If you are losing 20% of your finished products as waste, the cost of this problem is visible to management. On the other hand, the cost of financial analysts reworking the numbers five or six times in the budgeting process until management is willing to accept them is invisible. You cannot look at standard financial reports and immediately see that huge amounts of analysts' time (and therefore huge amounts of money) are being wasted through "rework," because it is not being measured.

The second way that better measurement systems make application easier in manufacturing is that after you begin the Six Sigma project, the data needed for analysis are more readily available. In most factories, for example, a measurement system for waste is already in place for accounting purposes. This will help bring visibility of the waste problem to management, as noted above. In addition, when a Six Sigma project is chartered, the team will be able to hit the ground running on the project because the data they need are readily available. Conversely, if you want to work on reducing rework in your budgeting process, you must first figure out how to measure the time spent on rework and implement a measurement system.

Implementing measurement systems is rarely easy, especially when people are involved. Often people are suspicious that "big brother" will be watching them, and managers sometimes worry that the data collected will expose the inadequacies of their operations. Without strong leadership, there will likely be stiff resistance to implementing the measurement system. BBs with manufacturing experience may become frustrated and suggest, "Hey, why don't we do something back in manufacturing?"

One suggestion for dealing with the measurement issue in non-manufacturing applications is to begin projects in areas where good measurement systems already exist, and where the savings are immediately obvious. Accounts payable and accounts receivable are good examples. To satisfy accounting needs, there are generally good measurement systems not only for the amounts in these accounts, but also on the timing of billing and payment. Another advantage of applications in these areas is that there is usually lots of money to be made by improving the process, all of which is easily quantified because of the existing measurement systems.

For example, by collecting faster in accounts receivable you can benefit from the time value of money and avoid costly delinquencies and defaults. One BB project in collections at GE (Hahn et al. 2000) produced just under $3 million in annual savings. By paying your invoices just in time to receive early-payment discounts in accounts payable, you can hold your money longer on average, but still receive all available discounts. This typically amounts to huge savings, and as previously noted, these savings are easily quantified.

Another typical technical difference relative to manufacturing is the fact that many processes are not well defined or standardized. If you ask several underwriters how they decide whether to approve an insurance application, for example, they may have trouble agreeing on a specific set of steps in this decision-making process. They will all likely look at the same data, but may not do so in exactly the same way. A similar situation might occur if you ask several surgeons how they decide whether a patient needs back surgery. The lack of a common decision-making process is one reason why most managed health-care plans require a second and perhaps third opinion prior to major surgery. Our point is not to criticize underwriters or surgeons; we could have chosen many other examples. Instead, our point is that many important processes in the real economy have not been well defined and standardized.

Manufacturing processes, on the other hand, involve physical hardware such as extruders, reactors, stamping machines, mechanical robots, and so on. The layout and operation of this hardware basically defines the process. It is typically very easy for anyone to visualize the process by just observing the flow of materials through the equipment. In addition, the layout of the equipment provides a certain degree of standardization; it is hard for anyone to significantly alter the process. Even in manufacturing there are often standardization issues, however, because some operators will run the equipment differently from others.

BBs in health care, financial services, and so on can overcome this hurdle by ensuring that key processes have been well documented through process maps and flowcharts (Hoerl and Snee 2002). Developing procedures at the appropriate level of detail can help people utilize the process in a more consistent manner, providing increased standardization. For example, a procedure that defines the specific steps to go through when dismissing patients from a hospital can provide a smoother experience for patients, while still gathering all information needed by the hospital, such as insurance coverage.

As previously noted, real economy processes often have a greater human element than do manufacturing processes. Manufacturing processes certainly have an important human element, but service processes often have an even greater one. For example, improving recruiting processes in *human resources* (HR) is likely to involve a greater emphasis on the work done by people than on better use of equipment. Although the emergence of e-commerce has closed the gap between manufacturing and real economy processes in this regard, through such things as electronic job applications and employment Web sites such as Monster.com, there is still a gap in HR (and in many other areas).

Another aspect of this human element is the fact that the customer is often directly involved in the process (in health care for example). Studying the process is therefore inherently linked with studying the customer. In other situations, the customer may also be the supplier. One example is dry-cleaning operations. It can be challenging to complain to customers that their inputs are not what you require!

This human element presents technical challenges because it is much easier to improve the work of a machine than a person! To the extent that human factors are key inputs or process variables, these will be harder to control. Machines tend to be less resistant to change and don't get their feelings hurt easily. With proper motivation and empathy, however, people's work can also be improved. When people understand the need for change, and are allowed to participate in determining the specific ways they will change, they are more willing. Many companies utilize some type of organizational-effectiveness approach to address the human element. Chapter 3 mentions the *Change Acceleration Process* (CAP) used at GE to address the human element.

The fourth common technical difference is that real economy businesses and functions typically lack "engineers," a group that generally provides the improvement expertise in manufacturing. It is not unusual in process industries for plants to have technical groups consisting primarily of engineers whose job it is to work on improving the performance of the plant's manufacturing processes. It is interesting to note that these groups rarely work on improving the other processes needed to operate the facility.

Engineers come in many types and from many fields, such as mechanical, electrical, chemical, industrial, aeronautical, and so on, so we are admittedly generalizing here. However, it is fair to say that virtually all engineers are trained in advanced mathematics and the use of the scientific method, that most have studied statistical methods, and that these disciplines have earned reputations for process thinking and having improvement cultures. Engineers in manufacturing facilities look for potential improvements in yield, quality, productivity, and so on, on a daily basis, almost by second nature.

When improvement initiatives such as Six Sigma come along, engineers are often first in line for selection as BBs, *Master Black Belts* (MBBs), and other technical roles. Their mathematical and statistical background makes it relatively easy for them to pick up the statistical and engineering methods required, and their process orientation and improvement mindset fit right in to the framework of Six Sigma projects. Because of these advantages, engineers often form the backbone of Six Sigma deployment in manufacturing organizations. Recall that selecting the right people and taking a systematic approach were discussed as key aspects of Six Sigma in Chapter 1. But what about a bank or accounting firm; where do they find engineers?

Obviously, banks don't generally hire engineers in a big way; nor do accounting firms, hospitals, or Wal-Mart branches. Yet these types of organizations will still need solid BBs, *Green Belts* (GBs), and even MBBs if they are to successfully implement Six Sigma. Fortunately, the statistical methods needed to close the books faster are not nearly as complex as those needed to optimize a chemical distillation process. This principle is true in general, although some exceptions can be found; the level of statistical rigor needed in real economy Six Sigma projects is less than that needed in manufacturing and engineering. Chapter 7 discusses some of the exceptions, such as logistic regression and discrete event simulation.

BBs, and especially MBBs, will still need solid technical and statistical skills, however. Therefore, selection will still present an important challenge to organizations deploying Six Sigma. One option is to find employees with technical backgrounds. In insurance, for example, actuaries typically have strong statistical backgrounds. The same is true of many doctors and nurses. Some MBA and finance programs in academia are quite quantitative in nature. Therefore, employees with the needed technical backgrounds are often available within the organization. When they are not, one approach is to hire a few MBBs or BBs with relevant experience to help "kick-start" deployment. Of course, one must be careful to hire external resources that can make the transition to the real economy. Some Six Sigma providers offer experienced BBs on a temporary basis as part of their overall offerings.

Another option is to designate employees who have the desired non-technical skills (see Snee and Hoerl 2003) as BBs, and then develop their technical skills as rapidly as possible. Technical skill building is part of the Six Sigma training received by the BBs and GBs. Training and mentoring from an experienced Six Sigma provider can prove extremely helpful here. Experience can be an excellent teacher, so under the right circumstances these BBs will learn quickly, and some may become candidates for MBB positions. In summary, this lack of engineers is a valid concern, but there are many options available to overcome it.

Some key modifications that organizations beyond the factory floor may need to make to be successful in projects, and in use of the methods and tools, include the following:

■ Use availability of good measurement systems as a criterion for project selection. This is also a valid criterion in manufacturing, but is typically not as critical as in real economy applications.

■ Consciously plan for time needed on projects to introduce new measurement systems.

- Utilize process mapping tools early on projects to identify key work processes, and consider a preliminary step of "freezing" the process so that it can be more easily studied and improved. Freezing the process means defining how to operate a potentially poorly defined process, perhaps subjectively, even though this may not be the best way to operate it long term. For example, we could agree on a common approach to collections, even though some do not believe this is the best approach.

- Consider the use of organizational-effectiveness approaches in conjunction with Six Sigma, such as the GE CAP process, to help address human issues.

- Be creative about selection of BBs and MBBs for projects that require deep technical skills, such as finding technically trained employees, hiring externally, developing internal candidates with strong non-technical skills, or utilizing BBs or MBBs from an external supplier.

What's Similar?

We have just discussed important differences, both conceptual and technical, between real economy businesses and functions, and manufacturing operations. As noted previously, although these differences are real, they can be addressed, and none provides a valid excuse for missing the potential benefits of Six Sigma deployment. We now point out some important similarities with manufacturing, including the following:

- All work occurs through processes.

- Processes provide information and data that can be used to improve them.

- All processes have "hidden factories" that add cost and reduce output.

■ All processes involve people, equipment, materials, measurement, methods or procedures, and operate in an environment.

■ Undesired variation is a common source of process problems.

The following discussion shows that the similarities are more important than the differences.

Perhaps most noteworthy is the fact that all work—whether done in manufacturing, financial services, health care, e-commerce, or anywhere else—occurs through processes, typically a system of interconnected processes. Just as there are assembly-line processes to manufacture automobiles, there are processes, or sequences of steps, used to acquire other companies, conduct a sales transaction, predict future earnings, perform brain surgery, or pay an insurance claim. Those experienced in applying Six Sigma to diverse application areas have learned how to identify the key elements of any process. When these elements have been identified, all processes begin to look very similar, at least at a high level. This is the key to holistic application of Six Sigma.

An appropriate analogy would be to compare an 80-year-old man with a 1-year-old girl. Certainly they appear very different to the casual observer! To trained medical professionals in an *emergency room* (ER), however, they both have a similar circulatory system, respiratory system, skeletal structure, and so on, and these medical professionals need to be prepared to treat both on the same ER shift. The advanced training that doctors and other medical professionals receive allows them to look past the obvious differences between the 80-year-old man and the 1-year-old girl and focus on the similarities. Of course, the differences will also be taken into account in determining treatment, but the similarities are key. The next section discusses the critical role of developing a process viewpoint.

A second similarity, obviously related to the first, is that these processes provide information and data that can be used to study and improve the process. Data on operating conditions and productivity at a manufacturing facility can be used to better understand the variables that influence quality or productivity (and how to modify them to drive improvements). Similarly, careful study of the cycle time of each step in the process of closing the books, as well as the source of any delays, can be used to streamline and improve the closing process. Florence Nightingale (Cohen 1984) is credited with utilizing data to study and reduce mortality at military hospitals during the Crimean War. Of course, many processes are *not* producing such information currently. The point is that they *can*, if you choose to collect such information. Six Sigma helps you identify what data to collect and how to analyze it to drive improvements.

For example, you can track the time it takes to prepare a hospital room for the next patient after the previous patient has been released. This metric could be compared to others, such as number of nurses or other employees available, type of patient, day of week, and so on, to study causes of cycle time and identify potential improvements. In e-commerce, you can track the percent of repeat visitors to your Web site, how long they stay (measured in time or pages viewed), and what percent are actually buying. In supply-chain management, you can track such things as the size of your inventories, total delivery time, and stock-outs. In finance you can track cash flow or the time it takes to close the books. These are simple examples, but hopefully make the point that all processes can produce information that will help improve them.

Another similarity is that all processes involve mistakes or inefficiencies that require additional work to fix, or perhaps cause irreparable damage. In manufacturing, the additional work is called *rework*, and the irreparably damaged goods are called *waste*. The effort required to handle waste and rework are often lumped together and referred to as *non–value-adding work*. For example, the work required to disassemble, fix, and then reassemble a cell phone that is not working properly after original assembly is rework. It is rework in the sense that the cell phone should have worked the first time; because it didn't, you have to do the same work over again. Obviously, such work adds additional costs, and in some cases additional opportunity for quality problems or safety incidents. If any components have been damaged beyond repair, these will be discarded and written off as waste.

Processing the rework and waste often requires the purchase of additional capital equipment, additional employees, and often significant charges for disposal of such things as toxic waste. Because all these costs of rework and waste are, at least in theory, avoidable, such activities often present excellent opportunities to make improvements through Six Sigma. First, of course, you have to find them! The physical location where the rework and waste processes are found is often referred to as the *hidden factory* or *hidden plant.* This is because most factories do not want visiting customers or managers to see such activities, and therefore often locate them in remote parts of the facility, where they are literally hidden.

Importantly, all processes, in manufacturing or not, have some type of hidden factory involving waste and rework. We have not seen a process that didn't have a hidden factory. For example, we previously noted that financial analysts often have to rework the budget several times before management is willing to accept it. There is no legitimate reason why these analysts could not have developed an acceptable budget the first time, given appropriate direction and information. Note that we are not suggesting that the rework is the fault of the financial analysts; the root cause may be lack of required information, lack of clear direction, a poor budgeting process, unreasonable management, or a host of other potential issues.

Six Sigma provides the rigor and discipline to objectively identify the root causes of such rework and eliminate them. Tables 2.1 and 2.2, adapted from Hoerl and Snee (2002), list examples of rework and waste in various types of business functions and various types of businesses, respectively.

TABLE 2.1   Examples of Rework and Waste Activities by Function*

Function	Rework and Waste Activities
Sales	Making repeat sales calls because we did not have all the information requested by the customer on the first visit.
Marketing	Changing a product image because the original image was rejected by the consumer (e.g., the Nova automobile introduced in Mexico—in Spanish, "No va" means "it doesn't go").

Function	Rework and Waste Activities
Engineering	Designing out flaws in a product after they have been detected by customers who have lodged complaints.
Manufacturing	Disposing of waste, or performing rework on defective products.
HR	Conducting second, third, or fourth interviews, because we have not gotten enough information previously to make a decision about a candidate.
Logistics	Shipping the product from site A to site B and then to site C prior to eventually getting it to a customer.
IT Support	Solving employees' hardware or software problems two or three times because we didn't totally solve the problem the first time.
Accounting	Performing manual account reconciliation to close the books.
Finance	Revising financial forecasts three or four times until senior management is willing to "accept" the numbers.
Procurement	Holding second, third, or fourth meetings with our vendor's sales force because we haven't properly documented our requirements.
Legal	Preparing extensive documents for a litigation, only to find out that a decision has been made to settle out of court.
Environmental	Paying fines, and preparing additional documentation, because of being found in violation of environmental standards.
Quality	Responding to customer complaints.
R&D	Beginning a research project, and then abandoning it because funding was cut.

*Adapted from Hoerl and Snee (2002)

TABLE 2.2 Examples of Rework and Waste Activities by Business Type*

Type of Business	Rework and Waste Activities
Health care	Second medical opinions, obtained because we are not confident in the first opinion.
Financial services	Fixing errors in credit card bills or mortgage statements.
Food service	Disposing of spoiled food.
Transportation	Rescheduling passengers from a canceled flight.
Catalogue sales	Paying postage twice (to the customer and back) for goods returned because they were not what the customer ordered, or were damaged in shipment.
Internet commerce	Restoring a "crashed" server.
Retail sales	Restocking returned merchandise.
Chemicals	"Blending" batches of finished chemicals, because one or both did not meet physical property standards.
Microelectronics	Disposing of inventory that has gone from "state of the art" to "antiquated" while sitting in the distribution pipeline for a year.
Automobiles	All activities and expenses associated with recalls.
Telecommunications	All activities and expenses associated with reassigning area codes to existing phone numbers.

*Adapted from Hoerl and Snee (2002)

Still another similarity is that all processes involve some combination of people, equipment (possibly computers), materials (possibly in the form of information), measurement, and methods or procedures. Sometimes environment is added as an additional component of the process. As noted above, the human element tends to be even more critical in many real economy processes. Certainly the type of equipment involved in hospitals is very different from the equipment in a plastics plant, but both rely on equipment. Even banks rely heavily on equipment, such as ATM machines and, of course, computers. Because all processes have these common elements, we can conduct Six Sigma projects in financial services, manufacturing, or e-commerce using the same conceptual approach, although the details will be quite different in each case.

This same conceptual approach enables us to look in the same categories of root causes for problems, regardless of the application area. For example, Figure 2.1 shows a cause-and-effect diagram from Hoerl and Snee (2002) that depicts causes of high cycle time in paying corporate property taxes. This diagram focuses on causes within the generic categories of people, equipment, methods, and materials.

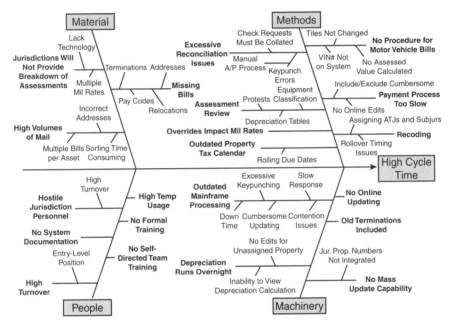

FIGURE 2.1   Cause-and-effect diagram for high-cycle time in paying corporate property taxes.

Further, undesired process variation is a predominant source of problems in all the application areas known to us. Just as an operator in a factory becomes frustrated with variation in raw material lots from a supplier, distributors in the supply chain become frustrated with variation in delivery times, treasurers become frustrated with variation in cash flow, and retail store managers become frustrated with variation in capability and attitude of their employees. In each of these application areas, and all others that we are aware of, many problems are not caused by too much or too little of something—that is, delivery times that are consistently too high or too low—but are caused by undesirable and uncontrolled variation somewhere in the process. Therefore, a common improvement strategy in Six Sigma, and other improvement initiatives, is to identify and eliminate causes of variation, regardless of the application area.

In summary, one can see that there are noteworthy differences between real economy businesses or functions and manufacturing, but there are also some important similarities. We have found that each of the differences can be successfully overcome when properly understood and accounted for. The similarities can then be exploited to apply a common conceptual approach in any application area. It should be obvious at this point that process thinking is critical to employing such a strategy. The next section discusses process thinking in more detail. Our experience is that when all facts are considered, finance, e-commerce, health care, and so on are much more similar to manufacturing than they are different, at least in terms of deploying Six Sigma. As noted previously, the most difficult hurdle to overcome is the attitude that "we're different."

Process Thinking: The Key to Overcome a "We're Different"
Attitude

When discussing the similarities between real economy businesses and functions and those of manufacturing, we began by pointing out that in both arenas the work occurs through processes. The process is not generally your primary interest, the "product" or output is. However, the best way to improve the outputs is to improve the process. Therefore, process thinking, including identifying, studying, and improving processes, is at the heart of any successful improvement initiative, including Six Sigma. Note further that the other important similarities, those attributes previously discussed that enable you to utilize a common approach between the real economy and manufacturing, are all related to processes. For example, we discussed using information generated by the process to improve it, eliminating the hidden factory in the process, exploiting the fact that all processes share common categories of elements, and the need to identify and eliminate undesired process variation.

Also note that process thinking, which we have already identified as a key, was integral to overcoming the differences noted previously. In fact, lack of process thinking was one of the major differences! By learning to take a process viewpoint, you not only overcome this hurdle, you naturally lead to organizational recognition that processes can be studied and improved—that is, to an improvement mindset. This addresses another key conceptual difference. As discussed later in this chapter, process thinking clarifies the fact that all processes have some output, or product. This clarification addresses the first key conceptual difference noted previously. We noted that the most difficult barrier to overcome is the "we're different" attitude. Fortunately, when people can view all work as a process, it becomes obvious that their work, although unique, does share important similarities with other processes and, therefore, that Six Sigma can be applied by them as well.

This leads to consideration of the technical differences noted previously. One of these was the fact that there is a lack of standardized work processes, which hinders improvement efforts. Of course, it is difficult to standardize something that is not recognized or understood! When people have a process mindset, and can readily see the underlying processes at work, it becomes not only easier, but also desirable to standardize them. Because people will now want to study and improve processes, they will recognize the need for measurement systems to collect appropriate data to enable improvement.

When the entire organization is thinking this way about process improvement, and utilizing data to do so, they have become the equivalent of a corps of "engineers," the final technical difference discussed previously. This is not to suggest that financial analysts or nurses will have the same technical training as engineers, but it is to suggest that they will begin to think the same way. Proper BB or GB training will provide them with the technical skills needed to successfully complete their projects.

Although a process mindset does not directly address the remaining technical issue of the greater impact of human issues, it does make it easier to tackle. When people learn to study their work processes with the intent of improving them, and understand that people are a key element of processes, they are usually more willing to objectively evaluate the human element. They are also less likely to be intimidated by, or suspicious of, efforts to study people-intensive processes, such as comparing decisions between underwriters using the same insurance applications.

Given the above discussion, we believe strongly that if you can develop process thinking in your workforce, you have won 80% of the battle. You can then address all the differences and take advantage of all the similarities. Although we do not want to over-simplify deployment of Six Sigma in the real economy, we are confident in stating that this mindset change is the key to success. Certainly, process thinking is also key in manufacturing; in that environment it is much easier to develop, however, because the processes tend to be visible. Developing process thinking is a much greater challenge beyond the factory floor, and also a greater potential competitive advantage.

What Is Process Thinking?

So what exactly is process thinking, and how does one develop this mindset in an organization? Chapter 3 of Hoerl and Snee (2002) is devoted to identifying, studying, and improving processes; hence we will not repeat all of that material here. Instead, we focus on a conceptual model for studying processes and share our thoughts about developing process thinking skills. The model we refer to is the SIPOC model, which is a common model for process-improvement efforts. Figure 2.2 shows this model. It shows that all activities, including work activities, can be viewed as an example of this model. All work activities take some type of input from suppliers and transform this input into outputs, which are utilized in some way by customers. Note that *suppliers* and *customers* are general terms; they could be the person down the hall, and in some cases the supplier and customer may be the same person or organization.

People rarely struggle applying this model to manufacturing because they can physically see the process, including the inputs and outputs. In marketing, transportation, or human resources, however, it is not always obvious. Although it may not be obvious, there certainly is a process at work. For example, consider the hiring process for a research and development organization. In this case, the output is fairly obvious: new hires. Who needs these new hires? In this case, it is the managers doing the hiring, so they are the primary customer group of the hiring process, although there could be others who rely on this process as well.

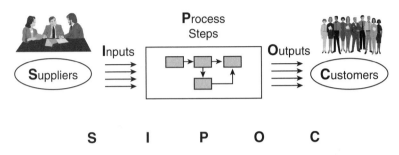

FIGURE 2.2   A series of activities that converts inputs into outputs.

What inputs or materials does the hiring process need? Certainly information is needed, such as resumés, input from previous employers and professors, responses to ads or employment Web pages, and so on. The people who supply these inputs, including candidates themselves, are the suppliers in the SIPOC model. The work you actually do on these inputs, such as conducting interviews, evaluating references, making offers, and so on, forms the process itself. Obviously, the process should transform the inputs into the desired outputs. Use of this model is particularly helpful outside manufacturing, because it enables you to put all processes on the common ground of one framework. Regardless of whether you are working on cancer-screening exams in health care, financial forecasting, or managing the supply chain, you can discuss outputs, inputs, customers, process steps, and so on. The SIPOC model enables you to take a common approach to understanding any process.

The SIPOC model also enables you to develop process-thinking skills more easily in others. This model is a very effective tool for helping people see the process at work in any situation. After people gain a little experience developing flowcharts or process maps to document their work processes, this will become second nature to them. People will begin to view any activity as a process and see the various process steps at work, even before developing a process map. You will begin to hear people say things like, "Can you describe your acquisitions process?" or "We're investigating the processes that impact cash flow" or "We're making improvements to our hiring process." These are actual statements we have overheard in the workplace after people developed process-thinking skills. When a critical mass within the organization develop these skills, virtually all the barriers to Six Sigma deployment discussed above begin to fade away on their own. This is why we feel process thinking is so critical in Six Sigma deployment in the real economy.

The Role of Leadership

As previously noted, any new initiative will face some degree of resistance, and Six Sigma is not immune to this phenomenon. This resistance may be particularly strong outside manufacturing, where employees and managers are not familiar with improvement initiatives, especially those based on statistics and quantitative methods. The previous section discussed the fact that process thinking is the critical skill that can help address the barriers to Six Sigma deployment. This is true, but of course it will not happen by itself. Strong leadership is typically required to make this happen on a broad scale. Again, leadership is key to all Six Sigma applications; because of the typical increased resistance beyond the factory floor, however, it is even more critical here.

We discussed leadership roles in Six Sigma deployment at a high level in Chapter 1, and in more detail in Snee and Hoerl (2003). We focus here on the leadership required to overcome the "we're different" mindset. We noted earlier that this mindset could be due to honest ignorance, denial, or is perhaps being used as an excuse to avoid change. Our experience is that the appropriate response from leadership depends on which of these root causes is at work. Therefore, the first, and perhaps most critical role of leadership in dealing with this resistance is to diagnose the root cause behind it. This approach requires business leaders to be actively involved in the Six Sigma deployment and know the people leading the effort well. Clearly, Six Sigma cannot be implemented by simple edict; it must be led.

If it appears that the "we're different" attitude is due to honest ignorance, the logical response is to provide appropriate education and training. This education should include healthy doses of successful case studies outside manufacturing, especially in the application areas of the organization in question, and of process thinking. Executive overviews of Six Sigma, or perhaps brief general educational sessions for employees, may suffice. Of course, this response requires involvement of people, either external Six Sigma providers or appropriate employees who have experience applying Six Sigma in these application areas and who can answer the difficult questions that will be asked. Too strong a response by leadership to honest ignorance can poison the atmosphere and lead to the impression that Six Sigma is being rammed down people's throats. Process thinking may be new for many people, and they should be given time to understand it.

If education and training have been given to clarify how Six Sigma can be deployed in these application areas through process thinking and some people are still resisting out of denial, another approach is called for. Firm, consistent messages that the organization is indeed going to deploy Six Sigma are helpful. Repetition of the message, using various media, is often needed to overcome denial. Assistance and support should be offered to those who appear to need it. This process is in some ways analogous to the grieving process, in which one of the early stages is denial. For example, upon hearing of the tragic death of a loved one, perhaps in a car accident, people often initially refuse to believe the news. Emotional support enables those grieving to eventually accept the reality of the situation.

During this time it is critical that the message is unwavering. If people in denial hear a tentative message about Six Sigma, this will only encourage their denial and resistance. In one specific case study mentioned in Snee and Hoerl (2003, 33–35), a company communicated that it was going to pilot Six Sigma in one area to see whether it worked. Further deployment was dependent on the success of this pilot. Unfortunately, this approach led to some people working hard to make the pilot successful, while others worked hard to make sure it failed. Ultimately, the pilot achieved only minimal success, and implementation stalled. Conversely, strong, clear, and unwavering messages from senior leadership facilitated acceptance of Six Sigma deployment at companies such as Bank of America and GE.

Unfortunately, in some cases people won't understand how Six Sigma can be deployed in their organization and will continue to utilize the "we're different" attitude as an excuse to avoid change. After people have been educated about this, and have received support and reinforcement that the organization is going to implement Six Sigma, it is time to move on and begin deployment. This is especially true of leaders. Leaders should openly debate whether to deploy Six Sigma; after a decision is made, however, the time for debate is over: Leaders have to lead. At GE, Jack Welch made it clear that if leaders could not support Six Sigma 100%, GE was simply not the right company for them. Several leaders at GE who could not or would not support Six Sigma moved on, one way or the other.

Although such measures may seem severe, it is critical that there not be an ongoing debate after deployment has started. We can state from our experience that any improvement initiative—TQM, Six Sigma, Lean manufacturing, and so on—that is subject to ongoing debate after deployment has started will achieve minimal success at best, and complete failure at worst. The continuing debate drains time and energy that should go into the deployment itself. We prefer a culture that encourages people to express their opinion and that allows for disagreement while an issue is being debated, and we also believe that after a decision is made everyone should be expected to fully support the decision. If leaders allow griping and whining about the decision to deploy Six Sigma to continue, it may grow and fester until it eventually sabotages the initiative. Of course, it should be fair game to continue debate as to *how* to deploy Six Sigma.

Summary

The most common reason given for not deploying Six Sigma in the real economy is the belief that "we're different" and therefore "Six Sigma doesn't apply to us." In our experience, this is the fundamental barrier beyond manufacturing. There is certainly a kernel of truth to this belief, in that collecting on overdue credit cards is certainly different from making refrigerators. However, we also point out that refining gasoline is totally different from making refrigerators. In other words, every process has some unique aspects, even in manufacturing, but these unique aspects have not prevented organizations from deploying Six Sigma.

Upon closer examination, there are certainly some consistent differences between typical manufacturing processes and real economy processes. These do require some modification in our approach to deployment, to specific projects, and to application of the methods and tools. Fortunately, however, there are also important similarities, and in our opinion these similarities more than outweigh the differences. Chief among these similarities is the fact that all work occurs through processes that can be studied and improved. Therefore, process thinking and related tools such as process maps, SIPOC analyses, and measurements are critical to overcoming such resistance. Leadership is also critically important; leaders have to ensure that after a decision to deploy Six Sigma is made, they do not allow ongoing whining and sniping to sabotage the effort. If leadership ensures that process thinking skills are developed across the organization, deployment will be significantly facilitated.

References

Arndt, M. 2002. Quality isn't just for widgets. *Business Week* (July 22).

Cohen, I. B. 1984. Florence Nightingale. *Scientific American* (March) 128–137.

Dusharme, D. 2003. Six Sigma survey. *Quality Digest* 23 2 (February) 24–32.

Hahn, G. J., N. Doganaksoy, and R. W. Hoerl. 2000. The evolution of Six Sigma. *Quality Engineering* 12 3:317–326.

Harry, M., and R. Schroeder. 2000. *Six Sigma: the breakthrough management strategy revolutionizing the world's top corporations*. New York: Currency Doubleday.

Hoerl, R. W., and R. D. Snee. 2002. *Statistical thinking: improving business performance*. Pacific Grove, CA: Duxbury Press.

Stahl, R., B. Schultz, and C. Pexton. 2003. Health care's horizon. *Six Sigma Forum Magazine* (February) 17–26.

Snee, R. D., and R. W. Hoerl. 2003. *Leading Six Sigma: a step-by-step guide based on experience with GE and other Six Sigma companies*. Upper Saddle River, NJ: FT Prentice Hall.

Velocci, A. L., Jr. 2002. Full potential of Six Sigma eludes most companies. *Aviation Week & Space Technology* (September 30) 56–60.

PART II

ENSURING SUCCESSFUL DEPLOYMENT

3

DEPLOYMENT CASE STUDIES

"Experience gives you the test before it gives you
the learning"
—Anonymous

Chapter 2 discussed how to address the fundamental barrier to deployment in the *real economy*, the attitude that "we're different," leading to the belief that "Six Sigma doesn't apply to us." In this chapter, we review some actual deployment case studies from organizations that have successfully overcome this barrier. We present deployments from several application areas, such as financial services, research and development, and health care. The health care case study is from a non-profit organization, illustrating how Six Sigma can be effective in non-profits. We focus on deployment rather than project case studies at this point because deployment success is the focus of Part II of this book, consisting of Chapters 3 and 4. In Chapter 4 we present a road map for Six Sigma deployment in the real economy, based in part on the lessons learned from these successful case studies. In Part III we then address the more detailed topic of keys to success on individual projects, and in Part IV we address common technical challenges associated with application of the methods and tools of Six Sigma beyond the factory floor.

Although it proves particularly helpful to see deployments in one's own application area, presenting a comprehensive set of all such deployments in one book is impossible. Therefore, we focus on a few application areas beyond the factory floor that we see driving the growth of Six Sigma deployment in the future, such as health care and banking services. Based on our own experience, as well as trends in current Six Sigma literature and conferences, we believe that health care and financial services are beginning to experience the explosion of implementations that occurred within manufacturing around the turn of the century. Of course, we are also starting to see growth in other application areas as well, such as supply-chain management, e-commerce, and even education and government.

After discussing two deployment case studies of businesses that do not manufacture, we present two cases from deployments in real economy organizations within companies that do manufacture products. As noted in Chapter 1, the real economy, as we use the term, includes both businesses that do not manufacture and all the processes and people in manufacturing companies that are not directly involved in the manufacturing process. This includes the finance organization, sales, marketing, human resources, and research and development. These are also growth areas for Six Sigma within manufacturing companies. For example, companies implementing in manufacturing will need to move on to design to provide true Six Sigma products, requiring the involvement of research and development. We begin with cases from banking and health care.

The Bank of America Story

Bank of America began its quality journey several years prior to its Six Sigma deployment, a journey undertaken simply because senior leaders realized that inefficient, error-prone processes were costing the company money through non–value-added rework. Unfortunately, according to quality leader Milton

Jones (Jones 2004), these efforts had minimal lasting effect because they lacked systematic implementation and often lacked executive support. This led to a perception by some in the company that quality approaches were nothing more than another "flavor of the month."

This situation changed radically when Ken Lewis became CEO in 2001. Lewis announced a major strategic shift in the company, from growth through acquisitions to organic growth. Realizing many of its customer satisfaction metrics were still at poor levels, and realizing that organic growth would require significantly enhanced customer loyalty, Lewis decided to get serious about quality improvement. In particular, he felt the need for a disciplined, rigorous, and comprehensive approach to process improvement. Based on the results he had seen others achieve, he chose Six Sigma as his approach. Then he hired Chuck Goslee as the first Bank of America quality executive, reporting to Lewis.

It is particularly noteworthy that as CEO, Lewis took on the first Green Belt project in the company, setting the expectation for others. This project involved resolution of customer complaints that had been elevated to the executive level. In a talk given at the *American Society for Quality* (ASQ) annual Six Sigma conference on February 2, 2004, Lewis described his experiences on this project:

> Some of you may wonder why the CEO would get involved in a Green Belt project. The answer is three-fold: First, I wanted to send a clear message to the entire company that Six Sigma had the support of the company's most senior leadership. Second, I wanted to have a useful command of the terms, tools, and techniques that we would be adopting throughout the company. And third, this was a problem that really needed to be solved. Let me elaborate.

> I felt it was critical to our success that everyone in the company get on board with this effort. When we began our quality journey back in 2001, there were skeptics—some of them inside the company—who wondered whether we could use disciplines, methods, and tools from the factory floor and apply them at a large financial services company.

I knew we had to get the message out, loud and clear, that we were very serious about quality and that Six Sigma would be our methodology. We hired a seasoned quality executive, Chuck Goslee, and I made him a member of my executive leadership team. That sent a message.

Then I took my Green Belt training, and I asked each executive on my leadership team to complete Green Belt training as well. That sent a message, too.

Today, I'm proud to say that every member of my leadership team has Green Belt certification, and about 95% of leaders in the next two levels have completed their Green Belts as well.

I knew that in many companies, Six Sigma professionals were frustrated with the "bottom-up" implementation of quality, and the absence of executive sponsorship. At Bank of America, our leaders have made the effort to understand the language of Six Sigma—its tools and techniques. They support its implementation across our company, and everyone in the company knows it. My other reason for wanting to look at this particular Green Belt project, as I said, was that this was a problem that simply needed to be solved. We were getting 20,000 of these complaints per year, and the actual and potential losses were in the millions of dollars.

A lot of those letters were on my desk. So I took it personally.

Other executives would do well to take customer complaints as personally as Lewis did! Lewis stated later in his talk that the ultimate result of this project, which included efforts of many others beyond his own, was a doubling of Bank of America's customer delight metric, and a financial impact of more than $2 million.

Deployment Strategy

As discussed in Chapter 2, it is often difficult to find the appropriate technical resources for *Master Black Belt* (MBB) and *Black Belt* (BB) roles when launching a deployment beyond the factory floor. Bank of America decided to address this by using internal *Green Belts* (GBs), but aggressively recruiting MBBs and BBs externally, especially from Six Sigma successes such as

Motorola and GE. In addition to providing needed technical skills right away, this also helped to "seed a culture of quality throughout the company" (Jones 2004, 15).

Another important aspect of deployment was to have all Lewis's direct reports conduct their own GB projects. This approach not only ensured that leadership was driving the initiative personally, but also that critical, strategic issues were being addressed. The list of executive projects included the following:

- Increased customer delight with problem resolution

- More precise control over payments to suppliers

- Increased productivity of new hires via training

- Elimination of significant travel expenses

- Enhancement of enterprise e-mail governance to improve productivity

- Reduction of credit-risk assessment that was considered biased

- Elimination of significant numbers of electronic information subscriptions

- Increased associate retention in key areas

- Increased collections by reducing abandoned inbound calls

- Improved ability to detect and prevent fraud at banking centers

Further, new quality executive Goslee established an enterprise-wide customer delight metric, replacing product- and channel-specific measures. Bank of America benchmarked externally to identify world-class performance in several areas, including a 90% goal for customer delight. They also obtained extensive voice-of-the-customer data to identify the key processes that needed to be improved to enhance customer delight, which included deposits and payments. Cross-functional teams began working on projects to improve these critical processes.

The results that Bank of America was achieving through Six Sigma were impressive. For example, missing items on customer statements were reduced by 70%, and through a series of focused projects, defects in electronic channels (ATMs, online banking, etc.) decreased by 88%. One project on mortgage applications reduced average cycle time by 15 days. Non-credit losses, including fraud, were driven down by 28% on a per-account basis, whereas the number of accounts increased by more than a million in 2003 alone. Same-day payments have been improved by 22%, and deposit processing has been improved by 35%. The cumulative financial benefits exceeded $2 billion by the end of 2003, and the customer delight metric had increased 25% across the company. Six Sigma was generating the same magnitude of benefits at a bank that have been seen in manufacturing organizations.

Next Steps

When Chuck Goslee retired in April 2003, Lewis asked Milton Jones to lead the Bank of America Six Sigma effort and take it to a new level. In particular, Jones was asked to focus the effort on driving revenue growth. As in other application areas, including manufacturing, initial efforts often produce more bottom-line cost savings than top-line revenue growth. In the next phase of Six Sigma, Lewis wanted to have the same impact on top-line growth. In addition, the application of Six Sigma was expanded along the entire value chain, including suppliers and the sales force. Many of the sales projects focused on new revenue generation. Lewis and Jones now require key vendors to apply Six Sigma and to partici-pate in Bank of America's training.

In his talk at the ASQ annual Six Sigma conference, Lewis noted the beneficial impact Six Sigma had on the merger with Fleet Bank and how it would continue to drive improvement in this part of the business. He stated:

> And when we agreed last Fall to our pending merger with
> FleetBoston, we did so expecting that Six Sigma would be a
> key to unlocking the full value of the merger. We plan to
> accelerate the existing Six Sigma effort underway at Fleet,
> including a training center there. We are also using Six Sigma
> in the very process of organizing the transition itself—the

first time to my knowledge Six Sigma has been used to
execute the merger of major financial institutions.

According to Jones (2004), Bank of America has trained
more than 10,000 Champions, MBBs, BBs, and GBs in DMAIC as
well as *design for Six Sigma* (DFSS), Lean, Hoshin Planning, and
other quality methods. He also pointed out that there are currently more than 100 open senior leadership positions that require BB
certification as a prerequisite. In summarizing the keys to success,
Jones stated (2004, 17): "Quality and Six Sigma have become part
of the culture at Bank of America, thanks to senior commitment, a
robust internal training program, aggressive and ongoing external
recruiting, and results that excite everyone in our company." As discussed at the end of the chapter, this statement captures the keys
to success that we have seen here and elsewhere, both in manufacturing and beyond.

Some key lessons learned from this case study are as follows:

- The critical importance of strong leadership (again!)

- The huge potential benefits available in many financial
  services

- How obtaining top technical resources externally can help
  obtain momentum early in the deployment, when such
  resources are not readily available within the organization

- The ability to drive top-line growth as well as bottom-line
  savings with Six Sigma

Commonwealth Health Corporation

Health care is another arena, like financial services and
research and development, where Six Sigma has much to offer on
a broad scale. In addition to being a significant component of the
U.S. economy, health care also impacts each of us individually, at a
personal level. Successful implementation of Six Sigma in health
care improves not only the bottom line, but our life expectancy
and quality of life as well. Fortunately, a number of health-care
providers have initiated Six Sigma deployments, producing

significant results. We briefly review the experiences of one such health-care provider, *Commonwealth Health Corporation* (CHC). This case is based on information provided by Jean Cherry, executive vice president, and Lisa Douglas, Six Sigma Champion.

Getting Started

CHC is a non-profit organization committed to meeting the health-care needs of south central Kentucky residents. It is located in Bowling Green, and is the area's leading employer, with more than 2,000 employees. CHC has 3 medical centers with about 518 beds in total, and has annual revenue of more than $350 million. Although CHC is a non-profit organization, its leaders realized that effective use of their financial resources was extremely important. This was particularly true for CHC because it spends almost double the percentage of total operating expense on indigent and free care in comparison with other hospitals, both for-profit and non-profit. In other words, CHC chooses to spend more money on providing care to those who are unable to pay for it. In addition, CHC was under increasing pressure to deal with lower reimbursement rates, mitigate the impacts of the Balanced Budget Act, and respond to increased consumer awareness and expectations.

Perhaps even more important than financial impetus, CHC leadership wanted to increase employee motivation, build more effective teamwork, and transform the organizational culture. These objectives were not necessarily related to financial benefits, but were more directed toward customer satisfaction and quality of care provided. Interestingly, CHC had experience with various quality initiatives, all of which delivered a measure of success, and some of which are still in use. None entirely fulfilled the organization's objectives for excellence, however; therefore, many at CHC still felt a need to take performance to a new level. Six Sigma would become the missing "capstone to the pyramid of quality we've built over the years," in the words of president and CEO John C. Desmarais.

Desmarais had learned about Six Sigma at a conference in late 1997 where Jack Welch, CEO of GE at the time, spoke. Desmarais had several conversations with Welch about Six Sigma and its potential applicability in health care. In March 1998, CHC signed a contract with Healthcare Solutions, a division of GE Medical Systems, to help it launch a full-scale Six Sigma initiative. Desmarais held an initial visioning session with his staff during which long-term objectives were determined, including becoming a true Six Sigma organization by the year 2004. This leadership team identified four key priorities for Six Sigma deployment:

■ Customer satisfaction

■ Quality of care/service

■ Timeliness/speed/convenience

■ Cost

Following the development of a long-term deployment plan, the initial technical training sessions began. Two unique aspects of the training GE Healthcare Solutions provided for CHC were the *Change Acceleration Process* (CAP), which is a change-management process intended to help facilitate the organizational change required for Six Sigma to be effective, and WorkOut, which is a participatory problem-solving process designed to address bureaucracy and other organizational issues (rather than technical issues). These methodologies integrated into the effort well by addressing the "soft" issues, while Six Sigma was used to address the "hard" issues.

Deployment Strategy and Initial Results

CHC leadership identified a four-phase deployment strategy for Six Sigma:

■ **Phase one**—Radiology

■ **Phase two**—Management training and projects

■ **Phase three**—Billing

■ **Phase four**—Internal capability

The radiology department became an initial point of focus for deployment, to draw on GE's expertise in diagnostic imaging and to accomplish some "quick hits" to develop momentum. Initially, 12 employees focusing on radiology took GB training, including CAP and WorkOut. At this point, GE Healthcare Solutions employees fulfilled the MBB role, providing technical support to the CHC GBs on their initial projects. The tangible results of these early projects were impressive: a 25% increase in radiology throughput using fewer resources, and a decrease in cost per procedure of more than 20%. These results were obtained by reducing waiting times for patients, providing faster turnaround for radiology reports, and increasing productivity in several areas. Table 3.1 lists some specific projects conducted in the radiology department.

TABLE 3.1   Sample Projects in Radiology

Reducing time between report dictation and report signature

Reducing patient wait time from arrival in radiology to time of exam

Reducing time between patient dismissal and dictation completion

Reducing patient wait time for radiology registration process

Enhancing radiology scheduling process

Reducing time from radiologist signature to report distribution

Increased efficiency in the MRI ordering process

Optimizing the content quality and delivery of pre-exam patient education

Reducing time for dismissal of radiology patients

Enhancing film jacket retrieval process

Decreasing MRI report turnaround time

Improving general radiology staff scheduling

Increasing efficiency of ultrasound exam scheduling and reducing overtime

Utilizing special procedures inventory more efficiently

Augmenting radiology exam scheduling and preregistration process

Reducing CT order to taken time

Decreasing IVP exam time

Improving utilization of nuclear medicine radio-pharmaceuticals

The training in phase two did not include high-level training for senior leaders; this had been done previously. Instead, phase two was an enterprise-wide intensive training initiative for 74 managers over a period of 6 months. Their 10 days of Six Sigma training, which included heavy doses of CAP, WorkOut, and team effectiveness, were immediately applied to improvement projects in such areas as the following:

- Patient registration

- Employee empowerment

- Communication flow

- Customer service

- Human resources

- Medication process

These processes tended to be under management versus worker control, and senior leadership felt that managerial action would be required to resolve issues in them. This approach had the fringe benefit of getting various layers of management actively involved in deployment, rather than passively observing from the sidelines. One result was a perceptible culture shift toward greater teamwork and visible support of Six Sigma. In terms of more tangible benefits, the medication process team project received honorable mention from Abbott Labs at the annual meeting of the American Society of Health Systems Pharmacy. Abbott rated the team's project, "Using Six Sigma Methodology to Impact Medication Errors," in the top 10 of 130 submissions and awarded CHC an institutional grant on the basis of it.

Phase three focused on the billing process. Obviously, billing in health care involves collecting large amounts of money, and small improvements in effectiveness can have huge payoffs. The first wave of GB training here, begun in November 1998, involved 15 participants from various departments, allowing the group to look at the entire billing system. To assist the GBs in their efforts and to ensure managers learned more about Six Sigma "from the trenches," senior leadership designated 16 "Shadows," who participated in the training and observed the flow of the projects first hand. This team worked together to identify potential high-impact projects for the GBs by employing such project-selection methods as these:

- Identifying key indicators for the billing process vision

- Developing high-level billing system maps

- Defining high-level CTQs (*critical to quality variables*)

The Shadows thereby helped provide direction to the GBs and pinpointed areas of greatest opportunity via the key indicators. In many companies implementing Six Sigma, project identification is the responsibility of Champions, allowing the BBs and GBs to focus on project execution. Recently, CHC has appointed formal Project Sponsors to fulfill this project Champion role, as well as an overall Champion to lead day-to-day deployment (Lisa Douglas). Sample projects included reducing the billing cycle time, improving the efficiency of charging procedures, and reducing the number of bills returned by the postal service.

The intent of phase four was to enhance CHC's internal ability to drive the initiative and deliver tangible improvements. Until this point, GE Healthcare Solutions was providing technical support via MBBs, whereas CHC resources were primarily in Shadow or GB roles. Now CHC named their first two BBs, as well as facilitators of the CAP and WorkOut processes. These internal resources further developed their abilities and experience levels, eventually taking over the "train the trainer" duties, work typically associated with MBBs. As noted below, CHC MBBs were eventually named. CHC was now becoming self-sufficient to drive improvement throughout their organization.

Awareness training was given across the board, and "lite" training was given to individuals who participated on Six Sigma project teams. The lite training consisted of 3 days of instruction and was intended to enable participants to understand Six Sigma well enough to effectively contribute to projects as a team member.

As CHC moved through these deployment phases, tangible results began to roll in. For example, within 18 months of beginning the deployment in radiology, CHC's cost per procedure went from about $68 to $50. With more than 100,000 radiological procedures a year, this amounts to about $1.68 million in savings, a benefit that will be enjoyed year after year! Targeted projects reduced the errors in the MR ordering process by 90%. In terms of intangible benefits, overall employee survey results improved by 20% within 6 months of beginning deployment. Areas of particular improvement were teamwork, patient-centered decision making, and understanding of the organization's direction. Clearly, Six Sigma was having a profound impact.

Expansion of the Effort and Current Status

Encouraged by these results, CHC leadership expanded the focus of Six Sigma deployment to additional functional areas, such as admissions and documentation, as well as to clinical service areas, such as maternity care. Table 3.2 shows sample projects in these additional application areas. As Figure 3.1 shows, the financial benefits from Six Sigma deployment grew as the deployment expanded. These impressive results led to publications in industry journals such as *Diagnostic Imaging* and *Radiology Management* and to visits from other health-care providers, including some from Asia, to benchmark CHC. In addition, CHC has been invited to give talks to share their success story at health-care conferences around the world.

TABLE 3.2   Sample Projects in Expanded Application Areas

Functional Service Areas

Admissions

- Patient identification bands
- ER admissions process

Documentation/charge entry (billing)

- Pyxis projects (Pyxis machines automatically dispense medication.)
- Charge capture in outpatient (accurate billing amounts)

Human resources employment processes

- Hiring process
- Employee evaluations
- TB skin tests

continues

TABLE 3.2   Sample Projects in Expanded Application Areas (*continued*)

Clinical Service Lines

Pulmonary-related illnesses

- Length of stay for congestive heart failure
- Pulmonary-function tests
- Pneumonia patients switched from IV to oral medication

Maternal care

- Decision to incision time for emergency C-sections
- Urine screen vs. urinalysis testing for moms

Surgery processes

- Surgery scheduling process
- Time from holding to inpatient & outpatient surgery
- Operating room suites turnaround time
- Surgery staffing patterns

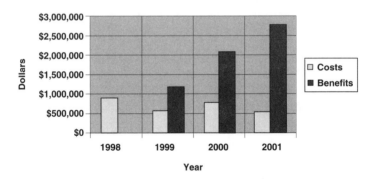

FIGURE 3.1   CHC's benefits from Six Sigma.

As with anything new, there was some initial resistance to Six Sigma in the organization. Some may have had a perception that Six Sigma would be a short-lived "flavor of the month." Others may have been suspicious that Six Sigma was just a well-camouflaged scheme to reduce the workforce. Another group may have been concerned about loss of influence when data-based decisions replaced functional decisions. The CAP tools proved particularly helpful in addressing resistance because they provide tools designed for human rather than technical issues. CEO Desmarais's unwavering leadership was also critical. In his own words, "Frankly, Six Sigma was made non-negotiable." As people began to see the positive benefits of data-based decision making, such as quicker, less-bureaucratic decisions, the resistance gradually turned to support. Belief in data-based decision making also helped pave the way for acceptance of statistical methods.

Organizationally, CHC has named a full-time Six Sigma Champion (overall leader), a logistics coordinator for all Six Sigma training, and has designated MBBs. The logistics coordinator position was a temporary position needed to help the organization get over the training "hump" when ramping up Six Sigma. The MBBs have taken over the responsibility for all Six Sigma training and have developed their own materials. One particularly noteworthy addition they created is a computer simulation of the patient registration process. This simulation enables students to immediately apply what they are learning to a relevant process. The simulation is structured so that students can walk through each phase of a Six Sigma project on it, enabling them to better understand project flow and how the output of one tool forms the input to the next.

Figure 3.2 illustrates the current organizational structure for Six Sigma at CHC. Reporting to the CEO are three *executive vice presidents* (EVPs), each responsible for a key aspect of Six Sigma results. Improvement in these three areas—customer satisfaction, cycle time, and cost effectiveness—is the focus of Six Sigma efforts at CHC. Each of these areas is rigorously tracked via quantitative metrics. Jean Cherry is the EVP responsible for customer satisfaction and has overall accountability for the Six Sigma initiative. Lisa Douglas, the Six Sigma Champion, reports to Jean Cherry and leads the day-to-day deployment of Six Sigma at CHC.

CHC began referring to their GBs as "Brown Belts," due to their BB-level training, but part-time duties. These Brown Belts execute targeted projects to drive improvements in each of the three areas of strategic focus. The Brown Belts are supported by Project Sponsors (Champions), MBBs, and Change Agents, who are specialists in the CAP and WorkOut methodologies. The Six Sigma

Champion oversees this entire structure. Note that this figure should be read from a process rather than hierarchy point of view. It is focused on the flow of improvement work, not on the power structure.

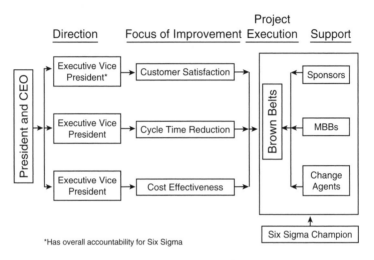

FIGURE 3.2 CHC Six Sigma organizational structure.

Some key lessons learned from CHC's experiences, relative to succeeding with Six Sigma, are as follows:

■ Commitment from the top is critical.

■ Identify and address pockets of resistance.

■ Ensure that top-talent employees are selected for Six Sigma roles.

■ Focus on project selection and make sure projects are tied to strategic goals.

■ Emphasize the need for tangible financial results, and validate them.

■ View Six Sigma from a holistic perspective, as a culture change versus a quality methodology.

CEO Desmarais summed up CHC's Six Sigma experiences by stating, "I only wish we had done this five years earlier... the competitive edge the organization has gained through this process is incredible." It is interesting to note that CHC's vision statement specifically states that it wishes to have a major influence in reshaping health care. Based on its pioneering work applying Six Sigma holistically, and freely sharing its experiences with others, it appears to be accomplishing this objective.

We now present two case studies from organizations within manufacturing companies: finance first, and then research and development.

Motorola Finance

It is well known that Six Sigma originated at Motorola in the 1980s. It is perhaps less well known that Motorola deployed Six Sigma in its corporate finance organization, not just in its manufacturing operations. According to Stoner and Werner (1994), this deployment was not easy. Initially, many in finance thought that Six Sigma was a "production technology" and not relevant to them. Sound familiar? There was widespread skepticism as to whether the decision to deploy in finance made sense. Fortunately, however, senior management provided the leadership required, ensuring deployment continued. Motorola developed a six-step action plan, called the Six Steps to Six Sigma, for non-manufacturing organizations, and this was utilized by finance:

1. Define the major functions or services performed by a unit of the company.

2. Determine the internal customers and suppliers of these services.

3. Identify the customer's requirements, along with quantitative measures to assess customer satisfactions in meeting such requirements.

4. Identify the requirements and measurement criteria that the supplier to the process must meet.

5. Flowchart or map the process at the macro (interdepartmental) level and at the micro (intradepartmental) level.

6. Continuously improve the process with respect to effectiveness, quality, cycle time, and cost.

It is interesting to note the degree to which process thinking underlies the steps in this action plan! Motorola had the advantage of having utilized *total quality management* (TQM) previously, which makes heavy use of process thinking.

Deployment Within the Audit Staff

To implement this six-step action plan within the audit staff, part of corporate finance, a task force of two audit managers and four new auditors (less than 24 months experience within the audit staff) was formed. Senior management pulled this task force off their schedule for 2 weeks, and sequestered them in a conference room. These leaders challenged the task force to come up with a plan to implement Six Sigma quality improvement within the audit staff, including a measurement system for implementation. The direction emphasized that the task force could not conclude that Six Sigma couldn't be done, nor could it suggest something bureaucratic that would "drag us to our knees." Further, the task force was to develop a written report of recommendations and be prepared to train other members of the department in whatever new processes and systems they chose to recommend.

Interestingly, senior manager of internal audit Larry Grow gave them the following advice (Stoner and Werner 1994 p. 162):

> My view of administrative processes is that they are all really
> factories. Whether you are in a banking institution clearing
> checks or whether you are a secretary worrying about your
> own in-box and out-box, you can view your operation as a fac-
> tory. The secretary gets things from a supplier, does something
> with it, and then ships the goods out to a customer. What she
> is doing is running her own little factory. I urged them to
> think horizontally not vertically.

We find it noteworthy that audit staff leadership was crystal clear on their direction concerning Six Sigma and stressed the importance of process thinking.

In two weeks the task force reported its recommendations. It defined the audit staff's customers and "products," defined the audit process, defined what a defective product was, developed hard metrics on audit quality, and produced a series of recommendations to enable the audit staff to implement a Six Sigma quality initiative. Their depiction of the audit process, with its five major steps, and substeps listed for each of these major steps, is shown in Figure 3.3. This type of process map is called a top-down flowchart (Hoerl and Snee 2002, 197). One of the most important learnings from rethinking the audit process was the gradual realization that the audit report generated for each audit was not the most important product of the audit process. In reality, evaluating and promoting an internal control environment was their most important product; the audit report was "simply the box they ship it in."

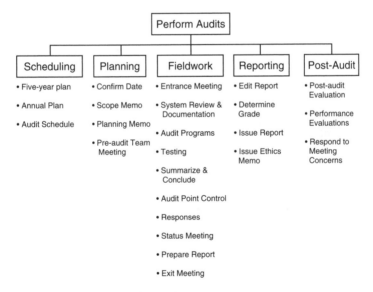

FIGURE3.3   Motorola's audit process.
Adapted from Stoner and Werner 1994.

The task team mapped the audit process into five macro steps: scheduling, planning, fieldwork, reporting, and post-audit. Further, they brainstormed specific areas where errors were likely to occur, identifying 56 such areas. They grouped these 56 areas into 4 major categories: administrative errors, technical errors, work-paper documentation errors, and personnel-related errors. The team developed two questionnaires to measure audit quality: one to be filled out by an audit department peer as an independent professional evaluation, and one to be filled out by the customer who was being audited. Numerous individual improvement projects emanated from the task force's written report.

After a few years of Six Sigma deployment, errors in performing audits dropped from almost 10,000 errors per million opportunities in 1988, to about 20 errors per million opportunities in 1991. The cycle time for completing and issuing the final audit report dropped from 51 days after completion of fieldwork to 5 days. Much of this improvement came not from better report writing, but from improvements to earlier steps in the audit process that greatly simplified final report writing. "Defects" reported by customers on the post-audit questionnaires dropped by a factor of 94.

Improvements in the internal audit also carried over to the independent external audit performed by the accounting firm KPMG Peat Marwick. In 1983, Motorola's revenues were about $4.8 billion, and the external domestic audit took about 24,000 person-hours. In 1991, the company's revenues had grown to $11.3 billion, but the external domestic audit only took 12,000 person-hours. This improvement produced a savings of $1.8 million dollars in avoidance of additional audit fees.

Broader Deployment Within Finance

Cycle time reduction in closing the books was one of the initial improvement projects in finance. Initially, it took approximately 9 days to close the books, resulting in an updated financial forecast coming out 11 or 12 working days into the new month, and an operating committee meeting to review the last month's results and the current month's plan on the 18th or 19th working day. The month was almost over by the time leadership was beginning to plan for it! An ambitious goal was set: closing the books within 4 days by 1990, and 2 days by the end of 1992.

Stoner and Werner (1994) quote assistant chief financial officer David Hickie's explanation for such an ambitious goal:

> If you tell people to close the books in seven days instead of eight, they will figure out how to do it very easily. They will work a little overtime over the weekend. If you say do it in six days, they will work on Sunday. But they would not change what they were doing. When we told them to do it in four days and that we would not let them use the weekend as a crutch, they had to look at a fundamental change in the process.

Six Sigma methods led Motorola to a key root cause of cycle time in closing the books: journal-entry errors, resulting in manual account reconciliation—that is, manually tracking down the reasons why the numbers didn't "add up." Previously, Motorola's journal-entry accuracy rate of more than 98.6% was considered enviable. However, upon further examination via Six Sigma, people realized that with 600,000 entries per month, this accuracy rate would produce more than 8,000 errors each month, errors that would later have to be identified and corrected to close the books.

A second cause was also identified: the number of signoffs required as data originating overseas was reported up through local organizations into U.S. headquarters. Data went from international factories to local headquarters for approval, then to U.S. international headquarters, then to U.S. sector headquarters, and finally to corporate offices. At each step, the information was held up for approval prior to being sent on. Interestingly, investigation discovered that it was extremely rare for any changes to be made prior to approval.

The net result of Motorola's improvement projects was that monthly closing time went from averaging 9 days to just 2 days, with much less variation, as of July 1992. This was about 6 months ahead of plan for this critical goal. Motorola had documented annual savings of $20 million from reducing closing time from 9 to 4 days, and when it was reduced to 2 days Motorola anticipated saving an additional $10 million per year.

To drive Six Sigma quality improvement throughout finance, Motorola created three quality councils to provide infrastructure to lead and manage the effort:

- **The Financial Metrics Council**—To evaluate new and evolving financial metrics for potential adoption by Motorola

- **The Internal Controls Council**—To evaluate and improve the internal financial control systems within the company

- **The Accounting Policy Council**—To ensure worldwide consistency in accounting policy and practices

This type of supporting infrastructure enabled Motorola to extend the Six Sigma benefits from initial application areas, such as the closing process, to many other financial areas. For example, improvements to the expense account processing system, which allowed rapid checking for errors in expense accounts and automatically converted foreign currency into local currency, cut a reimbursement check in only 4 hours, long before the employee's credit card statement arrived. Significant improvements were made in accounts receivable, allowing faster collection and realization of revenue.

David Hickie, assistant chief financial officer, stated of these improvements (Stoner and Werner 1994, 171):

> Our receivables are interesting. For years we always said
> as our international business goes up, our total receivables
> should keep increasing in terms of weeks of receivables. But
> they have not because the quality improvements in the order
> entry system and the billing system make it easier for the
> customers to pay us—so they pay us. When we quote 30 days
> and they pay us in 6 weeks it is because of their saying things
> like "We don't know who to call" and "I don't agree with the
> bill."

In summary, beyond all the tangible and bottom-line results noted above, which of course are only a small sampling of all that was accomplished through Six Sigma, *Financial World* named Motorola's accounting department as the U.S. benchmark in 1991, providing external corroboration of what was being experienced internally. Interestingly, many of Motorola's experiences applying Six Sigma to their corporate audit staff parallel those of GE's corporate audit staff as it implemented Six Sigma in a big way beginning in the late 1990s (Snee and Hoerl 2003, 25–27).

Some key lessons learned from this case study are as follows:

- As previously noted, strong leadership is critical to overcoming resistance and the "we're different" syndrome.

- Process thinking is fundamental to holistic deployment of Six Sigma (that is, what Larry Grow called horizontal versus vertical thinking).

- Beyond manufacturing, "products" exist, but are less obvious. Formally asking the question "What outputs do we produce?" can actually help answer this important question.

- Creating an integrated set of councils to lead and manage implementation helped drive the initiative broadly.

GE Research and Development

Just as many in financial organizations think that they are different and that Six Sigma doesn't apply to them, many in technology organizations, especially those in *research and development* (R&D), feel the same way. These detractors point out that R&D organizations don't "produce" things the way manufacturing does, but they certainly have important outputs and deliverables. Other detractors fear that the rigor and discipline of Six Sigma will stifle the creativity required for innovation. Fortunately, although Six Sigma is certainly disciplined, there are key phases in the process where creativity is not only permissible, but also absolutely mandatory. GE had to address these and other concerns in the late 1990s as it was deploying Six Sigma across the company. The following case study is based on Roger Hoerl's experiences at GE Corporate Research and Development (now known as the Global Research Center), beginning with GE's decision to pursue Six Sigma in late 1995.

Corporate Research Gets Into the Act

As discussed in Chapter 2 of Snee and Hoerl (2003), Jack Welch announced GE's decision to dive into Six Sigma in the fourth quarter of 1995. Senior leadership asked all salaried employees to view a short videotape Jack made to explain this decision internally, and the research center was no exception. After we watched the video, there was considerable discussion and debate as to how this would affect us. As might be expected, a number of scientists saw no role for us to play, because the research center wasn't a factory. Others understood that we made significant earnings from services businesses and were concerned that making better products and services might hurt rather than help the company, because there would be fewer defective products on which to sell parts and service. Yes, they actually said this!

Global Research joined the Six Sigma initiative by sending three people to the first MBB training session within GE. Much of the initial effort of MBBs focused on serving as technical resources to "mission-critical" projects within the GE businesses. Other efforts included thinking about applying Six Sigma to the design process, so that new products would be Six Sigma from initial product launch and not require a series of improvement projects to get them there. At this time there was still no still clear vision for Six Sigma in R&D or a dedicated organizational structure to develop and implement such a vision.

A Strategy Takes Form

Toward the end of 1996, this situation changed dramatically when a dedicated Quality Leader was named at the research center. This person was a seasoned and respected engineering department manager, at what most organizations would consider a "director"-level position. He also created a dedicated quality organization of six people, who came from a variety of disciplines and backgrounds at the research center. It is important to note that each of these members brought a distinguished technical track record and a strong interest in Six Sigma. A budget was also created to support the team's initiatives. Senior leadership was clearly supporting the effort.

The initial focus areas for the quality organization were as follows:

- Developing a unique GE approach to applying Six Sigma to design (that is, DFSS)

- Developing a Six Sigma training curriculum tailored for the research center and delivering the training

- Conducting improvement projects on internal research center processes, such as the patent application process and recruiting

- Providing technical support for mission-critical projects within the GE businesses

- Understanding how Six Sigma could be applied in non-manufacturing processes, such as in finance or marketing

The focus on DFSS became the most significant of these focus areas, and is discussed in greater detail below. Development of a training curriculum was a challenge because of the uniqueness of the research center audience. More than 50% of the scientists had Ph.D.s, and many had already studied statistics. The problem was not in conveying statistical concepts and methods, as it often is, but rather how to position Six Sigma in the context of what a scientist actually does. In addition, looking at Six Sigma from a scientific context, people tended to see only the technical aspects, such as the engineering and statistical tools, and overlooked the leadership and customer-centric aspects. In addition, a Six Sigma course was developed for hourly employees at the research center, such as electricians, pipe fitters, and other crafts. Six Sigma training could not be forced on these employees, but many took the course and conducted projects voluntarily.

We found many internal processes at the research center in need of improvement, which turned out to be ripe projects for Six Sigma. These included our patent application process—critical for any research organization, recruiting processes, and even the process for moving scientists from one office to another. On the patent application project, there was considerable frustration among scientists, administrators, and patent attorneys because the process seemed to take so long and because we often ended up submitting incomplete patents to meet legal deadlines. These incomplete patents not only caused financial penalties, they also led to a great deal of "rework" (when we had to go back and complete them at some point in the future).

One GB project in this area was able to identify critical bottlenecks in the process, such as a reward system that encouraged incomplete submissions, and reduced the percent of incomplete submissions by 60%. This percentage could have been higher, but the project revealed that there were occasionally legitimate reasons to submit incomplete applications, such as international patents where laws typically favor "first to file" versus "first to invent."

Relative to the focus area on non-manufacturing, it should be kept in mind that in 1996 there were very few published Six Sigma case studies outside manufacturing, and many people viewed Six Sigma as a purely manufacturing initiative. GE, on the other hand, made roughly 40% of its profits from financial services businesses, not to mention NBC and the service activities within the engineering businesses, such as GE Aircraft Engines, GE Power Systems, and so on. Successful application of Six Sigma beyond manufacturing was clearly critical to success of the overall initiative. Because of its technical expertise, the research center was a logical organization to focus on this problem, to augment the efforts of the financial and services businesses themselves.

Design for Six Sigma

As noted above, DFSS became the number one priority of the quality organization at the research center. This made perfect sense given that we devoted such a large percentage of our efforts not to production of current products, but rather to design and development of future products. Unfortunately, at that time we were unable to find any commercially available approaches to DFSS that we thought were complete and holistic—that is, that offered a step-by-step process to go all the way from customer needs to the start-up of a Six Sigma product and process design. Therefore, we ended up developing our own approach. This approach borrowed considerably from the *define, measure, analyze, improve, control* (DMAIC) process used to improve existing processes; as well as from traditional engineering design processes; and from methodologies we obtained externally.

One such external methodology was a well-developed process for a critical aspect of DFSS. This involved taking requirements for system-level performance and determining what requirements lower-level components in the system would need to satisfy to meet the higher-level requirements, a process known as CTQ flow down. Similar approaches have been applied with Quality Function Deployment, and other design engineering methods. As an example of this particular approach, you might want to minimize vibration in a motor below a certain threshold to satisfy customer expectations. In CTQ flow down, you would determine the components of the motor that significantly impact vibration, such as a measure of structural integrity of the motor, size and uniformity of the gap between the rotor and stator (the rotor is the part that rotates, and the stator is the stationary part that the rotor rotates within), and so on. You would determine the critical specifications that these metrics would need to satisfy in order to meet the vibration specification.

Then you would determine the key variables that impact structural integrity, size and uniformity of the rotor-stator gap, and so on. For example, rotor roundness might have a significant impact on uniformity of the rotor-stator gap. The next issue to determine would be what requirements the rotor roundness would need to meet for the gap uniformity requirement in order to satisfy the vibration specification. Depending on the complexity of the design, you might need to continue flowing down requirements to lower and lower levels of detail.

Eventually, you will get down to basic measurements, such as steel hardness. An important point to note is that there is a clear "line of sight" from each lower-level requirement to the ultimate customer specification. In other words, it is clear why you need to satisfy each requirement and how it relates to product performance. Figure 3.4 illustrates the concept of CTQ flow down using a simpler example: cycle time to complete an audit, using the audit process depicted in Figure 3.3. All numbers shown in this example are hypothetical, but illustrate the concept.

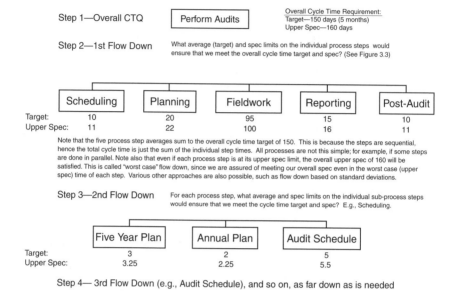

FIGURE 3.4   CTQ flow down for audit process cycle time.

If the mathematical relationship between the higher-level requirements and the lower-level requirements (that is, the transfer function) is complex, this task is not necessarily clear and straightforward and requires an understanding of transmission of variation. GE obtained a specific methodology for CTQ flow down from independent consultant Maurice Berryman, who had experience with DFSS at Texas Instruments and several other companies. To verify the manufacturing capability to achieve the lower-level requirements, organizations could evaluate historic data from manufacturing and "flow up" actual capability. That is, they need to use the transfer function to predict how well they will be able to meet higher-level requirements, based on the data for lower-level requirements.

This results in a two-step process of flowing down requirements—that is, what is needed; and then flowing up capability, or what is possible. As might be expected, this often results in several iterations going back and forth between flow down and flow up until a desirable compromise is reached that both satisfies customer needs and can be manufactured. By integrating this CTQ flow-down and flow-up methodology, along with accompanying design scorecards that predicted final system performance, with the tools and methodologies we already had, we developed a framework for DFSS, analogous to the DMAIC framework for improving existing processes.

At about the same time, resources from the GE financial services businesses (known as GE Capital at the time) were working on a DFSS approach for financial services processes. This group originally developed the acronym DMADV, which stands for *define, measure, analyze, design, verify.* The two groups worked together to ensure an equivalent approach, although the financial services businesses maintained a separate version of the DMADV training course tailored to financial services. Figure 3.5 depicts the key elements of DMADV, which apply both to the engineering and financial services approaches. GE leadership standardized this approach across GE. More recently, several other companies are now using the DMADV approach or similar processes based on it.

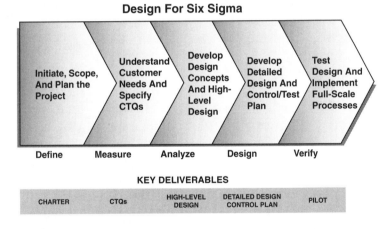

FIGURE 3.5   The DMADV methodology.

The LightSpeed CT scanner from GE Medical Systems was one of the first GE products developed using DFSS to hit the market. It has been an unqualified success. By utilizing a multislice CT approach, it reduced the time required for full-body scans from 3 minutes to less than 30 seconds. Not only was this a major enhancement for patients, who no longer had to sit perfectly still for 3 minutes, it also dramatically increased the throughput of people through the scanner for hospitals, which provided a significant reduction in their cost per scan. The image resolution was also unparalleled relative to competitive products. Not surprisingly, GE Medical Systems sold orders worth more than $60 million in the first 90 days that this scanner was available.

Some Unique Challenges

As noted previously, the engineering curricula itself was a challenge, in that most scientists had already learned basic statistics and the DFSS projects often required more advanced tools than those traditionally taught in Six Sigma. A very unique curriculum was needed, and this is what we developed. It included an introduction to Six Sigma concepts and the DMAIC methodology (Tier 1). Then it augmented DMAIC with instruction on our approach to DFSS (Tier 2). The curriculum also included more advanced courses that were not needed by everyone, but which were needed on specific projects (Tier 3). These were taught on an "as-needed" basis and included specialized topics such as mixture experimentation, reliability tools, and three-dimensional tolerancing. This curriculum has been constantly evolving since its inception.

Another major challenge has been the difficulty in documenting hard benefits from DFSS projects. If a manufacturing plant is producing 20% waste, and a DMAIC project reduces this to 2%, it is relatively straightforward to document and justify the financial benefits from the project. Suppose, however, that the production process is initially designed via DFSS so that it starts up producing .1% waste. What is the savings from this DFSS project? Because there is no history to directly compare the .1% to, it is impossible to come up with an exact savings figure. This issue made it virtually impossible to justify DFSS projects on a purely financial basis. After much discussion and debate, it was finally decided to not claim any hard financial benefits from such projects. There could be cost avoidance or other "soft" savings, but GE has standardized on hard savings for official reporting. This is one reason why we believe that the official Six Sigma savings numbers published by GE are perhaps understated.

Some key lessons learned from GE's implementation of Six Sigma in research and development are as follows:

- DFSS is particularly relevant in R&D because there is such a strong emphasis on new product development.

- An integrated approach including both DMAIC and DMADV projects will help maximize the benefits of Six Sigma deployments.

- Significant progress did not occur until management dedicated resources, provided a budget, and so forth (for instance, until they introduced supporting infrastructure).

- As in the Motorola case, initially there was a challenge identifying "products" and processes in R&D.

Key Deployment Lessons Learned

Although each of these case studies is in a unique application area, and faced unique challenges, some important commonalities help explain the success achieved. Interestingly, these commonalities are very similar to the key deployment lessons learned from manufacturing companies (Snee and Hoerl 2003). This reinforces our belief that although modifications are necessary to tailor Six Sigma deployments in different environments, the fundamentals and critical success factors stay the same. We briefly highlight these important lessons learned here, and then in Chapter 4 discuss a deployment strategy based on these success criteria (but also tailored to real economy deployments).

The critical success factors are as follows:

- Committed leadership

- Top talent

- Supportive infrastructure

Beyond the factory floor, we add widespread process thinking, including the ability to identify "products" from real economy processes, as a key success factor. Recall that we discussed in

Chapter 2 process thinking as a key to overcoming the "we're different" attitude; therefore, we do not repeat that discussion here.

By committed leadership, we do not mean leaders who provide passive support, such as encouraging speeches at kick-off meetings. Many improvement efforts that had supportive leaders have failed. Rather, we mean leaders who devote their personal time to ensure success of the effort. It really must become a personal obsession with them. This is particularly true in non-standard application areas, such as those discussed in this chapter, because there will be additional resistance. Note that in the four case studies in this chapter, there was initially strong resistance to Six Sigma, on the basis of the belief that "we're different; Six Sigma doesn't apply to us." Only personally committed leaders would have been able to overcome such resistance, and drive the organization to successfully deploy Six Sigma in these areas. John Desmarais has certainly supplied such committed leadership at CHC, and Ken Lewis appears to have used a similar leadership style to GE's Jack Welch in deploying Six Sigma at Bank of America.

Top talent is important to the success of Six Sigma, as with any human endeavor. However, it is even more critical in a major change initiative, for several reasons. In addition to the obvious fact that top talent will be able to deliver the best results, it is also true that many people, especially those "sitting on the fence" relative to Six Sigma, will judge the effort by those with leading roles. If those taking Champion, MBB, and BB roles are viewed by the organization as top talent, others will conclude that the effort is serious and will want to be involved, to be associated with the top talent. On the other hand, if those leading the effort are not viewed as top talent, the effort will be viewed as a losing cause, and others will not want to be involved.

Another important reason for involving top talent is that these people will become the future leaders of the organization. If these men and women have experienced Six Sigma first hand and seen the results it can deliver, they will ensure that it becomes a lasting part of the culture. In essence, they will take the Six Sigma mindset into the boardroom. In the case of Motorola Finance, the auditors involved were generally experienced auditors who had come from the "Big Six" accounting firms—respected and talented individuals (Stoner and Werner 1994, 159). In the case of GE Global Research, it was critically important that the Quality Leader selected was already a respected technical manager and that those selected for his staff had distinguished technical careers. This gave the effort credibility.

Milton Jones mentioned the need for top talent indirectly when he noted that Bank of America made a conscious decision to bring in external technical resources for MBB and BB roles initially, because such top technical resources were not originally available internally (although they are now).

Supportive infrastructure is critical to maintain momentum over time, by providing the Six Sigma effort with needed resources and attention. The infrastructure elements that we refer to are such things as these:

- A formal organizational structure

- Planning systems to develop budgets, human resources plans, key focus areas, and so on

- Project selection and review systems

- Training systems

These are simply the standard infrastructure elements that support business units, but are often overlooked in improvement efforts. Without such supporting infrastructure, however, each dollar spent on the effort must be justified, each personnel decision becomes a battle, and each project must be fought for individually. The time and energy required to obtain this support on a project-by-project basis becomes overwhelming, so that little time and energy is left to actually make improvements. This has been one of the key differentiating factors between successful and unsuccessful deployments of Six Sigma, and real economy deployments are no exception.

Recall that GE Global Research set up a dedicated organizational structure. This quality group had a budget and formal HR support, and soon developed planning and training systems to deploy Six Sigma across Global Research. This deployment would have been virtually impossible to accomplish without a formal organizational structure or these managerial systems. Similarly,

Motorola Finance freed up four auditors and two managers from their regular work to develop their Six Sigma strategy. They then set up three quality councils to provide needed infrastructure to three key areas of deployment: financial metrics, internal controls, and accounting policy. CHC modified its organizational structure to better support Six Sigma and named an overall Champion as well as a logistics leader. Milton Jones specifically mentioned the importance of a tailored training system in Bank of America's success.

Summary

We have seen that Six Sigma can be, and in fact has been, very successful beyond a manufacturing environment. This is true even for non-profit organizations, such as CHC. In each of the cases discussed in this chapter, unique situations and circumstances needed to be addressed in a thoughtful manner. In other words, the unique environments of finance, research and development, and health care needed to be taken into account in the deployment strategy. Just trying to follow a "cookie cutter" approach that worked in manufacturing is likely to be minimally successful in these environments.

Fortunately, we do find that the same key factors that lead to success in manufacturing also lead to success in real economy deployments. Regardless of application area, strong leadership commitment and involvement, utilization of the top talent in the organization, and implementation of supporting infrastructure— for example, to aid selection of appropriate projects—are critical. The presence or absence of these success factors essentially determines how much impact Six Sigma will have. This is reassuring, in that many organizations have learned, and some have documented, how to do each of these well. Therefore, those implementing Six Sigma in the real economy can take existing best practices and adapt them to their own unique environments. The next chapter provides more specifics on how to do this.

References

Hoerl, R. W., and R. D. Snee. 2002. *Statistical thinking: improving business performance*. Pacific Grove, CA: Duxbury Press.

Jones, M. H. 2004. Six Sigma… at a bank? *Six Sigma Forum Magazine* (February) 13–17.

Snee, R. D., and R. W. Hoerl. 2003. *Leading Six Sigma: a step-by-step guide based on experience with GE and other Six Sigma companies*. Upper Saddle River, NJ: FT Prentice Hall.

Stoner, J. F., and F. M. Werner. 1994. *Managing finance for quality*. Milwaukee: Quality Press.

4

A PROVEN DEPLOYMENT ROAD MAP

"Six Sigma works if you follow the process. If Six Sigma is not working you're not following the process."
—Allied-Signal Manager

In the first three chapters of this book you learned about the emergence of the *real economy* and the need to take an integrated view of improvement to keep an organization viable and growing. We then introduced you to the Six Sigma approach to improvement—what Six Sigma is, the benefits, and some insight as to how to deploy it beyond the factory floor. You also gained some insight as to how Six Sigma was different from previous approaches and how to overcome resistance. The central role of process thinking and the need for committed and involved leadership to initiate and sustain improvement were also discussed.

This was followed by some deployment case studies in different areas of the real economy, including finance, health care, and research and development. A key conclusion was that, with respect to improvement, the real economy businesses are similar to manufacturing in many more ways than they are different. Now that you understand the need for improvement, and have some understanding of the Six Sigma approach, you are likely ready to think about how you would deploy Six Sigma in the real economy and what a deployment road map might look like. This is the subject of this chapter.

We begin by elaborating on the keys to successful deployment identified at the end of Chapter 3, based on the presented case studies. Then we provide a proven deployment road map based on these success factors. We identified these keys to success and this road map in Snee and Hoerl (2003), hence here we will only summarize key points and highlight unique concerns for real economy deployments. We then provide some insights we have learned about deploying Six Sigma in specific environments, such as finance and e-commerce. This chapter concludes by identifying some important pitfalls that should be avoided to prevent derailment of the initiative and offering a suggestion to help launch Six Sigma successfully.

Keys to Success

In our studies of Six Sigma deployment beyond the factory floor in Chapter 3 we identified three major keys to successful deployment:

- Committed and involved leadership
- Top talent
- Supporting infrastructure

Our conclusions are corroborated by many other companies' experiences, not to mention current research in organizational change. See, for example, Harry and Schroeder (2000) and Weisbord (1989).

Committed and Involved Leadership

By committed and involved leadership, we mean leaders who are involved in the deployment of Six Sigma and have the conviction to make a difficult decision and then personally lead the organization in the chosen direction without wavering. Such commitment goes well beyond "being supportive" or "in favor" of Six Sigma. History provides many examples of committed leadership. For example, historians tell us that when Hernan Cortez landed in Mexico in 1519 to begin the Spanish conquest of the Aztecs, there was considerable dissention in the Spanish ranks as to whether it was possible for 500 soldiers to defeat the entire Aztec empire.

Most soldiers, and even Cortez's senior officers, felt that the more prudent course of action would be to sail back to Cuba to obtain additional troops. Cortez's solution to this dilemma was not to hold a prolonged debate, but rather to burn and sink his own ships! With the Spanish ships destroyed, there was no choice but to go forward toward the Aztec empire; there would be no more debate or indecision.

Although we do not find Cortez's mission of conquest and destruction praiseworthy, he did provide a classic example of leadership commitment. In his mind, there was no alternative to conquest and no thought of ever turning back. Senior leaders should realize that this is the level of commitment required to make Six Sigma successful.

Table 4.1 provides a checklist for measuring leadership commitment. As discussed, if there is not a clear "burn-the-ships" commitment for Six Sigma, the effort will gradually be sabotaged until it loses all momentum, especially in real economy deployments. If the financial and human resources are not provided, it will never get off the ground. Similarly, lack of a strategic deployment plan is an indication that senior leadership does not view Six Sigma as being strategically important.

TABLE 4.1   Key Aspects of Committed Leadership

- Clear, unwavering direction on deploying Six Sigma
- Commitment of required resources, including personnel
- Development of a strategy for deployment (that is, a "game plan," including tangible goals and objectives)
- Frequent and clear communications to the organization
- Personal involvement
- Willingness to revise company policies and procedures to be supportive (for example, management bonus plans)
- Reward, recognition, and celebration of successes
- Insistence on tangible results

At a high level, leaders of Six Sigma have to do four things well:

1. Provide direction by creating strategy and goals for the organization.

2. Communicate clearly, concisely, and consistently why Six Sigma is needed, what its benefits are, and the progress that has been made.

3. Enable the organization by providing the needed resources, training, coaching, and counseling.

4. Provide the recognition, reward, and celebration needed to recognize and reinforce the desired behavior.

Further details on these leadership needs are explained later in this chapter in Table 4.6 and its associated discussion.

Reviewing these leadership responsibilities makes it clear that much personal time and involvement is required of the leader. The issue of personal involvement is a critical one. Many feel that dollars measure senior leadership's commitment—that is, the more funding they provide, the more committed they are. Although there is some truth to this, we have found that personal time is an even better barometer of leadership commitment. Leaders can always get more money, but their time is the most precious commodity that they have. Even CEOs only have 24 hours in a day; they can't get any more time than that. Given the many demands on their time, they are forced to prioritize, and only the most critical issues receive their commitment. Six Sigma either makes the grade or it doesn't.

Most companies have found that some systems and policies need to be revised to be consistent with the direction on Six Sigma. One obvious example is GE revising its reward and recognition system so that management bonuses would be heavily weighted by Six Sigma results. Other examples include allowing additional headcount to backfill for *Black Belts* (BBs) and *Master Black Belts* (MBBs), rethinking career progression paths, incorporating Six Sigma as a criterion in performance evaluations at all levels, and adding Six Sigma as a line item in budgets. This last point also relates to the last bullet in Table 4.1.

Just as financial resources need to be provided to properly implement Six Sigma, financial benefits also need to be expected as a return. Having financial savings from the Six Sigma effort as a line item in the budget sets clear direction that to whom much is given, much is expected. Conversely, if leadership does not demand financial benefits, the organization will quickly see that this is an optional initiative. Why worry about Six Sigma if there are other things that you might actually get fired for not delivering?

Top Talent

There are three major reasons why top talent is so important to the Six Sigma effort:

1. The better the talent, the better the results.

2. Top talent become the next organizational leaders.

3. Top talent attract more top talent.

The first on the list is fairly obvious—the better the talent involved, the better results we will achieve with the effort. This is true in any initiative; for example, sports teams with the best records tend to have the most talented players. If this is obviously true, why don't improvement efforts tend to obtain the top talent in general?

One answer is that assigning top talent to Six Sigma causes significant stress to the system, because these folks have to stop what they are currently doing, their work needs to be reprioritized, and replacements have to be found. Naturally, the replacements will often not perform as well as the top talent on these important projects.

Weak leaders generally follow the path of least resistance, even if it is not the path to success. It takes committed leaders to choose the more difficult and stressful path. Our experience has been that only companies that have taken the more difficult path have fully benefited from Six Sigma. Certainly GE and other successful Six Sigma companies followed this path and accepted the additional stress and difficulties it required. Note also that obtaining top talent applies to filling not only the full-time roles, such as MBBs and BBs, but also the roles of other members of the BB and GB project teams, and to finding functional support needed to address root causes identified by the team.

The second reason for selecting top talent for Six Sigma roles is to utilize the effort to develop the future leaders of the company. Today's top talent will likely become tomorrow's leaders, and you need to ensure that these leaders fully understand and embrace Six Sigma. Having ex-BBs and ex-MBBs in senior leadership positions will help ensure that the culture change is permanent and is a major element of making the transition from an initiative to the way we work. Further, the experience of being dedicated to disciplined continuous improvement will make them better leaders. Consider what Jack Welch wrote in his autobiography (Welch 2001, 339):

> We've always had great functional training programs over the years, particularly in finance. But the diversity of the company has made it difficult to have a universal training program. Six Sigma gives us just the tool we need for generic management training since it applies as much in a customer service center as it does in a manufacturing environment.

There is a growing body of evidence to suggest that organizations are using Six Sigma to develop leaders. We see press releases announcing Person X has received a new position, and in the detail we find that the Person X was a Six Sigma leader (Champion, MBB, BB) at some point in his or her career. Companies such as GE, Honeywell, DuPont, 3M, and American Standard now require BB or GB experience for managerial advancement. W. R. Grace, whose Six Sigma deployment was discussed in our earlier book (Snee and Hoerl 2003), recently reported on a number of BBs returning to management positions, all with increased responsibilities and most with promotions (Rodebaugh 2004).

The third reason that selection of top talent is so critical is somewhat subtler. If top talent is selected for key roles, this sends a very clear message to the organization that management is serious about Six Sigma, and it creates suction for the initiative. By suction, we mean that people will naturally be drawn to Six Sigma, will want to be involved with it, and may even start to compete with one another for MBB and BB positions.

We are not fans of internal competition, but we do think it is healthy to have more people vying for Six Sigma roles than there are positions to fill. It is generally true that the organization knows the talent, so no words leadership may say here make a difference. When the names are announced, the organization will immediately know whether top talent has been selected. The names will speak for themselves.

Supporting Infrastructure

The presence of a supporting infrastructure was a key reason that Motorola Finance, *Community Health Corporation* (CHC), and other organizations achieved major success. Based on our experience, lack of a supporting infrastructure is a key reason why some organizations have achieved minimal success. Even committed leaders and top talent will have difficulty succeeding without a proper infrastructure. In practice, of course, these items tend to go together, because committed leaders will ensure that the required supporting infrastructure is developed; uncommitted leaders won't.

Table 4.2 lists the infrastructure elements that we think are most critical.

TABLE 4.2   Critical Infrastructure Elements

- An organizational structure for Six Sigma deployment that includes overall leadership of the effort, a Six Sigma Council, and dedicated positions for key roles (MBBs, BBs, and so on)

- Six Sigma planning systems; that is, development and managerial review of implementation plans, budgets, human resources plans, and so on, on at least an annual basis (a process typically done for each business unit in a major corporation, but often overlooked for improvement initiatives)

- Project selection and review processes

- Training systems for key roles

- Modification of human resources, reward and recognition, business planning, financial, and other business systems to support Six Sigma implementation, as needed

---

First there need to be formal roles, assigned leadership, and dedicated resources to get the initiative going, overcome inertia, and maintain momentum. No major corporation operates its finance department without a designated leader or a finance committee, with unclear roles, or with resources doing finance in their spare time. If such a disorganized approach fails for finance, why would we expect it to work for Six Sigma?

When Six Sigma becomes ingrained into the organization, it will be possible to scale down the level of dedicated resources, similar to the safety department in a well-managed company, which typically has few full-time resources because everyone in the company works on safety every day.

The second item in Table 4.2 addresses the need to have Six Sigma formally managed like any other activity of the company. The Six Sigma effort needs to plan, to develop a budget, to have clear objectives, to obtain resources, and so on. Similarly, if leadership takes Six Sigma seriously, they will want to review and potentially revise these plans. Good companies spend a lot of time planning, which in turn means less time has to be spent fighting fires and solving crises. As UCLA basketball coaching legend John Wooden noted, "Failing to plan is planning to fail." The same principle holds for Six Sigma.

A set of formal mechanisms for communication, which collectively form a communication system, are also important. As the old saying goes, "Out of sight, out of mind." The mechanisms can include anything from formal periodic newsletters, to regular e-mails from the CEO, to rotating posters placed in strategic places, or to informal "meet-the-troops" interactions. At GE, company leaders have discussed Six Sigma progress in each annual report since 1995.

As you have seen, project selection is a critical component of success. Project selection should align the Six Sigma initiative with the strategic direction of the organization. We consistently see projects that aren't supported by the organization are typically not linked to the strategic direction of the organization. In Snee and Hoerl (2003), we report on two companies whose Six Sigma deployment was not successful, with poor project selection being a significant contributing factor.

Many people believe that Six Sigma should begin with good project selection and put it near the top of their list of key success factors. Often the battle is lost before we have even begun due to selection of poor projects. You also need a formal project review process. The review process ensures that the projects are continuing to move in the right direction at an appropriate pace. Without a regular drumbeat of reviews, projects often get bogged down and move at a glacial pace. The reviews also give leadership an opportunity to make midcourse corrections and to quickly learn of barriers. In addition, the reviews provide a visible symbol that leadership is personally involved.

Training systems may at first glance seem obvious. Everyone who gets involved with Six Sigma receives training to build the needed skills. However, there is a big difference between establishing a formal training system and conducting a wave of mass training. A training system is not a one-time event, but rather an ongoing set of interconnected processes. It will evaluate and document the business needs, develop or obtain tailored training courses to meet those needs, and then deliver the appropriate type and depth of training to those who need it (and at the most appropriate time). This may require a more complex curriculum with several courses of varying breadth and depth, rather than a single one-size-fits-all course. It will also require that new people joining the organization be trained promptly.

A common problem in real economy deployments is the use of manufacturing-oriented training materials. Such materials are easiest to obtain, so using them is certainly tempting to management. However, putting financial analysts or computer scientists into a training course that focuses on improving manufacturing processes typically results in disaster. Not only will people not understand how it applies to them, they will likely develop an attitude that Six Sigma is a manufacturing initiative irrelevant to finance or e-commerce. In other words, it reinforces the attitude that "we're different; Six Sigma doesn't apply to us."

We have commented previously on the need to modify systems, policies, and procedures to be consistent with Six Sigma direction. For example, to attract top talent to the effort, career progression paths need to be modified so that MBB and BB roles are clearly seen as accelerators, rather than hindrances, to career advancement. Similarly, managerial bonus programs, annual performance-appraisal systems, communication processes, and the like need to be modified to help drive Six Sigma. These points illustrate why the three key success factors of leadership, top talent, and supportive infrastructure must be tightly linked.

Road Map for Leading Six Sigma

We now provide the major steps in our road map, including the objectives for each step. Subsequent chapters provide more detailed, step-by-step advice for succeeding in each step. The overall deployment process is flexible (as are the individual steps) and can be applied to organizations of different sizes, industries, cultures, and so on. Figure 4.1 shows the recommended deployment process. This road map is not the only road map that can be used, but it has been applied in a number of situations and utilizes the experiences of many types of companies, including lessons learned about the key success factors.

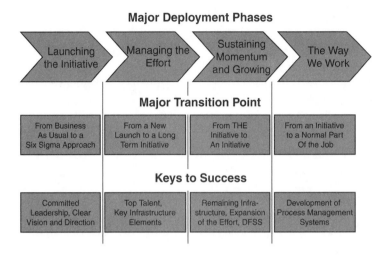

FIGURE 4.1   High-level deployment process for Six Sigma.

The deployment process shown in Figure 4.1 consists of four major steps or phases:

1. Launching the initiative

2. Managing the effort

3. Sustaining momentum and growing

4. The way we work

Our experience has been that all organizations successfully deploying Six Sigma go through each phase, although each progresses through the phases differently. Each phase has unique challenges and issues, and, of course, there may be overlap. Some organizations may have to recycle through previous phases if they have not been properly addressed. We have found these steps to be common to all companies implementing Six Sigma, but each organization is likely to experience them in a unique way.

These four steps have been carefully chosen to align with the major transition points in Six Sigma deployment. Unfortunately, no one has gone immediately from being a non-Six Sigma company to being a Six Sigma company in one big step. Everyone has had to go through an evolutionary deployment over several years, resulting in several transitions. This is true for real economy organizations as well as manufacturing organizations. Organizational transitions often provide major opportunities for breakthroughs as well as for pitfalls.

During transitions, direction changes, roles change, often circumstances change, and there is always some level of anxiety in the organization, if not confusion and fear. It is therefore very important that the transitions in Six Sigma deployment be planned properly and take into account the key success factors discussed at the end of Chapter 3:

- Leadership commitment

- Top talent

- Supportive infrastructure

Without proper planning, these transitions could turn out to be full of landmines and derail deployment.

Quarterly reviews of the overall Six Sigma deployment in each organizational unit (facility, business unit, function, etc.) by senior management of the unit are key to the successful deployment of Six Sigma. Transition between phases and changes in direction are much easier to make if these reviews are done properly. Every fourth review is frequently used to focus on deployment strategy for the coming year.

It should not go unnoticed that by deploying Six Sigma you are creating a management system that will enable the organization to make systematic improvement an integral part of how you run your business. You are creating a business process that you plan for, set goals for, assign resources to, and assess the effectiveness of each year just like you do for all your other business processes. Although such processes to manage improvement are common in manufacturing, they are much less common in finance, health care, and other areas beyond the factory floor.

The following sections provide an overview of each deployment phase of Six Sigma, with special focus on real economy organizations. Let's take a closer look at each of them.

Launching the Initiative

The first transition occurs when the organization makes the decision to implement Six Sigma. Implementing Six Sigma will cause significant change to the status quo of the organization. There may be current managers who are philosophically opposed to Six Sigma, or who want to jockey for position based on political motivations. Individual contributors in the organization will no doubt have a lot of serious questions. This is particularly true outside manufacturing, because people may feel that "we're different; Six Sigma doesn't apply to us," as discussed in Chapter 2. Opinions at this point may be based on hearsay or sound bites from the media that may or may not be accurate. The organization will be looking for clear vision and direction at all levels.

Some of the key issues that will need to be addressed in the launching the initiative step are as follows:

- Setting the overall vision, strategy, and justification for deployment of Six Sigma

- Selecting an external Six Sigma provider for training, project mentoring and consulting, project management, and so on, if needed

- Developing a long-term deployment plan, including objectives

- Developing a short-term implementation plan based on the long-term deployment plan, including selecting the initial set of projects and resources

- Writing a clear communication plan to explain this direction to the entire organization, including expected benefits

Of the key success factors discussed earlier, committed and involved leadership is particularly relevant during this step, especially in the real economy. As noted in Chapter 2, strong leadership is needed to overcome the "we're different" mindset. Committed and involved leaders provide the compelling vision and strong leadership required to ensure that each of the issues is properly addressed, whereas supportive leaders likely hope that someone else takes care of these issues while they focus on whatever they consider to be critically important to the organization. It is imperative that everyone in the organization understands why the organization is deploying Six Sigma and has a clear understanding of the long-term vision. Understanding the rationale for change and seeing where the organization is headed are crucial to any change initiative (Weisbord 1989).

Managing the Effort

After the Six Sigma initiative has been formally implemented, the next key transition occurs when the first set of projects are being completed and people start wondering where we go from here. If Six Sigma is properly implemented, there will likely be a wave of enthusiasm that will carry the effort through the first set of projects. It is at this crucial transition point that Six Sigma will either fizzle out as just another short-lived fad or it will be properly managed as a long-term business priority.

To successfully move through this transition, you need the second set of projects and the involvement of the organization's top talent (change is tough!), as well as initial elements of the supporting infrastructure.

Key requirements at this step are as follows:

- Strong leaders in Six Sigma roles
- An effective project selection system including the all-important second set of projects
- A multilayered project-review system
- An approved Six Sigma budget
- Good communication processes
- Formal recruitment and career progression processes for MBBs and BBs
- Reward and recognition systems

The issue of top talent is particularly challenging outside manufacturing and engineering. In those organizations, large pools of engineers are trained in advanced mathematics and the scientific method; these people make logical candidates for BB and MBB roles. As noted in Chapter 2, most organizations outside manufacturing and engineering don't have engineers, so finding candidates who can pick up the scientific method and statistical techniques quickly is more challenging. As noted in Chapter 2, organizations should consider the following options:

- Finding quantitatively skilled existing employees (e.g., actuaries in insurance)

- Hiring external, experienced BBs and MBBs to "kick-start" the initiative

- Utilizing BBs or MBBs from a Six Sigma provider on a temporary basis

- Developing the technical skills of candidates with the right non-technical skills

The success factors of having top talent involved, and also several aspects of the supporting infrastructure, are particularly relevant in the "managing the effort" step.

Sustaining Momentum and Growing

Even after a successful introduction of Six Sigma, and a good transition to ongoing management of the effort, there is still a tendency to lose steam after a couple of years. Virtually all organizations implementing Six Sigma have experienced such difficulties, including in manufacturing. The reasons for this phenomenon are based on business realities and human nature.

One of the realities of business is that the environment is constantly changing due to economic fluctuations, new government regulations, technological breakthroughs (e.g., the Internet), or even world political events, such as the fall of the Berlin Wall and the subsequent opening of Eastern Europe and Russia.

With Six Sigma progressing well, leadership's attention will naturally be distracted toward emerging trends and opportunities in the marketplace. For example, Internet commerce exploded onto the business scene in the middle of Six Sigma deployment at GE and other companies. Similarly, it is only human nature to be attracted to the latest hot topic in the business world, even at the expense of successful initiatives that may be viewed as yesterday's news.

These reasons help explain why so many corporations go through a series of flavor-of-the-month fads without reaping sustained benefits from any of them. If these natural impulses are not checked, Six Sigma will gradually slip in organizational importance. The participation of leadership will fade, Six Sigma will struggle to attract top talent, and it will slowly become a second tier or backburner initiative. After the leadership presence, top talent, and infrastructure fade away, so will the benefits. Analysts will eventually ask, "Whatever happened to Six Sigma?" An embarrassed leadership team will likely either claim that the organization is still driving Six Sigma or that it has been successfully integrated into daily operations. Customers and employees will know better.

An alternative to this scenario exists. Certainly business leaders have to respond to multiple issues and various crises in the marketplace. They do not have the luxury of having only one thing to worry about. The tragic terrorists attacks upon the United States on September 11, 2001, and the subsequent economic impact, are unfortunate examples of an unexpected crisis to which management must respond. Even under the best of circumstances, the organization will have to transition from Six Sigma being *the* initiative to *an* initiative. The key to maintaining momentum and growing Six Sigma during this transition is the proper functioning of the rest of the supporting infrastructure.

A good infrastructure will ensure that Six Sigma gets the nourishment it needs when the organization must focus attention on other issues as well. To grow, you also have to continually expand the effort to include all aspects of the organization, including using Six Sigma to grow revenue.

To successfully get to this point, organizations will have already implemented good project-selection and review systems. Other components of the supporting infrastructure that become key in this step are as follows:

- Well-defined organizational structure, especially a functioning Six Sigma Council. The council will develop annual objectives and budgets, manage the Six Sigma systems and processes, and provide leadership for the overall effort.

- A training system that provides the required skills to new employees, as well as continuing education and training for experienced MBBs, BBs, and *Green Belts* (GBs).

- A system of audits to ensure that previously closed projects are continuing to reap benefits (the purpose of the control phase in the DMAIC process).

- Quarterly management reviews of the Six Sigma system at the business and corporate levels to make sure that the system is performing as desired.

These systems are equally important, perhaps even more important, to real economy organizations than they are to manufacturing.

The Way We Work

The last transition point in deploying Six Sigma is perhaps the most difficult. This is the point at which you need to move Six Sigma from being an initiative to being the way you work. In other words, the concepts and methodologies of Six Sigma must become standard operating procedures rather than a separate initiative.

Organizations can't go on indefinitely with Six Sigma being their primary focus—nor should they! If Six Sigma is deployed properly, it will fundamentally change the way leaders lead and the way work is done. If it can be effectively institutionalized, the organization can continue its benefits without maintaining a separate Six Sigma infrastructure, or continuing the significant demands on leadership's time and energy. This allows leadership to focus on other strategically important issues, such as its e-commerce strategy, or rethinking safety and security systems after the terrorist attacks of September 11, 2001. It will bring a continuous improvement culture based on scientific, disciplined approaches, something that is often unique and a competitive advantage in accounting, logistics, marketing, and other real economy organizations.

We believe this is the most difficult transition phase. First of all, it is rarely addressed well in the corporate world, for any initiative, not just Six Sigma. Business journals and textbooks are full of case studies where a variety of methodologies have been introduced and produced significant savings. In most companies, however, there are few traces of the initiative (or the benefits) after about 5 years. Examples include *total quality management* (TQM), reengineering, *activity-based costing* (ABC), benchmarking, Lean manufacturing, and so on. Contrary to some commentators' opinions, this fact does not indicate a deficiency in any of these methodologies. In reality, each of these initiatives can reap huge benefits for organizations that deploy them properly.

The deficiency that generally causes this phenomenon is the organization's inability to successfully integrate the key concepts and methodologies of the initiative into its normal mode of operation—that is, to make it the way we work. If this is not done, as soon as the separate infrastructure is dismantled, and leadership moves on to other issues (which they need to do), the initiative dissolves.

In fact, given the relative newness of Six Sigma, we do not feel that any organization has successfully made this transition. GE is perhaps the furthest along, but would likely admit that it has not yet fully institutionalized Six Sigma. Based on conversations we have had with Six Sigma resources at Motorola, it does not appear to us that they succeeded corporate-wide in this transition. Fortunately, there are some positive counter-examples from other initiatives.

For example, GE launched an initiative called WorkOut almost 20 years ago. WorkOut was originally a series of town meetings in which rank-and-file employees got together to address bureaucracy and other issues in the workplace. This initiative was hugely successful and helped GE get through a key transition early in Jack Welch's tenure as CEO. There is no longer a WorkOut initiative at GE, nor is there a WorkOut infrastructure with dedicated resources, budget allocations, and so on. However, WorkOut is still very much part of the GE culture, and the term is used on a regular basis when teams get together to tackle routine problems. The safety management system at DuPont is another outstanding example of a major initiative being successfully institutionalized for long-term benefit.

The key to such successes has been the ability to integrate the initiative into the culture of the organization, so that it is no longer seen as a separate initiative. How can this be done with Six

Sigma? The best way that we know of is to migrate the Six Sigma improvement effort into an ongoing process management system. Six Sigma relies on formal projects and the allocation of dedicated, trained resources. When the separate infrastructure of Six Sigma matures, we need to integrate these key components into the existing infrastructure to create a new way of working, as shown in Figure 4.2.

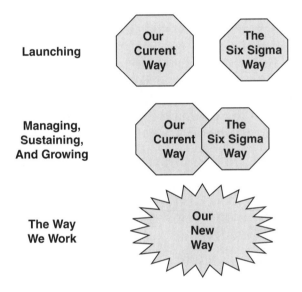

FIGURE 4.2   Stages of change.

We use the term *process management system* to refer to an enrichment of the old infrastructure that incorporates measurement of key process metrics, response to out-of-control conditions, identification of key improvement opportunities, and assignment of resources to capture these opportunities. A key point is that this system is part of normal operations—that is, people just doing their jobs, not a separate initiative. By making it a formal business system, we minimize the need for a separate infrastructure. Formal process management systems are difficult to institute in manufacturing environments, but perhaps even more difficult to implement in the real economy, simply because such systems are less common there. Use of process management systems is discussed in greater detail in Chapter 6.

Now that you understand the generic road map and its four key phases, you are ready to plan how you will adapt the road map to your organization. Tailoring the road map and its associated success factors and pitfalls are discussed in the next section.

Tailoring the Road Map for Your Organization

As you begin to think about how to tailor the high-level road map described in Figure 4.1, you need a framework to help you think about what the road map should look like for your organization. This can be effectively accomplished by developing a deployment plan specific to your organization. The key elements of such a plan are summarized in Table 4.3. As you develop the deployment plan, consider at the beginning the unique characteristics of your organization. Primary in your consideration should be the following:

- The organization's goals and objectives

- The unique characteristics of the organization's culture

- The nature of processes, and background and skills of the employees

- Existing infrastructure and management systems

The organization's goals and objectives will influence the specific goals for Six Sigma, the initial projects the BBs or GBs will work on, and the timing of the deployment in the organization—which departments and in which order (that is, who leads and who follows). Manufacturing organizations generally begin in operations (that is, manufacturing facilities) and then gradually expand to other functions. The decision of where to focus initial efforts is less clear and requires more careful thought in an insurance company, a non-profit, or a consulting organization.

Key to the culture of the organization is its language. Because you will be bringing Six Sigma methods from other companies and disciplines, you must ensure that aspects of the initiative—communications, workshop and training materials, examples, etc.—are in the language of the organization and its industry.

Some of the unique characteristics of real economy processes and the people who work in them are summarized in Table 4.4. These characteristics, discussed in more detail in Chapter 2, must be taken into account if the initiative is to succeed. The characteristics of your people, processes, and measurement systems must be taken into account as you design your Six Sigma deployment. Training systems need to take into account organizational language, learning styles, thinking preferences, and personnel backgrounds and education. Process measurements and some financial measurements will likely be deficient or non-existent and have to be created. Many process improvements will focus on reducing complexity, reducing non–value-added work, reducing human intervention in the work, and simply building good processes.

TABLE 4.3   Six Sigma Deployment Plan Elements

- Strategy and goals for Six Sigma
- Process performance measures
- Project selection criteria
- Project identification/prioritization system
- Deployment process for Champions, MBBs, BBs, etc.
- Roles of management, Champions, BBs, MBBs, and functional groups
- Curricula and training system
- Project and Six Sigma initiative review schedule
- Reporting and tracking system
- Audit system for closed projects
- Reward and recognition plan
- Communication plan

Finally, an assessment of the organization's management systems, including communications, project tracking, recognition and reward, and so on, should be made because changes will be needed in these systems to support the Six Sigma initiative and to integrate Six Sigma within your culture and operating procedures.

TABLE 4.4 Key Characteristics of Typical Real Economy Processes

- Culture doesn't think in terms of *process, variation*, and *data*.
- Work requires considerable *human intervention*.
- *Processes* are often complex and not well defined.
- Process output is often intangible and can be unique.
- *Nonfinancial measurements* are often nonexistent or ill defined.
- Large amounts of "*paperwork*" (perhaps electronic) are often generated.
- Similar activities are often done in different ways.
- Processes usually not planned or designed; have frequently never been subjected to rigorous study.
- A large number of ways to make mistakes and a high frequency of errors and rework.
- Errors and delays have serious downstream cost consequences.

Deployment Plan Elements

The deployment plan elements shown in Table 4.3 must be addressed regardless of the type of deployment approach that is used, or the type of organization involved. However, the elements are not all implemented at the same time. Some are critical at launch, others in the second phase of deployment (managing the effort), and others in the third phase (sustaining momentum). The launch elements need to be covered in detail from the beginning, but the other elements can be defined at a high, strategic level. Details of these elements will be added at the appropriate time.

Although seasoned planners may feel the need to define all deployment elements in detail from the very beginning, our experience is that trying to do so delays implementation, and can result in paralysis by analysis as you try to cross every *t* and dot every *i*. This is particularly true beyond the factory floor, because it is important to deliver results quickly to defuse the "Six Sigma won't work here" attitude among detractors. We now briefly describe each deployment plan element, and then go into detail on the critical launch phase items.

Strategy and Goals

Strategy and goals make up the first key element. This element is the responsibility of senior management and sets the overall vision for Six Sigma deployment. A key element of the strategy is choosing where to initially deploy Six Sigma, and what the rollout sequence and timing will be. Six Sigma cannot be successfully rolled out in all business units and all functions at the same time. A sequential approach that enables you to learn as you go works much better. High-volume transactional businesses, such as insurance, e-commerce, or consumer credit, typically begin Six Sigma in operations. By operations, we mean the core "bread-and-butter" activities of the organization that provide a product or service to customers, such as processing applications for credit cards or preparing and mailing bills in consumer credit. Broader business projects and DFSS would typically begin 6 to 8 months and 1 year after operations implementation, respectively.

There are two reasons for starting in operations—and both relate to the fact that operations tend to have the best measurement systems. These systems are typically implemented for financial rather than improvement purposes (for example, for accounting purposes). The first reason is that it is much easier to achieve quick hits if you begin with a good measurement system, instead of having to take time to create one. The second reason is that the existence of good measurements usually means that everyone is aware of the huge potential savings available in operations and is anxious to go after them.

Conversely, many people will need to be convinced that huge savings are available in the marketing or finance functions, and data to convince them may be hard to come by. For example, few companies rigorously track the total number of person-hours required to develop the annual budget. Starting Six Sigma in operations sets up the initiative for success by enabling quick hits. Success in operations builds confidence that Six Sigma will work, as well as producing bottom-line results that help pay as you go, thereby enabling deployment throughout the organization.

Of course, the concept of "operations" is less clear in low-volume or non-transactional organizations, such as in an engineering consulting business. In such cases, we recommend initiating Six Sigma in those areas that are considered "core processes" to the organization, particularly those with existing measurement systems. In the case of engineering consulting, this could be negotiating contracts or conducting the technical work of the contract.

Another decision is when to start GB training—typically initiated 8 to 10 months after BB training starts. BBs, preferably dedicated to Six Sigma projects 100% of their time, are needed to get the initiative moving quickly. GBs typically receive less-intense training than BBs and work on Six Sigma projects in addition to their normal accountabilities. Some companies have a goal of training the entire professional staff as GBs as soon as it can be managed.

It is also important that 1- to 2-year goals for Six Sigma be developed and broadly communicated in an initial Executive Workshop. The goals, which generally include financial targets, should be communicated for the organization as a whole and reinforced within each major part of the organization.

A goal not stated in financial terms is often an indication that management is not serious about making Six Sigma successful. A financial goal tells the organization's members what is expected of them. For example, in the case of a $1 billion revenue company, a goal of $2 million to the bottom or top line from Six Sigma communicates a far different message than a goal of $10 million or $20 million. At $250,000 per project, $2 million translates into 8 projects, whereas $10 million and $20 million translates to 40 and 80 projects, respectively. Clearly, much more effort (people, time, and money) is required to complete 40 to 80 projects than to complete 8.

The financial goals and focus of the projects will likely be revised over the course of deployment. For example, Six Sigma can be used to improve customer service, marketing, sales, and other processes that result in projects with a longer-term payback. Projects related to growth typically take longer to produce bottom-line results than do productivity-improvement projects. Projects with longer-term paybacks are usually undertaken later in the deployment after the effectiveness of Six Sigma is well established.

Process Performance Measures

Process performance measures define what's important for success and are used to select projects. A pitfall to be avoided is selecting each project independently. This is analogous to spending

5 minutes starting to clean 10 different rooms in a house, versus spending 50 minutes to completely clean 1 room. In the first case, it is difficult to see what impact the effort has had; in the second case there is a visible, tangible success that will now be ready to be leveraged elsewhere. It is preferable to launch Six Sigma by focusing on a few strategic areas, rather than 10 or 20. The process performance measures determined by senior leadership help everyone focus the initial projects strategically.

One model for key measures is *quality*, *delivery*, and *cost* (QDC). This model provides three strategic focus areas for the initial projects. If all the projects affect one of these three key measures, you will have significant tangible results when they are completed. Quality obviously relates to customer satisfaction, and an emphasis on it will almost always have the fringe benefit of saving money because you will reduce the costs of performing rework (reissuing inaccurate bills and so on), dealing with customer returns, shouldering warranty costs, and so forth. The only exception is likely to be the case where delivering the desired quality level requires significant upgrade to equipment or materials. Surprisingly, this is rarely the case. In many applications beyond the factory floor, the quality metric of interest is some type of accuracy measure, such as accuracy of information on credit card bills.

Delivery relates to the procurement, inventory, distribution, and other logistics systems. We do not restrict delivery here to a physical product; we are also referring to such things as providing rapid turnaround on mortgage applications, responding to customer requests for investment advice, and so on. Again, improvement almost always enhances customer satisfaction, while reducing internal costs. (After all, less time usually equates to lower cost.) Reducing the cycle times of individual steps in the process allows for quicker realization of revenues, and of course, reduces the overall cycle time. Improving the key processes almost always results in better products and services, which ultimately benefits both the customer and the shareholder.

Although cost is always important, our experience is that reducing cost is usually a result of doing other things well. For example, if you are able to improve accuracy and reduce cycle time, your costs will naturally decrease. Therefore, in the vast majority of cases, attempts to define internal cost metrics ultimately result in some measure of accuracy or cycle time. We keep cost on the list of key metrics because it is important to always keep cost and financial benefits visible to leadership.

Project Selection Criteria

The process metrics are also used to develop a set of more specific criteria to select projects. Some of the project selection criteria used by *Commonwealth Health Corporation* (CHC), discussed in Chapter 3, are summarized in Table 4.5. These criteria define areas that are important to improve and will produce significant tangible results. Often, organizations develop targets such as *savings per project*, and *expected time to project completion*. Project-selection criteria also communicate what types of improvements are important to the organization. Recall that CHC is a non-profit organization, and therefore non-financial criteria are also important. By communicating these criteria, you alert the organization as to what your objectives are and as to the kinds of projects on which you want to focus. This increases the probability that large numbers of people in the organization help identify improvement opportunities. As noted, you want to select projects strategically rather than haphazardly.

TABLE 4.5   Project Selection Criteria Used by Commonwealth Health Corporation

Priority metrics to improve

- Customer satisfaction
- Quality of care/service
- Timeliness/speed/convenience
- Cost

Initial application area

- Radiology

Doable within reasonable timeframe (quick hits)

Methodology

- Identify key indicators
- Develop high-level system maps
- Define high-level CTQs

Project Identification and Prioritization System

These project-selection criteria are typically used in the Champions Workshop to develop a set of initial candidate projects. The projects are put in the "hopper" and prioritized for assignment to a BB or GB. In later deployment phases, it is important to develop an ongoing system to identify potential projects, rank them, and place them in the project hopper, so that there is a continuously refreshed list of good projects. In some cases, GBs choose their own projects in their own functional area, while BBs work on the strategically identified projects in the hopper.

Nothing establishes the credibility of Six Sigma better that the rapid accumulation of hard bottom-line results. Wall Street is only interested in hard financial results. Our view is that the first wave or two of projects should focus completely on hard bottom-line results. We recognize that there are important improvement opportunities (for instance, cost avoidance) that produce soft savings or gains that are difficult to link to the bottom line. We believe that a few of these projects can be included in each of later waves of improvement projects (< 20% of the projects in each wave) after the usefulness of Six Sigma has been established. For example, W. R. Grace reported in their first year of Six Sigma deployment $26 million in bottom line results and $7 million in cost-avoidance savings (Snee and Hoerl 2003). The best strategy is to manage your project hopper as a "project portfolio," the composition of which matches the improvement and financial needs of the organization (Snee and Hoerl 2003, Snee and Rodebaugh 2002).

Deployment Processes for Leaders

Lists of the Champions, BBs, MBBs, and GBs are also part of the deployment plan. In later deployment phases, these lists are expanded to become a system for selection, deployment, and advancement for each of these roles. The list of initial Champions will be developed at the Executive Workshop. At the Champion Workshop, the Champions develop the list of initial projects and, based on this, develop a list of candidate BBs to lead these projects.

In Chapter 1 you learned that Six Sigma is about improvement—not training. It is strongly recommended that the projects be selected first, and then the BBs and GBs identified for these projects. The Champions should be selected at the Executive Workshop based on the areas targeted for improvement. Selecting the Champions and BBs before identifying specific projects increases the risk that important projects will be overlooked. This critical issue is discussed further later in the chapter.

Finding the right people for the key Six Sigma roles is another ingredient for success. This is particularly important in the launch phase, and is a key ingredient throughout the deployment of Six Sigma. Leadership is the key characteristic to keep in mind when selecting the people who are to be involved in Six Sigma. The need for leadership is evident in the typical roles of the Management Team, Project Champion, BB, and MBB, summarized in Table 4.6. See Snee and Hoerl (2003) for more specific advice on finding the right people for key Six Sigma roles.

Roles of Leadership and Others

Although there are generic job descriptions for Six Sigma titles, such as Champion, MBB, BB, GB, and so on, there is considerable variation in the actual role that these people play in different organizations. Table 4.6 shows typical roles, but organizations should take the time to consider the specific roles that each of these positions play in their deployment. Within reasonable boundaries, leadership can tailor the roles for a specific function or business. The roles of the Leadership Team, Champions, MBBs, BBs, and Functional groups should be defined in the Executive Workshop and communicated to the organization.

Curricula and Training System

An overall training system for each of the Six Sigma roles is a key element of the deployment plan. At launch, a training schedule is needed only for the initial wave of BBs. As more and more people in various roles become involved in Six Sigma, new employees are hired, and the need is found for advanced training in certain areas, a functioning training system with diverse curricula will need to be developed. A wave of mass training does not make a

TABLE 4.6 Six Sigma Roles

Corporate Leadership	Unit Leadership	Project Champions	Black Belts	Master Black Belts	Functional Support Group
Create and deploy strategy and goals.	Establish project-selection criteria.	Facilitate project selection.	Learn and use Six Sigma methodologies and tools.	Develop and deliver Six Sigma training.	Provide data and aid in data collection.
Define boundaries (what's in and what's out).	Approve projects; ensure linkage to strategy and key needs.	Create project charter.	Develop and maintain project work plan.	Assist in project selection.	Provide team members.
Communicate purpose and progress.	Select project Champions.	Facilitate identification of resources (BB team, $$, functional resources).	Provide leadership for team.	Coach and counsel BBs.	Support with expertise in the department, such as financial value of projects.
Provide resources (people, time, and $$).	Provide needed resources and training.	Remove barriers.	Meet weekly with the Project Champion.	Ensure the success of "mission-critical" projects.	Identify opportunities for Six Sigma projects.
Ensure training plan is in place.	Review BB and GB projects monthly.	Review projects weekly.	Communicate support needs to functional groups.	Support the efforts of Champions and the management team.	Help with benchmarking.
Ensure recognition plan is in place.	Establish and use communications process.	Verify project deliverables for each phase of DMAIC.	Ensure that the right data are collected and analyzed.	Share project learnings and best practices across the organization.	Set boundaries (legal, company policy, environmental).
Review overall initiative quarterly.	Review the entire process every 3 to 6 months.	Communicate purpose and progress of projects.	Identify and communicate barriers to Champion.		Provide reality check, diversity of ideas, perspective.
Review plant and business initiatives periodically.	Establish reward and recognition structure.	Approve project closure.	Provide monthly updates to Champion and MBB.		
Support initiative with rewards and recognition.	Link rewards to performance.	Identify the next project for the BB/GB.	Responsible for delivering results ($$).		
Publicly celebrate successes.	Be accountable for success of the effort.	Celebrate, recognize, and reward BB and team.			

training system; mass training is an event that usually has no lasting impact. What is needed is a well-thought-out system that identifies all the training needs of all the roles and puts together a sustained, ongoing system to continuously satisfy these needs in the most efficient means possible. This will be a tremendous amount of work, but fortunately the complete training system is not needed at the launch of Six Sigma. Manufacturing organizations typically have an existing training system, but many real economy organizations do not, and they will need to implement one.

Project and Six Sigma Initiative Review Schedule

A project review schedule for the deployment plan is key. Experience has shown that an effective schedule involves short (30 minute) weekly reviews by the Champion, and monthly reviews with functional leaders, local management, or business leaders as appropriate. These are needed soon after the kick-off of the initial projects. Regular reviews not only demonstrate management's commitment, they also provide real-time feedback on how the projects are going and enable floundering projects to obtain needed assistance.

A review of the Six Sigma deployment should be done quarterly by the corporate or business unit leaders, as appropriate. All the elements of the deployment plan, and the associated goals, are appropriate agenda items for the quarterly reviews. This review focuses on how well the overall initiative is going; it does not focus on review of individual projects. This review is critical to sustaining momentum of the Six Sigma effort long term and to quickly detect any evidence of the initiative becoming bogged down.

Project Reporting and Tracking System

This system documents the results of the projects and provides valuable managerial information. Development of a formal system is not required in initial deployment, and this system is typically emphasized later in the deployment process, such as in the "managing the effort" phase. The project reporting and tracking system will keep a record of all the Six Sigma projects, providing a corporate memory of what has been accomplished to date. The system will generate managerial reports at several levels to keep management informed of progress.

The reports will include financial results taken from the tracking system as well as non-financial information, such as number of projects completed or in progress, time to completion of projects, status reports, and so on. The tracking part of this system is intended to document the financial benefits of closed projects. Obviously, this system needs to be designed with rigor so that the claimed financial benefits are accurate and credible. For small organizations, or to get started, a simple Excel spreadsheet will do the trick. Dedicated computer systems are eventually needed for larger organizations.

Audit System for Previously Closed Projects

When your organization gets to the "sustaining momentum and growing" phase, there will be a large number of completed projects, many of which will claim perpetual benefits; that is, benefits that will recur year after year. For example, if billing accuracy levels improve from 99% to 99.5%, and this improvement is maintained, cost savings from lower error levels will be reaped every year. Unfortunately, in many improvement efforts these lower costs begin to creep up over time, much like weight lost due to dieting. To some degree this is to be expected, because it is human nature to revert to old habits when the additional resources and focus brought by Six Sigma move on to other priorities.

Of course, you will need to preempt the natural digression back to old ways and rework levels if your efforts are to have lasting impact. Six Sigma has the advantage of a formal step in the DMAIC process, the control phase, which is specifically targeted to implement controls that prevent backsliding to the previous performance. As a second layer of protection, an audit system for previously closed projects needs to be implemented. This is not primarily a financial audit system to ensure that claimed benefits are real—financial controls need to be implemented from the very beginning. Rather, this audit system is intended to audit the control plan of previously closed projects and ensure that the control plan is working. In other words, the audit system will check to make sure the benefits of this project are still being received. If not, action will be initiated to revisit the project, regain the benefits, and institute an effective control plan.

Reward and Recognition Plan

Human resources (HR) needs to develop a reward and recognition plan to ensure that the organization is able to obtain (and eventually promote) the best possible candidates for Six Sigma roles. We believe in the power of "intrinsic motivation" (the idea that people do something because they really want to do it), instead of solely relying on "extrinsic motivation" (people do something because they are coerced or "bribed" to do it). Therefore, those who have a "fire in the belly" for improvement will likely perform better in Six Sigma roles than those solely looking for money or promotion.

However, it must be recognized that a total lack of extrinsic rewards for involvement in Six Sigma is essentially a disincentive; therefore, consider rewarding these roles in such a way that top performers will be drawn to Six Sigma. Review and revise this plan as needed over time to ensure that the Champions, BBs, MBBs, GBs, and even team members are properly recognized for their contributions. Most successful Six Sigma companies have revised their reward and recognition systems to more effectively support the Six Sigma initiative. A balance of both intrinsic and extrinsic motivation is encouraged.

The form of the recognition and reward plan depends on the organization. What works in one organization will not necessarily work in another organization. The goal should be to provide a mixture of rewards and recognition options that will drive the desired behaviors. It is important that a recognition and reward plan be created to support the Six Sigma initiative. This will communicate the value of Six Sigma and the personal benefits that can be obtained by being a part of the initiative. Examples of recognition and reward plans are discussed in Snee and Hoerl (2003).

Communication Plan

A communication plan has to be developed to support the Six Sigma initiative. This will be a very important part of the deployment plan because it will significantly affect the impression that rank-and-file employees have of Six Sigma. Again, because of potential false impressions of Six Sigma within real economy organizations, clear and consistent communication is even more important than in manufacturing organizations. Communication about Six Sigma typically utilizes existing media, but sometimes new media have to be developed.

It is important to use a variety of media because people take in information and learn in different ways. There is variation in people as well as in processes. Some prefer personal contacts, either one on one or in groups. Others prefer to read newsletters or memos, whereas still others respond well to videos, Webcasts, or e-mails. Leadership needs to carefully communicate why they chose to deploy Six Sigma, how it applies to their business, what they hope to get out of it, and where it will take the organization. One example of such a communication plan was the video that Jack Welch made and which each exempt employee at GE was expected to watch. This was followed up with frequent e-mails to all employees with updates on the progress of the initiative.

In some cases, such as GE and AlliedSignal, the CEO makes a bold statement about Six Sigma at the very beginning. However, we have also worked with organizations that did not feel comfortable making such bold statements. There is often a concern that if too big a deal is made of Six Sigma at the very beginning, unrealistic expectations will be set. Every employee might expect to begin Six Sigma training the next week. Customers may expect better services immediately. Confidence in the initiative may fade if people's unrealistic expectations are not fully met. Therefore, many organizations choose to begin the initiative in a fairly low-key manner, without hoopla.

When actual projects are begun, and results are starting to flow in, the initiative will be more formally and broadly communicated. Leadership will be able to point to tangible savings that have already been accomplished and can communicate the sequenced rollout of projects and training. The decision of when to begin implementing the communication plan needs to be made at the Executive Workshop.

Experience and surveys have shown that every element of the deployment plan shown in Table 4.3 is important. All are needed for success; none is optional. Not paying attention to any of these items can seriously limit the effectiveness of the Six Sigma initiative. As previously noted, however, not all need to be developed to the same degree of detail in the launch phase. The items that comprise the implementation process are the most critical initially.

Application to Specific Businesses and Functions

As noted previously, this deployment road map has proven effective in a variety of settings, including manufacturing and beyond. We realize, however, that it can often be difficult to determine how best to apply a generic road map to a specific business situation. We therefore provide some advice on how to apply this road map to several specific types of businesses and functions. Because it would be impossible to provide complete, detailed advice for every potential environment, we only provide some high-level tips for getting started in common types of businesses and functions.

We discuss more functions than business application areas, because these functions tend to exist in every business, whereas the application areas are only relevant to specific businesses. Note that there is some overlap in the advice—for example, between e-commerce as a business and IT as a function; in this case, e-commerce is clearly IT-centric, and hence it is logical that some advice would apply to both. The business application areas and functions discussed are as follows:

Business Application Areas	**Functions**
E-commerce	Finance
Health care	Human resources
Consumer Finance	Supply chain
Non-profits	Distribution and transportation

continues

Business Application Areas	**Functions**
Insurance	Purchasing
	Information technology
	Research and development
	Sales and marketing

Specific Business Application Areas

E-Commerce

Keep in mind that all aspects of commerce apply equally well to e-commerce; the only difference is that with e-commerce it all happens a lot faster! For example, you still need good marketing, logistics (if physical products are involved), financial planning, and so on. Don't fall for the myth that all you need to succeed in e-commerce is a good Web page. Six Sigma can help in these other areas, such as fulfillment—the Achilles' heel of many failed dot.coms.

Six Sigma can help with Web page design also, to optimize the page for speed, "stickiness" (keeping people coming to the site), ease of navigation, and so on.

For software development projects, it is usually better to treat these as design projects rather than DMAIC projects. This is because a new piece of software is essentially the design of something new rather than the improvement of something that already exists.

The random variation in software comes from the variation in results that users under different usage conditions will experience. In other words, people operating on a standalone PC will likely experience different results than someone on a networked PC, where the software is actually running on a server. Such things as time of day and type of network architecture also cause variation. In 1950s technology, running the same software at different times would almost always produce the same result; this is no longer true today.

Health Care

In many ways, hospitals are very similar to factories; they tend to have high volumes, repeat many of the same procedures on a regular basis, and are very dependent on equipment and machinery.

Many methods developed to optimize factories work very well in hospitals, such as discrete-event simulation tools to understand how queues and bottlenecks develop, and how to design them out.

Health care is a natural place to apply Six Sigma because Six Sigma quality levels are typically required; utilize this fact when communicating the launch of Six Sigma.

Many projects related to treating patients will have quality-of-care CTQs rather than financial-savings CTQs. Ultimately, quality of care equates to savings through such things as reducing litigation, but these may not be directly verifiable in the short term on a specific project.

Don't forget to apply Six Sigma to all the activities in the overall health-care system, even those not directly related to giving care to a patient, such as collections, payroll, maintaining records, and so on.

Pharmaceutical research has a long history of application of statistical methods to clinical trials. However, Six Sigma can drive further improvement by accelerating the discovery process used to invent new drugs; this would typically involve design for Six Sigma projects. In addition, DMAIC projects can help streamline and improve how clinical trials are conducted, within the constraints of government regulation of these trials.

Consumer Finance

Some aspects of consumer finance, like many aspects of health care, have strong similarities to manufacturing, such as the creation, printing, and mailing of large numbers of bills on a regular basis. As in manufacturing, finding a minor improvement that saves a penny a bill will produce tremendous savings.

Account-level profitability is a key CTQ. For example, credit card customers who pay their bills in full each month are generally not profitable, even though they typically have excellent credit.

The credit approval process is almost always a critical driver of profit and loss. Bad decisions here can be very costly.

Collections is often an area of major opportunity; the measurement systems are already in place, and scientific approaches have rarely been taken previously.

Detecting, and hopefully preventing, fraud may also be a major opportunity for savings. Consumer fraud, such as fraudulent use of credit cards, costs businesses billions of dollars a year.

American Express found that they had to first address the cultural issues to enable Six Sigma projects to deliver the desired bottom-line savings (Young 2001); you may have this experience as well.

Non-Profits

Although non-profits are obviously not in existence to make money, money is still critically important. Virtually all non-profits run on "shoe-string" budgets, meaning that money saved from Six Sigma would directly lead to providing more services. Utilize this point with skeptical employees or volunteers when communicating the initiative.

To find the financial opportunities, "follow the money"—that is, track the flow of money from providers of support through to expenses for providing services. Wherever money is collected (fund raising) and spent (expenses) are opportunities for improvement.

If a financial analysis indicates that a large portion of expenses are fixed, such as salaries or office rental, DFSS projects may be called for to redesign the structure of the organization to enable a higher percentage of income to be spent directly on providing services. A key metric to optimize is the percentage of donation dollars spent on providing service to constituency groups, as opposed to internal expenses to operate the organization (overhead).

Given the non-financial purpose of the organization, look for opportunities to utilize Six Sigma to provide better services, in addition to saving money.

Six Sigma will drive the organization to develop measurements for intangibles, such as quality of service. Although such efforts may be painful, the resulting data can be used when soliciting donations, as well as for Six Sigma projects. Donors want to know that their contributions produce results.

Six Sigma can be used to improve fund-raising campaigns by helping target communications to the most likely donors in much the same way that targeted marketing techniques can improve the effectiveness of marketing in for-profit companies. Design-of-experiment techniques have been used in the improve phase of DMAIC to evaluate various approaches to fund raising and member recruitment.

Insurance

Different underwriters often come to different conclusions. This variation causes a variety of problems, including financial losses. Use Six Sigma to understand causes of undesired variation between underwriters, and then to reduce this variation.

The point above also holds for adjusters; Six Sigma can help understand and reduce variation here, producing bottom-line savings.

It is of course critical to price for the risk assumed in any insurance policy. Therefore, estimation of risk is a key driver of pricing, and profitability. Six Sigma can be used to evaluate the accuracy of risk models and to improve them. The Six Sigma control plan can help maintain accuracy of risk models over time.

When evaluating the overall pricing process, apply Six Sigma to both cost-based pricing models and to market-based pricing models (what the market will bear). Six Sigma can improve both and optimize overall pricing.

The investment of customer premiums can be a good opportunity for Six Sigma applications.

Actuaries have strong statistical backgrounds and provide a deep talent pool for filling key Six Sigma roles.

As with consumer credit, insurance fraud costs billions of dollars a year, and represents another savings opportunity for Six Sigma.

Specific Functions

Finance

Follow the money—that is, look at the flow of money from customers through internal processes and out to vendors and other expenses. The areas where money flows are good potential application areas for Six Sigma (for example, paying taxes).

Initially focus in areas that already have good measurement systems, such as accounts payable, accounts receivable, collections, and so forth.

Don't forget about cycle time as a key CTQ; for example, reducing the cycle time required to close the books. Cycle time equates to money when you realize that you are tying up valuable resources.

Accuracy is also important in finance, because inaccurate information will lead to problems later on, such as manual account reconciliation.

Because many people in finance may not think Six Sigma applies to them, it is particularly important to have strong, unwavering leadership from the CFO; he or she cannot simply be a cheerleader.

Human Resources

Typically, HR is the "owner" of the processes related to hiring, supporting, rewarding, retaining, and, where needed, firing employees. Therefore, contrary to what one might initially think, there are many relevant processes to be improved. Examples include recruiting, the annual employee-evaluation process, employee surveys, retention (minimizing loss of the most desired employees), compliance with federal and state employment regulations, and so on.

A challenge in HR is to ensure that projects such as these do not drag on for too long. For example, many companies have an annual recruiting cycle, and hence it would usually take a year to quantify the benefits of changes to the recruiting process. Although this is often true, the projects themselves should be kept to less than this timeframe; 3 to 4 months, if possible.

HR can also use DFSS to develop and implement new benefits packages or other new programs.

It is wise to involve employees from outside HR on key HR projects, so that the team can benefit from the "customer" viewpoint. (Employees should be the primary customers of the HR processes in question.)

HR often has the reputation of being bureaucratic; using Six Sigma to focus on improving key processes should change the culture to one of continuous improvement and service, rather than bureaucracy. In fact, one measure of the success of Six Sigma in HR should be the views of HR expressed by employees in employee surveys (that is, the views of those not in HR).

Supply Chain

Recognize that the overall supply chain encompasses a variety of functions, including purchasing, manufacturing, transportation and distribution, and warehousing. These functions often have conflicting goals. Be careful to avoid suboptimization (for example, improving transportation at the expense of warehousing).

The systems view should include sales, customer service and planning, and scheduling. The effect of incoming materials on the entire supply chain should be considered. Eventually all of these need to be addressed, but you can begin in individual functions, as long as success is always measured by overall system impact, not individual function impact.

The SCOR model is an effective tool for identifying opportunities for improvement and benchmarking. The SCOR model is a supply chain benchmarking tool develop by the Supply Chain Council (See www.supply-chain.org for more information).

Key output metrics to consider for project CTQs include order lead time, process cycle time, on-time delivery, order correct and undamaged, inventory levels, and total cost of product and service.

Put a system of metrics in place to monitor the inputs, activities, and outputs of your supply-chain processes. Again, this relates to viewing the supply chain as an integrated system.

Distribution and Transportation

There are big opportunities in delivery, inventory, and transportation. Delivery touches the customer. Inventory and transportation are often sources of large costs and large cycle time. Identify opportunities for improvement by "following the money" through the system.

Work at the customer interface, focusing on reduction of high variation in delivery times. Consistency in delivery times is often more important than the absolute level of delivery time. In many situations, "too early" is worse than "too late" because the customer is not ready to handle the early shipment.

Critical delivery times are date of request, promise date, and date of receipt of product or service. It is often enlightening to compare request date with promise date; sometimes people can convince themselves they are doing a good job in delivery when they are never actually giving the customers what they want.

Shipping contracts and warehouse handling errors are often fruitful sources of improvement projects.

Put a system of metrics in place to monitor the inputs, activities, and outputs of your distribution and transportation processes. These would likely be at a lower level than the overall supply-chain metrics, but would map to them.

Purchasing

Improve supplier performance by helping suppliers implement Six Sigma in their operations. Ultimately, your organization will benefit.

Understand the effect of the quality and cost of supplied products and services on your business, so you can better manage your supplier base. Focus on minimizing total cost of ownership versus purchase price. The reward system must encourage this philosophy.

Identify and apply for discounts for early payment of supplier invoices (ties to accounts payable).

Reduce the number of low-volume purchase orders, which tend to add significant complexity.

Perform a Pareto analysis to focus your supplier improvement efforts on the "critical few" suppliers and products and services that have the greatest effect on the cost of your supplied materials and the performance of your processes. Create strategic partnerships with these suppliers.

Put a system of metrics in place to monitor the inputs, activities, and outputs of your purchasing processes. Again, these would likely be at a lower level than the overall supply chain metrics, but would map to them.

Consider altering product and service requirements to meet supplier capabilities, when these do not sacrifice performance. In some cases, your organization's specifications may be out of date and not actually represent the needs of your processes.

In the improve phase of DMAIC projects, or in the analyze phase of DMADV (DFSS) projects, consider the use of supplier-managed inventory and consignment inventory of supplied products and services. A total cost of ownership analysis will determine whether this will be beneficial to your business.

Also in the improve or analyze phases, consider reorganizing the management structure and increasing the use of e-procurement. Digital systems may be able to minimize non–value-added work and streamline the overall system.

Information Technology

For software development projects, it is usually better to treat these as design projects rather than DMAIC projects. This is because a new piece of software is essentially the design of something new rather than the improvement of something that already exists.

The randomness in software comes from the variation in results that users under different usage conditions will experience. In other words, people operating on a standalone PC will likely experience different results than someone on a networked PC, where the software is actually running on a server. Time of day and type of network architecture also cause variation. In 1950s technology, running the same software at different times would almost always produce the same result; this is no longer true.

Six Sigma can also help with Web page design, to optimize the page for speed, "stickiness" (keeping people coming to the site), ease of navigation, and so on.

Candidate topics for projects include the following:

- Improving the response of user help desks

- Reducing time and resources required to create Web documentation

- Reducing hours worked by contract IT support, through prioritization and restructuring of tasks

- Reducing network and mainframe "gridlock" by billing users more directly; for example, charging users on a per-megabyte basis for e-mail usage

- Structuring the steps to negotiate IT contracts, and routinely measuring the performance of the contract process

- Reducing the costs of computer purchases by improving the processes used to make purchases and improving utilization of existing systems

Research and Development

Integrate the DFSS methodology with your product/process development stage-gate process (that is, the existing process your organization uses to develop and validate new technology prior to releasing it).

Keep in mind that R&D projects have a longer time line than process-improvement projects, and as such will take longer to get money to the bottom line than DMAIC projects.

Very large projects should be broken down into a set of smaller DFSS projects. In addition to each having its own leader and team, someone should own the overall set and bring the individual project leaders together on a regular basis to ensure that the entire set of projects is well integrated.

New product/process development will likely require both DFSS and DMAIC projects. For example, the development of GE's LightSpeed CT scanner in 1998, the first multislice CT to reach the market, required a number of DFSS and DMAIC projects to come to fruition.

Development of measurements is an integral part of both DFSS and DMAIC projects. Measurement development and validation are often overlooked when the DFSS approach is not used. Technology development is often enabled by measurement development, nanotechnology (the technology of nano-scale—one billionth of a meter—materials) being one example.

Market research and business-case development methodologies should be included in the DFSS approach. Otherwise, the voice of the customer may be given limited attention. Engineers often believe they know what the customer wants; sometimes they are right, and sometimes they are wrong.

Sales and Marketing

Process thinking is a new concept to many sales and marketing professionals; take the time to teach them, and make sure they understand.

Many sales and marketing professionals do not think in terms of measurements and structured approaches to problem solving and process improvement. Often, each sale is viewed as an event. Be prepared for resistance, and take the time necessary to transform the culture to utilize a disciplined approach. Quantitative marketing research resources can often help lead the way; they are used to taking a structured approach based on quantitative measurements.

Because many aspects of the sales process are under your control, and data are readily available, *design-of-experiments* (DOE) techniques can often be employed within Six Sigma projects to better understand and improve the sales process.

In addition to improving its own processes, sales and marketing can play a useful role for the organization by asking customers (current, past, and future) what changes the organization can make that would increase the volume of business from these customers. These suggestions become input to the improvement efforts and project selection of the organization.

Some potential project opportunities include the following:

- Sales lead management (managing the "funnel" from leads to final sales)
- Price quoting process cycle time reduction
- Various aspects of managing price quotes (maximizing margin)
- Reducing the sales process cycle time
- Returns and credit process
- Inquiry process
- Consignment process
- Targeted marketing campaigns

Pitfalls to Avoid

A bureaucratic focus for the initiative is perhaps the greatest pitfall we see in Six Sigma deployments today. When organizations fall into this pitfall, the primary emphasis is on the initiative itself, and not on the results it is supposed to generate. This often occurs when it is not recognized that Six Sigma is about improvement, not training. Indeed, training is needed to build the required improvement skills, but the desired result is better business results, not training per se. Business leaders learned from the deployment of *total quality management* (TQM), *statistical process control* (SPC), and other quality initiatives that focus primarily on training is a "low-yield strategy."

An organization focused on improvement talks about progress toward improvement goals and bottom-line results. A bureaucratic focus on training produces emphasis on the number of managers, BBs, and GBs trained, or perhaps the number of projects closed. Other examples of the differences between improvement and training mindsets, specifically the different languages used, are summarized in Table 4.7 (Snee 2001). Most people have a training mindset when they are first exposed to Six Sigma. You should work to shift their mindset and focus to improvement as quickly as possible. The objective is to produce tangible results, not to have a great Six Sigma initiative.

TABLE 4.7   Language Used—They Say

Training Focus	Improvement Focus
We monitor participant surveys and number of people trained.	We monitor bottom-line impact, participant surveys, and number of people trained.
Training projects.	Strategic improvement projects.
Homework assignments done.	Impact of projects completed.
Who should we train as BBs?	What projects should we work on to reach our goals? Who should the BBs and Champions be for these projects?
Here is my training plan for next year.	Here is my improvement plan for next year and the training plan that will provide the needed skills and knowledge.
They liked it and learned it.	They liked it, learned it, used it, and got the results they needed.
Training classes.	Improvement workshops.
This training is needed by everyone.	Train those who are leading and working on improvement projects.
More training is better.	Appropriate training is best.

Other common pitfalls include the following:

■ Lack of commitment from top leadership

■ Attempting to deploy Six Sigma in people's "spare time"

■ Utilizing less than top talent

■ Lacking key supporting infrastructure, especially

◆ Reward and recognition systems for Six Sigma

◆ Project tracking systems

Note that most of these are just lack of some aspect of the key success factors discussed earlier.

Lack of true commitment from top leadership will sabotage the initiative. As noted earlier in this chapter, leaders cannot passively support Six Sigma, they must proactively drive it with a "burn-the-ships" mentality. This pitfall is of particular concern in real economy deployments because there will likely be significant resistance based on the "we're different" attitude. Some senior leaders may want to "jump on the bandwagon," believing that simply announcing a Six Sigma initiative will improve the bottom line and increase the stock value. Obviously, nothing could be further from the truth; Six Sigma is not a get-rich-quick scheme, but rather requires a great deal of planning and hard work. Borrowing from a commercial from years ago, through Six Sigma you will make money the old-fashioned way—you will earn it.

Related to this pitfall is the approach of doing Six Sigma in people's "spare time." In today's economy, particularly beyond the factory floor, people just don't have spare time, and therefore Six Sigma deployment will slow down to a glacial pace. We recommend full-time MBB and BB resources; when this is not practical, 50% dedication is an absolute minimum in our opinion.

Of course, full-time resources will not be successful if they are not the right resources. Another pitfall is the use of less than top talent in critical Six Sigma positions. This point was addressed at length in the discussion of keys to success earlier in this chapter, so here we only remind the reader to resist the temptation to utilize those resources who happen to be available, or those who haven't been able to do other things well, and therefore need a new "home."

Another point addressed in the "keys to success" discussion was the need for supporting infrastructure. Lack of such infrastructure, even in one or two areas, can seriously derail the initiative. Keep in mind that supporting infrastructure for improvement efforts tends to be much less common in financial services, health care, e-commerce, and so on, versus manufacturing, which has for some time employed industrial engineers, and implemented process control computer systems. Of particular importance are systems for recognition and reward and project tracking.

"Begin with the End in Mind"—Take a Systems View

Two common problems encountered in launching Six Sigma deployments, particularly in real economy deployments, are lack of process measurements and difficulty in finding good projects. A root cause of this condition is an inability to tale a holistic view of the organization, and how the various parts of the organization work together to serve the customer. A remedy is to identify, early in the Six Sigma deployment, the key processes, the key measures of performance for these processes, and a systems map of how the key processes fit together. An example of a systems map for an IT company, IBM, is shown in Figure 4.3. You saw this map earlier in Chapter 1.

The systems map provides a focus for the work. It helps you decide where the best projects might be. It helps you see where you have concentrated your efforts in the past, and areas that have been left untouched. Responding to Stephen Covey's admonishment, the systems view helps you "begin with the end in mind." Six Sigma should move you to a process-centered organization (Hammer 1996) in which the focus is on managing the key processes using data-based control procedures. You should be thinking in these terms early in the Six Sigma deployment.

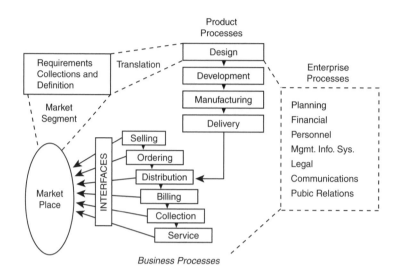

FIGURE 4.3 IBM core processes.

Six Sigma is fact based, driven by process metrics that enable both the selection of projects and the management and control of processes. Early on you should determine the baseline and entitlement values for the key process metrics. Baseline is the current level of performance. Entitlement is the level of performance that you are "entitled" to get from your processes, based on existing investment. Big gaps between baseline and entitlement are opportunities for improvement and sources of Six Sigma projects. Entitlement is determined by theoretical calculations based on the fundamentals of the process. When this information does not exist, historical data are analyzed and the "best observed performance" is used as the value of entitlement. Entitlement should be considered a working number that can be revised as new knowledge about the process is obtained.

Some organizations also begin work on a balanced score-card that typically has metrics in the following areas: financial performance, customer satisfaction, internal business process effectiveness, and organizational learning and growth (Kaplan and Norton 1996). It is critical in these situations to be able to link the metrics on the balanced scorecard with the key process metrics. Six Sigma projects focus on the improvement of the key process metrics.

Summary

Six Sigma deployments are greatly facilitated by using a proven road map. By definition, a proven road map has worked in the past and is likely to have incorporated the key learnings of its users. It is prudent to start with what has worked for others and then adapt the learnings to your organization in the form of a tailored deployment plan. The road map presented here has been used successfully by a wide variety of organizations in diverse application areas.

Successful Six Sigma companies have learned that there are three major success factors: committed and involved leadership, obtaining top talent, and building the needed infrastructure. All three are needed to be successful. It is also important to take a holistic view of the organization, identify core processes, and create a measurement system that enables you to monitor and improve the core processes. There are few, if any, shortcuts to successful Six Sigma deployment.

References

Hammer, M. 1996. *Beyond reengineering: how the process-centered organization is changing our work and lives*. New York: HarperCollins Publishers.

Harry, M., and R. Schroeder. 2000. *Six Sigma: the breakthrough management strategy revolutionizing the world's top corporations*. New York: Currency Doubleday.

Hoerl, R. W. 2001. Six Sigma Black Belts: What do they need to know? (with discussion). *Journal of Quality Technology* 33 4: 391–435.

Kaplan, R. S., and D. P. Norton. 1996. *The balanced scorecard*. Boston: Harvard Business School Press.

Rodebaugh, W. F., Jr. 2004. *The role of Six Sigma in enhancing leadership opportunities: a case study from W. R. Grace*. Transactions of the 58th Quality Congress. Toronto, Canada.

Snee, R. D. 2001. Make the view worth the climb: focus training on delivering better business results. *Quality Progress* (November) 58–61.

Snee, R. D., and R. W. Hoerl. 2003. *Leading Six Sigma: a step-by-step guide based on experience with GE and other Six Sigma companies.* New York: FT Prentice Hall.

Snee, R. D., and W. F. Rodebaugh, Jr. 2002. Enhance your project selection process: every company should be able to manage its project portfolio and create an overall organizational improvement system. *Quality Progress* (September) 78–80.

Weisbord, M. R. 1989. *Productive workplaces.* San Francisco: Jossey-Bass.

Welch, J. F. 2001. *Jack: straight from the gut.* New York: Warner Books.

Young, J. 2001. Driving performance results at American Express. *Six Sigma Forum Magazine* (November) 19–27.

Part III

Ensuring Project Success

5

PROJECT CASE
STUDIES

"A project is a problem scheduled for solution."
—Joseph M. Juran

This chapter begins Part III of this book, which focuses on keys to project success. Chapter 3 presented several deployment case studies within the real economy to illustrate successful Six Sigma deployment beyond the factory floor. Chapter 4 then discussed the keys to successful deployment. This chapter follows a similar format, but now focusing on individual project success rather than overall deployment success. Of course, these two are closely related, in that successful projects are critical to creating a successful deployment.

However, deployment is primarily a strategic issue, whereas an individual project is primarily a tactical issue. By this we mean that planning overall deployment requires one to think through strategic goals, overall human resources plans, reward and recognition systems, budgets, and so on. At the project level, you can typically focus on linking projects to business priorities and making specific projects successful without having to solve all the deployment issues within the organization. Therefore, this chapter and the next discuss how to succeed on individual projects, after which we turn to application of specific methods and tools in Part IV.

This chapter presents three successful projects from beyond the factory floor. The first is in the field of finance and involves prediction of corporate defaults in an investment portfolio at GE Capital, the financial services business of GE. This project is also unique in that it is a *design for Six Sigma* (DFSS) project rather than a *define, measure, analyze, improve, control* (DMAIC) project. The next two projects involve an application in legal at DuPont, and the tracking of pharmaceutical batch records for manufacturing and governmental compliance. These latter two projects involve applications in real economy functions within a manufacturing business.

These projects illustrate several keys to project success, such as careful selection of appropriate projects, following the right Six Sigma methodology, providing necessary support from functional groups (for example, IT), and assigning the right talent to the project.

Chapter 6 discusses the keys to success for these individual projects and presents a holistic project management approach based on these. We believe the principles contained in this approach provide specific guidance to help your real economy projects succeed. Chapter 7 then goes into more technical detail on the tools themselves. As noted in Chapter 2, real economy projects entail some unique technical challenges, such as the prevalence of discrete *critical-to-quality characteristics* (CTQs; for example, accuracy of financial figures) and skewed statistical distributions for typical continuous variables (for instance, cycle time). Fortunately, these unique technical challenges can be overcome with sound statistical approaches, as explained in Chapter 7.

We begin with the finance DFSS project, and then move to legal and pharmaceutical batch records projects. You can find additional details concerning the finance project in Neagu and Hoerl (2004).

A Six Sigma Approach to Predicting Corporate Defaults

The business world was shaken to its core in late 2001 and early 2002 because of the total collapse of energy conglomerate Enron and the fraud-induced bankruptcy at WorldCom. Enron, which had been number 5 on the Fortune 500 list, also took "Big 6" accounting firm Arthur Andersen down with it. The investigations resulting from the WorldCom bankruptcy led to discoveries of falsified accounting, fines, and criminal charges not only at WorldCom, but also at several other major corporations. These discoveries had a profound impact on investor confidence in equity markets in general, and in the opinion of many were one root cause for the significant declines in the stock market in 2002.

In addition to the losses experienced by individual investors and Enron pensioners, corporate investors also lost significant sums of money on investments in these companies. For example, Silverman (2002) reported that GE posted an after-tax loss of $110 million after downgrading the value of its WorldCom bond holdings. A key question that GE Capital, the GE financial services business that managed these accounts, asked itself at this point was whether such losses are simply the price of doing business with large investment portfolios, or if it might be possible to predict such corporate collapses ahead of time. Senior risk leaders in GE Capital asked a team at the GE Global Research Center to answer this question, and they decided to employ a Six Sigma methodology to do so.

To kick off the project, the Global Research team held an all-day planning meeting with the risk management group within GE Capital. The consensus of the group was that a DFSS approach using the DMADV (*define, measure, analyze, design, verify*) framework should be used for this project, because the intent was to design and implement an advanced warning system for corporate defaults rather than to improve an existing process. Of course, existing analytics were being utilized, but the group decided that none of these would satisfy the current need for a default predictor. The focus of the meeting was therefore on the define phase of the DMADV framework, because this is the phase that defines the overall objectives and approach used for the project.

Define

In the DMADV framework (Snee and Hoerl 2003), the major deliverable of the define phase is the project charter, which is basically a "contract" among all parties as to what the project will actually accomplish, a general timeline, roles and responsibilities, and so on. During the discussions, the group agreed that what was needed was an early warning system that would be based on publicly available information (no "insider information"). The system would need to give sufficient early warning to allow divestment of large (hundreds of millions of dollars) bond holdings prior to significant decline in value or default, and it would also have to minimize "false alarms"—that is, minimize the numbers of triggers to sell holdings that did not end up going into default in the near future. Note that the system was not intended to be a stock market predictor, just a predictor of default.

The dual focus on finding defaulting companies while avoiding false alarms is a common situation in statistics, usually referred to as *controlling both Type I and Type II errors*. However, this approach was itself an improvement, because previous efforts had focused primarily on finding defaulting companies only. The team determined that the scope of the project should be limited to North American, public, non-financial companies. The restriction to North American companies made the task of obtaining appropriate data more manageable, as did the focus on public companies, and thereby helped to create a realistic scope for the project. The restriction to non-financials was based on the belief that the modeling of financial companies' income, equity, and so forth presented a fundamentally different problem than modeling non-financial companies. Subsequent projects could address international and financial corporations.

Finally, the group agreed on an overall timeline with intermediate deliverables, a project budget, joint roles and responsibilities, and a path forward involving frequent communication via conference calls and face-to-face meetings. Part of the team was located in Bangalore, India; therefore, scheduling calls that allowed everyone to participate was not trivial. Figure 5.1 summarizes the key actions from the define phase and the other phases of this project.

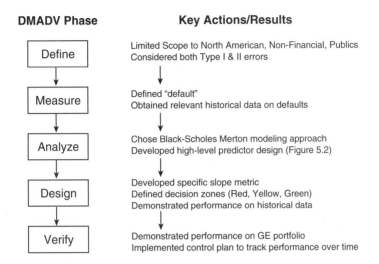

DMADV Phase   **Key Actions/Results**

Define
Limited Scope to North American, Non-Financial, Publics
Considered both Type I & II errors

Measure
Defined "default"
Obtained relevant historical data on defaults

Analyze
Chose Black-Scholes Merton modeling approach
Developed high-level predictor design (Figure 5.2)

Design
Developed specific slope metric
Defined decision zones (Red, Yellow, Green)
Demonstrated performance on historical data

Verify
Demonstrated performance on GE portfolio
Implemented control plan to track performance over time

FIGURE 5.1   Summary of default prediction project.

Measure

The main objectives of the measure phase in the DMADV framework are to operationally define the process CTQs, define performance objectives for them, ensure that they can be accurately measured, and, where needed, design a data collection and measurement system. As noted previously, in many applications beyond the factory floor, *Black Belts* (BBs) find that there is no measurement system currently in place and they need to design and implement one before the project can proceed.

In this particular case, the team discovered that it was using the term *defaulting companies* extensively, assuming that everyone knew what this term meant. However, upon closer examination, they discovered that there is no standard definition for *default*. For example, companies such as Moody's, *Standard and Poor's* (S&P), and *Dunn and Bradstreet* (D&B) report data on defaulting companies, but each uses a different definition of default. For example, if a company is delinquent in paying its bills, it may be classified as in default, even though it is not in bankruptcy proceedings and continues to operate.

Developing a formal operational definition of default was critical to success on the project. The team held several brainstorming meetings with the customer (risk management) to develop a formal, agreed-upon definition. What at first appeared to be a trivial task required a great deal of thought and discussion. This definition is considered GE proprietary, and therefore we do not provide the definition here.

After the team developed a definition of *default*, they were ready to define formal CTQs involving default. One CTQ was needed to monitor whether the system would be able to predict defaults ahead of time, with sufficient warning to allow countermeasures. For example, if the system provided 1 day of warning prior to WorldCom filing for Chapter 11 protection, this would be of minimal usefulness. By this time, the market knows that WorldCom is in serious trouble, and the value of bonds would already be discounted. The system would need to predict defaults with enough lead time that actions could be planned, and taken, prior to the market significantly discounting the companies involved. For significant bond holdings, in the hundreds of millions of dollars, this would require several months of lead time to completely divest. Therefore, again after significant discussions with the customer, this first CTQ was defined to be providing at least 6 months advance warning prior to a company going into default.

Investors within GE had another need—to avoid unnecessary sell offs that would drive up expenses and divert attention away from holdings that they really needed to divest. In other words, there was a need to limit the number of false alarms. Without such a CTQ, one could simply alarm every company all the time to satisfy the first CTQ 100%. Such a system would obviously be worthless.

Again, what sounded like a simple task—defining a false alarm—turned out to be nontrivial. To state that an alarm was a false alarm, the team needed to define a specific time window. In other words, after an alarm was sounded for a given company, the team needed to decide how long they would wait for an actual default before declaring this a false alarm. After more discussion and debate, the team decided that 2 years—24 months—was a reasonable amount of time to wait. If the company was still not in default after 2 years, the alarm was declared a false alarm. Therefore, the second CTQ was defined to be having alarmed companies actually go into default within 2 years.

The team now had two CTQs, one focusing on identifying defaulting companies early and the other focusing on ensuring that companies that generated an alarm actually went into default within a reasonable amount of time. These two CTQs seemed to fit well the objectives outlined in the define phase. In terms of capability to actually measure them, the definition of *default* used was based on information publicly available and reported by leading financial organizations such as D&B, S&P, and Moody's. The team was also able to obtain quantitative financial information on North American public companies going back about 10 years (as well as data on actual defaults for this same time period). However, the team was able to obtain financial data on many more companies (about 12,000) than those for which they could obtain actual default data (about 2,000). Initially, they focused on the 2,000 companies for which they had both financial data and actual default data.

This data provided a rich history that could be used to develop a default-prediction system and evaluate the historical accuracy of any system proposed. As is often the case, there were data quality issues with the quantitative financial data, and a significant amount of effort had to go into "scrubbing" the data to ensure it was accurate and useful. Although the team could not independently verify the measurement accuracy of the defaults reported by these organizations, they felt confident enough in published defaults to proceed with the analyze phase of the project. Figure 5.1 also shows the key actions from the measure phase.

Analyze

The analyze phase of a DMADV project is the most unique phase, relative to what is done in a DMAIC project. Because there is typically no existing process to analyze, this phase of DMADV focuses on developing a conceptual (high-level) design. In other words, the team attempts to think "outside the box" about potential design options, not limiting themselves to current design concepts. Because the team is thinking conceptually about alternative approaches, and there are at this point virtually no limitations (other than the scope from the define phase), this tends to be the most creative phase in Six Sigma. Critics who argue that Six Sigma is too technically rigid and inhibits creativity have generally never worked on the analyze phase of a DMADV project.

The conceptual design needs to include the entire system scoped out in the define phase, but does not yet need to include concrete technical details. For example, the conceptual design for a new customer service center could involve a Web-based system, but the team does not yet have to determine exactly how many servers, routers, or people in the center are required. These details will be added in the design phase, after the high-level design has been determined. It would obviously be a waste of time to work out technical details for a system that the team decides is not worth pursuing. In other words, it makes sense to screen out ideas that won't work prior to investing a lot of time and money in them.

Typically teams brainstorm ideas for potential design concepts, evaluate them to identify the most promising, and then use some type of formal evaluation methodology, such as a Pugh matrix (Ramaswamy 1996), to select the final high-level design. To ensure that all relevant elements of the system to be designed have been included, the team should consider each of the following categories:

- Product design (the output from the process, such as a loan, legal document, and so on)

- Process design (how the product will be produced)

- IT design (use of supporting information technology)

- Human design (what types of people will be needed, and how they will be organized)

- Materials design (what inputs will be required, such as information flows)

- Equipment design (what equipment will be needed, other than IT, such as medical equipment, phone systems, and so on)

- Facilities design (any physical facilities that will be needed, such as offices, warehouses, and so on)

In this case, the team evaluated various methodologies for default prediction. This is not a new problem, and extensive literature on the topic exists. After considerable research, the team identified the Black-Scholes Merton methodology as the most promising approach. This methodology is based on the Nobel Prize winning research of Merton (1996) and Black and Scholes (1973). The fundamental idea in this approach is to view the equity value (stock price) of a company as a stock option on the company's assets, and then to use stock option valuation theory to estimate the probability that this option will be called (have positive value). If the option is called, this implies that the company's assets remain greater than liabilities, meaning that the company remains solvent and does not go into default. See the references cited for a more detailed explanation of this approach.

Utilizing this approach provides a sequence of probabilities of default, updated each time new financial information is available. Theoretically, it would be possible to update these probabilities of default after each trade of a publicly held company on the stock market. Of course, most of the movement in the probabilities would be noise. Because other financial information, such as debt levels and asset volatility, are updated less frequently, the team chose to go with probabilities of default calculated on a monthly basis.

Finance theory suggests that equity-based metrics—that is, those based on stock market prices—are efficient, meaning that today's prices take into account all relevant information, and therefore historical values are not useful for prediction. In other words, if the price of a share of 3M stock is $150 today, it really doesn't matter whether yesterday's price was $140 or $151. Today's price of $150 incorporates this and all other relevant information. This theory therefore implies that there is no advantage to be gained from modeling changes in the stock market—it will simply wander from day to day reacting to changes in the economy and corporate performance.

Attempting to think "outside the box," as is expected in the analyze phase, and in response to noticing apparent trends in calculated probabilities of default, the team decided to try to develop some type of slope or "momentum" metric that would quantify whether a company seemed to be getting better or worse. Based on initial analysis of actual data, the team determined that some type of smoothing of the raw data, such as through moving averages, would be required to obtain a meaningful slope metric.

Then, each company would be plotted on a two-dimensional risk space, with one axis being probability of default and the other being the slope in probability of default. Companies in the upper-right corner (high probability, high slope) should be divested, companies in the lower-left corner (low probability, low slope) would be considered safe, and in between there would likely be a yellow alert zone of companies put on some type of watch list. Note that some level of vagueness in the ultimate system, as illustrated here, is acceptable in the analyze phase. These details have to be worked out in the design phase. Figure 5. 2 illustrates a high-level view of how this system might work, and Figure 5.1 summarizes the key actions from the analyze phase. The asterisk in Figure 5.2 indicates that the company in question falls in the No Action zone in this case.

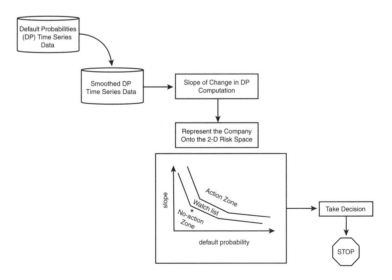

FIGURE 5.2   Depiction of high-level design.

Design

In the design phase, the focus is on providing the details needed to "flesh out" the conceptual design. The technical details that were not determined in the analyze phase, because they were not yet needed, now must be filled in rigorously. The goal at the end of this phase is to have a detailed system that meets the CTQs developed in the measure phase, and that is statistically validated and optimized. For the sake of brevity, we do not go into all the details of this design here. Rather, we focus on two key elements of the detailed design: the derivation of a specific slope metric, and the determination of the specific decision zones for the high-level design in Figure 5.2.

Obviously, the best choice of slope metric and the best choice of decision zones are dependent on one another. Therefore, the team actually considered these as one problem with two major aspects. As they developed alternative slope metrics, they evaluated the degree to which these could produce good decision zones (that is, decision rules). *Good* decision zones here means that they satisfy the two CTQs identified in the measure phase: providing early warning of true defaults, and minimizing the number of false alarms. The 10 years of historic data proved extremely useful here, in that any proposed slope metric or decision zone could be evaluated on these data to see how well it would have performed historically on the two CTQs.

Obviously, there is an inherent conflict between the two CTQs; the more sensitive the alarming system is, the fewer defaults it will miss, but the more false alarms it will produce. The team needed to identify a compromise that would provide satisfactory performance on both. The customers determined that missing defaults was a greater concern than false alarms, so they prioritized this CTQ. They set an objective of less than 20% missed defaults— that is, they wanted 6 months advance warning at least 80% of the time. For the second CTQ of false alarms, they were willing to tolerate a false alarm rate as high as 50% over 2 years. Of course, both the 20% missed defaults and 50% false alarm rate objectives are extremely high error rates for Six Sigma projects, in which you often seek part-per-million defect levels. Fortunately, the customers understood that these were atypical CTQs and that the way they had defined the CTQs would make it impossible to achieve part-per-million defect levels on both.

Figure 5.3 shows the results obtained using only a probability of default metric—that is, without using a slope metric—on historical data. The vertical scale shows the performance on CTQ 1 (missed defaults), and the horizontal scale shows performance on CTQ 2 (false alarms). Data for the 1-year, 2-year, and 3-year false alarm rates are shown. Each point represents the results obtained using a different "trigger value" for the prediction system. For example, the point in the lower-right corner of each curve represents the results obtained using a low probability as the trigger value for alarms. The exact values used are proprietary, so we shall assume this value in the lower-right corner was .02.

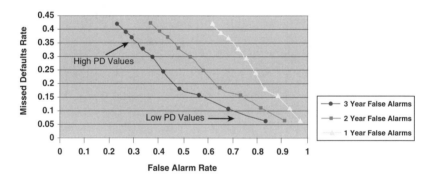

FIGURE 5.3   Results using only a probability of default (PD) metric.

Using a trigger value of .02, meaning that the system would "trigger" on any company whose probability of default exceeded .02, resulted in a missed default rate of about .06 (6%), and a 3-year false alarm rate of about .83, based on the historic data. (The 3-year false alarm curve is the leftmost curve in Figure 5.3.) For larger trigger values (say, .05), the system would trigger later, resulting in more missed defaults, but would likewise experience fewer false alarms. Therefore, the lines of points moving from the lower right to the upper left of Figure 5.3 represent increasing values of probability of default triggers. Clearly, the desired area to be in on this graph is the lower-left corner, which represents low error rates on both CTQs.

One might expect these results to form straight lines from the lower right to the upper left, indicating that any decrease in false alarms would result in an equal increase in missed defaults. Interestingly, this turns out not to be the case. Note that all three curves have a bend in the middle toward the lower-left corner. (That is, the curves are concave.) This implies that it is possible to decrease false alarms by, say, .05, but increase missed defaults by less than .05. The specific point that appears to be the cusp of the curve (closest to 0 missed defaults, 0 false alarms) is the fourth trigger value (counting from the lower right). Again, this value is proprietary, so we shall assume that it is .1. This analysis suggested that using a trigger value of .1 would produce an alarm system with the best balance of CTQ 1 and CTQ 2.

As can be seen in the 2-year false alarm rate graph in the middle of Figure 5.3, a trigger value of .1 resulted in a missed default rate of about .18 (CTQ1) and a false alarm rate of about .64 (CTQ2). This did not meet the objective of no more than 50% false alarms, but the 3-year false alarm rate of about .48 did meet this objective. The team therefore began investigating whether system performance could be improved through use of a slope metric. Interestingly, despite considerable effort, and a number of measures of slope applied, the team was unable to significantly improve on these overall results. This was disappointing, but the users felt comfortable with using a probability of default over .1 as the Red Zone trigger (Action Zone in Figure 5.2), and now wanted to see whether a slope metric could help define the Yellow Zone, which would be used as a watch list.

At this point the team decided to use migration into the Red Zone (PD >.1) as a sub-CTQ, for several reasons. First of all, they had hard evidence that most companies entering the Red Zone would eventually default. Therefore, predicting migration into the Red Zone would give an even earlier warning of default. Second, as noted earlier, they had much more data on financials than on actual defaults. By using a CTQ involving financials, and not actual default, they increased the sample size from about 2,000 to about 12,000.

The team utilized a variety of techniques to find and evaluate potential performance metrics, including logistic regression, classification and regression trees (CART), Markov chains, and simulation. These analyses had previously indicated that slope metrics were not effective in improving predictions of default, but now, with much more data, the team began to see evidence that slope metrics helped predict migration into the Red Zone. The conclusion that gradually emerged from several analyses was that very low probabilities of default clearly indicated corporate health, very high probabilities of default clearly indicated financial distress and likely default, but middle ranges of these probabilities provided insufficient evidence to draw definitive conclusions. In this area, slope metrics made a difference and enhanced predictability. CART analysis was particularly helpful in understanding this non-linear behavior.

Another interesting phenomenon discovered through Markov chain analysis was that if a company migrated into the Red Zone and then improved to move out of it, it was more likely to migrate back into the Red Zone than other companies with the same probability of default that had never been in the Red Zone. Technically, this implies that the system is not actually a Markov chain, but this analysis succeeded in detecting such behavior. Putting together all the information learned about migration into the Red Zone from these analyses, the team developed the rule system depicted in Figure 5.4. Note that above .1 probability of default, and below .01, no slope information is used. The slope metric did help in the middle ranges between .01 and .1, however. Each company was mapped into either the Red, Yellow, or Green (No Action) Zone based on its probability of default and slope. The key results from the design phase are shown in Figure 5.1. The next step was to validate that this system would actually work with a real portfolio.

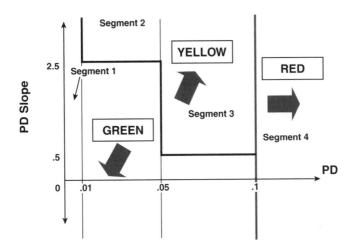

FIGURE 5.4   Rule system based on probability of default (PD) and slope of PD.

Verify

In the verify phase, the designers need to validate that the system will actually perform as expected under realistic operating conditions. By realistic operating conditions, we mean the same conditions that the system will see when implemented. For example, for a new IT system, you would not test it at 3 a.m., when computer traffic is at a low. Instead, you would test it during peak business hours, and would run it using the intended users of the system (nurses, accountants, and so on), not the computer scientists who developed the system. In this case, realistic conditions meant monitoring how the system would perform over time on a real investment portfolio, particularly one that was not used to develop the system in the first place.

Another deliverable of the verify phase is a control plan to help those who will own and operate the system and maintain it over time. This is similar to the control plan for a DMAIC project, but in this case it is developed ahead of time by the designers of the system, those who should be most knowledgeable about the details of how it works. A solid control plan aids implementation of the system and helps those operating it come up the "learning curve" quickly.

An actual credit (bond) portfolio of public North American non-financial companies (as per the original scope) was identified to evaluate performance. The team wanted to answer two specific questions:

1. Were the system predictions consistent with the price at which bonds were being traded—that is, would the market validate the predictions?

2. What financial results would occur from following advice from the system—that is, selling bonds in the Red and Yellow Zones, and buying bonds in the Green Zone?

To answer the first question, the team performed a "snapshot" analysis of the portfolio on 12/31/2001. Specifically, they calculated the market value of the bonds in the portfolio—that is, the value at which the bonds were currently selling in the market. This value was compared with the "book value" of the bond—that is, the value at which the bond is listed on the company's financial statements, or "books." In general, this is based on the original purchase price of the bond. If the default prediction system reflected market sentiment, the team would expect the market value of bonds for companies in the Red Zone to be lower than their book value. Similarly, they would expect the market value to be lower than book value for Yellow Zone companies, although not as much as for Red. Green companies should be approximately at their book value.

Table 5.1 shows the results of this snapshot analysis for the 1,016 bonds for which they could obtain market values. The bond markets are not as liquid as the stock market (that is, they do not trade as frequently), and therefore it is not always possible to obtain a valid market value for a given bond. In this table and the next, we segregate the Yellow Zone in the second segment in Figure 5.4 from the Yellow Zone in the third segment. Although both of these are in the Yellow Zone, the bonds in Yellow Segment 3 should be discounted more than those in Yellow Segment 2, simply because their probability of default is higher.

TABLE 5.1   Portfolio Snapshot on 12/31/2001 ($ Units Are Billions)

	Green	Yellow Segment 2	Yellow Segment 3	Red
Number of companies	897	21	38	60
Book Value	$47.1	$170	$1.02	$1.08
Market Value	$46.8	$170	$0.92	$0.81
Market-Book	-0.4%	0.5%	-9.5%	-24.7%

Note from this table that the market discounted bonds in the Red Zone by about 25%. Red definitely meant bad! The bonds in Yellow Segment 3 were also discounted, but not as much as those in the Red Zone (only about 10%). This was expected, and helped confirm the team's faith in the system. Interestingly, both the bonds in Yellow Segment 2 and the Green Zone were not noticeably different from book value (the -.4% and .5% variations were considered noise). This was noteworthy because it implied that the market had not yet discounted the Yellow Segment 2 bonds; in other words, the team knew something the market didn't know.

To answer the second question, these same companies were monitored until 3/31/2002—that is, for the next three months. The team determined the market value of these bonds on 3/31/2002, and then calculated the financial performance of each (its increase or drop in value). For reasons noted previously, they were only able to calculate market value for about half of the original bonds. They then segregated the financial performance by color coding as of 12/31/2001. This would indicate how well Red Zone bonds, Yellow Zone bonds, and Green Zone bonds performed.

If the market had already discounted the Red and Yellow Segment 3 bonds sufficiently, one would expect similar financial performance in each segment. Recall that the CTQs for this system involved predicting default, not bond prices. However, in the verify phase, the team didn't have time to wait for companies in this actual portfolio to go into default. They also assumed that companies headed toward default would decrease in value, and those not headed into default would maintain value, or increase. Therefore, monitoring financial results of the portfolio should tell a lot about ability to predict default.

The results of this analysis are shown in Table 5.2. Note that the Green Zone bonds decreased in value by about 1.5% over the first quarter of 2002, which is consistent with overall bond markets during that time frame. However, each of the other zones decreased more than this. Again, the Red Zone bonds decreased the most, even though they were already discounted by the market as of 12/31/2003, as shown in the snapshot analysis in Table 5.1.

TABLE 5.2   Portfolio Performance 1Q 2002 ($ Units Are Billions)

	Green	Yellow Segment 2	Yellow Segment 3	Red
Number of companies	501	16	17	19
Market Price 12/31/01	$25.3	$1.01	$0.35	$0.16
Market Price 3/31/02	$24.9	$0.96	$0.34	$0.14
Change	-1.5%	-5.0%	-2.1%	-8.5%

It was somewhat surprising that the Yellow Segment 2 bonds decreased in value more than the Yellow Segment 3 bonds, but this could be explained by a couple of reasons. First of all, it should be noted that with such small sample sizes, the observed differences could be due to random variation. Second, it could be due to the fact that the Yellow Segment 2 bonds had not been already discounted, whereas the Yellow Segment 3 bonds had. Therefore, the percentage decrease would be higher for those bonds in Yellow Segment 2. In any case, the value of the Yellow Zone bonds as a whole decreased more than those in Green, and less than those in Red. This analysis demonstrated the predictive powers of the system.

Theoretically, one would have liked to sell all the Yellow and Red bonds on 12/31/2003 and buy Green ones. Practically, this would be difficult to pull off, given the magnitude of the investments. However, if this had been done, the team's calculations indicated that GE would have saved more than $100 million in the first quarter of 2002. On an annual basis, this would amount to almost half a billion dollars. As Senator Everett Dirkson is reported to have stated, "A billion here, and a billion there, and pretty soon you're talking some real money." This team was definitely talking real money at this point!

Convinced that the system had predictive power, the final piece to the DMADV puzzle was to put in place a control system to maintain gains over time. In this case, it seemed probable that as macroeconomic conditions changed, the sensitivity of the system might change as well. After considerable discussion, the team decided to develop graphs of current missed default and false alarm rates (the performance on the CTQs) and update these each month. So long as these graphs were maintaining acceptable levels, there was no evidence that performance was deteriorating, or that the system needed to be retuned. If false alarm rates began increasing, however, it might indicate a shift in the underlying economy that would suggest a reevaluation of the triggers being used.

Discussions with intended users led the team to use simple run charts rather than control charts for these graphs. The main reason for this was the intended users' view that a change of practical rather than statistical significance would be needed to warrant modifying the system rules. This was particularly true given the very large sample size of companies the team was tracking, which would result in any standard control chart giving frequent out-of-control signals. They further agreed that a joint evaluation of the charts would be needed prior to modifying the system, involving both the developers and the users of the system, to convince themselves that any change was both real and of significant magnitude. Figure 5.1 shows the key actions from the verify phase.

Conclusion

The users were very satisfied with this system and integrated it into their formal procedures for approving large investments. In other words, anyone proposing a large investment was required to run the company through this system and document the color rating on the proposal. The chief risk officer of GE Capital (the name of GE's financial services business at the time) presented highlights of this system to Wall Street analysts during a presentation of GE's risk management procedures. Finally, GE leadership made a decision to patent this technology, and the researchers on this project have filed a patent application with the U.S. Patent Office. Future plans are to expand this system internationally (recall that it was developed based on North American, public, non-financial companies) and to develop a version for private companies, for which equity data is not readily available.

Interestingly, had this system been in place at the time, it would have predicted a problem with Enron 8 months prior to default and for WorldCom 5 months prior.

An Application to Legal Litigation

One of the "hardest nuts to crack" in company-wide Six Sigma deployment is often the corporate legal function. Many people have a difficult time seeing how Six Sigma could apply there. Of course, all major corporations have a legal function, and therefore deployment in legal is necessary to have a truly company-wide initiative. BB Julie Mazza, who is also a lawyer in the corporate legal function of DuPont, led the following project (Mazza 2000). To maintain confidentiality, some details of this case are omitted.

Background

Major litigation often produces massive amounts of documentation, sometimes measured in millions of pages. Such documents come from a variety of sources, but must be readily available if subpoenaed, or requested by the opposing counsel. Therefore, the problem of document management is both time-consuming and expensive, not to mention important for the legal case itself. This process is typically done manually, given the vast volume of documents that would need to be entered electronically. Such a manual process is obviously subject to human error, resulting in lost or incorrect documents. This project was based on the documentation required for one particular case, which for legal reasons Mazza did not name. In this litigation, an electronic database existed, which listed and classified all the relevant documents, but the documents themselves were still in hard copy form.

Define

In developing the charter for this project, Mazza recognized the DuPont legal team involved in the litigation as one customer and the legal function itself as another. The legal team needed a streamlined process to allow timely access to needed documents, with minimal errors. For example, if the legal team was not able to respond to a request for a particular document within 30 days, they would have to file for an extension with the court. Such extensions obviously undercut the credibility of DuPont's legal team, and if not granted could have dire consequences. The corporate legal function was a key customer in that it owned this process and was responsible for its costs. Specific objectives in the charter included reduction of non–value-added steps, reducing errors, improving cycle time, and reducing costs.

As an aside, such objectives might seem more appropriate to a Lean improvement approach, at least at first glance. However, as Chapter 7 explains, when the solution to the problem is unknown, Six Sigma provides a specific methodology to discover the solution, whereas Lean does not. In addition, because Six Sigma is a generic improvement methodology, it is straightforward to attack such things as cycle time reduction, error reduction, or waste elimination by just making them CTQs and applying DMAIC. Chapter 7 elaborates on how to improve Six Sigma by including Lean approaches in the toolkit.

The project team consisted of process owners, legal subject-matter experts, contract clerks, an IT professional, and Mazza (the BB). They began by mapping the entire document production process, including deciding where the project boundaries would be. Figure 5.5 shows the initial process map, including differentiating steps done by DuPont legal, outside counsel, and the outside document management company. This type of flowchart is often referred to as a *deployment flowchart* (Hoerl and Snee 2002, 197). This chart enabled the team to look at the process holistically and led to identification of redundant or non–value-adding steps, including inspection steps.

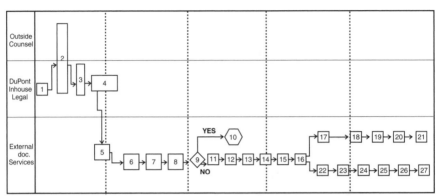

1. Document Request Received
2. Request reviewed for responsiveness, scope, timing staffing
3. Document database searched; list of potentially responsive documents printed
4. List provided to external doc. services "floor lead"
5. 2 copies of print request made: 1 for internal log; 1 working copy
6. Clerk assigned; given working copy of request
7. "Pull" sheet manually completed for each document
8. Document number(s) checked against Privilege Log
9. Is document privileged?
10. STOP
11. Document pulled from box, "pull" sheet inserted
12. Document pages manually reviewed for missing pages, gaps, etc.
13. Document production sheet manually completed; total pages calculated
14. Documents & tracking sheet given to "floor lead"

15. "QC" clerk assigned & given documents & tracking sheet
16. QC performed; documents returned to floor lead
17. Production tracking sheet sent to supervisor for updates
18. Request accuracy verified; new form created; form & tracking sheet sent to data entry clerk
19. Database updates made; form completed & returned to supervisor w/tracking sheet
20. QC clerk assigned; QC completed; report generated & attached to shipping boxes
21. Forms sent to production floor for filing
22. Copy center spec sheet manually completed & sent to copy center
23. Request logged in by floor supervisor
24. Copies made based on specs
25. Copies & originals sent to supervisor; QC clerk assigned
26. QC of copies v. originals made
27. Docs shipped to outside counsel via FedEx

FIGURE 5.5 Process map of document production process.
Adapted from Mazza (2000).

Measure

In this phase, the team formally defined the CTQs and measured the degree to which they were being met. CTQs were formally defined for cycle time, errors, and cost; the cost CTQ was a cost-per-page metric. To obtain measurements, the team reviewed data in the database mentioned previously, looked at actual invoices, including labor and copying charges, and also began looking into how frequently individual documents were being handled. Despite the existence of a "pull log" in the database, the frequency of handling variable turned out to be very difficult to measure accurately—that is, it was the most challenging measurement system issue.

The team documented the contributors to cost, including the following:

- Copying costs

- Time of people

- Fees for filing extensions to the 30-day limit for submitting documents to the court

- Data entry

- Document shipping

There were non–value-added costs in each of these categories (for example, when documents had to be recopied and reshipped because the wrong document had been copied and shipped originally). In addition, by digging through the details of the process the team discovered a number of opportunities for errors, such as allowing confidential documents to be copied. To protect confidentiality, Mazza did not list the specific levels of performance for each of these CTQs.

Analyze

In this phase the team worked with the data they had obtained and the existing knowledge of team members to identify root causes of errors and costs. Some of the most useful tools turned out to be knowledge-based tools, such as *failure modes and effects analysis* (FMEA) and cause-and-effect analysis. Both of these tools are discussed in more detail in Chapter 7. The FMEA analysis, shown in Figure 5.6 (with some details modified for confidentiality), highlights the most important issues that needed to be addressed to prevent potential failures of the system.

The RPN number is the *risk priority number*, which is just the product of the severity, occurrence, and detection numbers. The RPN provides one number to summarize the overall risk. QC in this document refers to a manual inspection loop. The cause-and-effect matrix is a form of *quality function deployment* (QFD), using a matrix format to identify the steps in the process most likely to impact the key process metrics of interest.

Process Step	Potential Failure Mode	Potential Effects of Failure	Severity	Potential Causes of Failure	Occurance	Current Controls	Detection	RPN
Pull Sheet Creation	Inaccurate Entries	Wrong Documents Pulled	9	Clerk Mistake, Inattention	8	QC	8	576
Priv. Log Check	Priv. Docs Not Identified	Wrong Documents Pulled	8	Clerk Mistake, Inattention	8	QC	8	512
Document Review	Miscounts, Wrong Documents	Wrong Documents Produced	8	Clerk Mistake, Inattention	7	QC	6	336
Tracking Form Creation	Inaccurate Entries	Wrong Documents Tracked	7	Clerk Mistake, Inattention	5	QC	6	210

FIGURE 5.6   FMEA of root causes of document process failures. Adapted from Mazza (2000).

In addition to application of Six Sigma tools, the BB team visited the people working in this process and interviewed them. These interviews were aimed at better understanding the way they did the work, the problems they faced, and how they felt about the job. It is common in applications beyond the factory floor to have an even greater human element in the process—that is, more human intervention than in manufacturing. Therefore, although meeting with the people working in the process is always a good idea, it is often even more important in real economy applications.

Based on these and other analyses, the team identified some key causes of errors and, ultimately, costs. These key root causes included the following:

- High turnover of contractor clerks

- Lack of adequate training

- Lack of ownership in the process by the clerks, leading to inattention

- Large numbers of documents.

After reviewing these causes, the team concluded that they would be difficult to eliminate or even mitigate with a manual process. This was particularly true because the clerks worked for a third party, not for DuPont. Therefore, the team reconsidered the option of a digital scanning system.

Improve

People had suggested scanning systems in the past. However, based on standard financial analysis, the investment had never been deemed worth the upfront costs. Fortunately for the BB team, their more extensive analysis had better captured total costs of the current solution, as well as the inability of a manual system to significantly reduce them. Based on this more detailed and quantified analysis, the team was able to successfully argue for a digital scanning system. There was still much work to be done, however, such as identifying the best digital option for DuPont's needs and agreeing on a price and schedule for scanning all the documents. The team also needed to develop an IT protocol for the scanning system consistent with existing IT systems.

The team remapped the document storage and production processes, based on a digital process, reducing these to four major steps in total:

1. Collect paper documents.

2. Image documents.

3. Index electronic documents.

4. Produce copies electronically when needed.

Based on the remapped process, the team ran a pilot study using a product called Virtual Partner, and found that they could reduce the unit costs of processing a page of documentation by more than 50%. This represents an annual savings of $1,130,000 for a similar-sized litigation. After full implementation, the electronic system was so successful that it is being migrated across DuPont legal, with total estimated savings of approximately $10 million.

Control

Despite the use of an IT solution, it was still important to implement a control plan to ensure the gains were maintained and that this solution did not lead to new problems. The IT system was designed to automatically track the estimated costs per document over time and provide real-time reports to quickly identify any emerging issues. The system also tracked performance on key CTQs and made this information available online to system users. Another aspect of the control plan was to forward invoices from the imaging contractor to the process owners, not for approval, but as a means of monitoring the costs on an absolute basis, in addition to a per-document basis. In addition, DuPont set up sessions to communicate the new roles and responsibilities people had with the new process and to provide training where needed.

Conclusion

The project delivered huge financial benefits to DuPont, and the solution is being leveraged across DuPont legal. Upon final examination, non–value-added steps were reduced by 70%. In addition to the hard financial benefits, this enabled the legal staff to become more productive and focus on what they were trained to do. For example, prior to this project, legal assistants spent considerable time on location at the document storage facility, expediting, checking up, resolving issues, and so on. Another benefit was that this system allowed DuPont legal to better comply with court requests for documents, enhancing the reputation of the organization.

As noted earlier, it is interesting that the ultimate solution of going to an imaging system had been suggested previously, but had been rejected based on assumed costs relative to assumed benefits. The detailed analysis done as part of the BB project demonstrated convincingly that the imaging system would not only be cost-effective, but that it also would likely be the only means of eliminating some of the root causes of defects (and subsequently, cycle time). Some might view this project to have migrated to a DFSS project after the decision to go with a digitized system was made. We acknowledge that in many cases, as seen here, the line between improving the existing process and designing a new one is somewhat fuzzy.

It should be noted that this was not the only Six Sigma project that DuPont legal completed; some additional Six Sigma application areas include the following:

- Records hold orders

- Employee termination

- Agreements management

- Online billing

- Legal charges to business units
- Continuing legal education

The Batch Records Case

A critical part of all pharmaceutical manufacturing is the creation and review of the records associated with the manufacture of each batch of drug product. Corporate manufacturing standards and governmental regulations require that detailed records be prepared for each batch of pharmaceuticals produced. These batch records track important information about various steps in the manufacturing process, including the manufacturing conditions under which the drug was made. The regulations require that prior to releasing any batch, the batch records be checked for completeness and compliance with *standard operating procedures* (SOPs). If anything is out of order, the batch is held until the issue is resolved.

In addition, government regulators could come in at any time to audit the records. As might be imagined, this system can create a huge bureaucracy, and often results in late or missed shipments. The required records could be as large as four feet when stacked on top of one another! Long batch review times result in millions of dollars of product in inventory, large floor space taken up by the inventory, and reduced customer satisfaction resulting from the long delivery times.

In this case study, Ajax Pharmaceuticals (a fictitious name used here to protect the confidentiality of the company) needed to increase production to serve a growing market. A major bottleneck was the poor performance of the batch review process. Ajax decided to use Six Sigma to improve the performance of the batch records review process, and Chris McKenna, a BB from Tunnell Consulting, was selected to lead the work on this important project. The results of this work are summarized in the following sections.

Define

Management started work on the project by developing a project charter. They narrowed the scope of the project to two specific products manufactured at the site, referred to here as Product A and Product B. The objective of the project was to simplify the process of developing and managing batch records, while fully satisfying all government regulations. Note that although this involved a manufacturing process, the scope of the project focused on the batch records review process, not the manufacturing process. As a result, this case is representative of many processes outside manufacturing that are essential for the effective operation of a manufacturing organization.

Key elements of the project charter included the following:

- The team would have 6 months to complete the project (given its complexity).

- The objective was to reduce batch record review time by 50%.

- A cross-functional team of seven people, including representatives from operations, quality assurance, and documentation, would work on the project.

- The investigation process (investigating issues in the batch records) was beyond the scope of this project.

Measure

In the measure phase, the team took a closer look at the process to develop an understanding of the process and to identify key measurement points. Figure 5.7 shows a flowchart of a part of the batch record process. The groups in the left column are the groups that get involved at one time or another in the batch record review.

- Labs create test results that are part of the batch record.

- Operator (production) is involved in creating the batch records.

- Supervisor ensures that the batch records are done properly.

- Manufacturing reviews the records from a manufacturing view.

- Quality assurance (QA) does the batch record review from the QA perspective.

- QA shop floor helps resolve questions arising from the batch records review.

- Investigation reporting process handles the incident reporting (things not meeting specifications or SOPs) as needed.

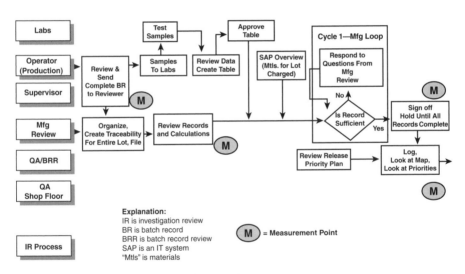

FIGURE 5.7   Flowchart of batch records process.

Note that there were two QA groups involved: one manufacturing oriented (QA shop floor), and one focused on the quality of the batch records (QA BRR—batch records review). The two related steps labeled "Review Release Priority Plan" and "Log, Look At Map, Look At Priorities" are listed as such because some batches would have higher priority for release than others. Often records for several batches would be in review at the same time, and according to business needs some batches would be given higher priority so they could be expedited, perhaps to meet a critical customer deadline. If the review process could be accelerated, the need for these "priority jumpers" would be greatly reduced.

The measurement points selected allowed the team to track cycle time through the process and determine which steps were causing problems with long review times. This strategy of identifying and monitoring subprocess cycle times has worked well in many other projects in monitoring process performance and identifying opportunities for improvement. They also helped track down root causes of errors in the records, which were the other key CTQ besides cycle time. Overall cycle time was defined as the time, measured in days, between completion of the manufacturing run and the completion of the batch records review.

The specific subprocess cycle times used to monitor the batch record flow from issuance to the time when the batch is approved are shown on Figure 5.8. In this process, manufacturing evaluates the records answering questions such as these: Are the calculations done correctly? Are the records complete? Have we complied with the specs? QA makes an additional overall assessment including these questions: Are the records generally complete? Are the calculations correct? Are the variances from specs and SOPs explained? Do the explanations make sense? Are there proper signoffs? QA sends the record back to manufacturing when a problem is found. QA has the final approval.

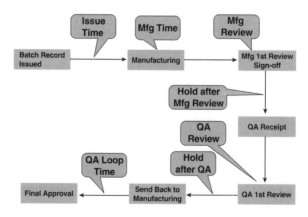

FIGURE 5.8   Document review process key CTQ variables.

Analyze

The team tracked and analyzed each of the subprocess cycle times and the overall cycle time. Figure 5.9 shows a control chart of cycle time for Product A batch record review time that the team constructed. (Product B had a similar chart.) This chart revealed that with a couple of exceptions, the cycle time was fairly stable, although it had wide variation, from about 12 to 54 days. This variation was obviously unacceptable, and the team set out to identify the drivers of cycle time. Data from the other measurement points in the process enabled the team to create Figure 5.10, a Pareto chart of the subprocess cycle times. Measured either in days ("index") or percent, this chart revealed that the manufacturing review was a key driver of overall cycle time. Note that in most cases a Pareto chart is not the most appropriate analysis for continuous data, but it was useful for the team in this case.

To dig deeper into the time required for manufacturing review, the team developed a cause-and-effect diagram (not to be confused with the cause-and-effect matrix—see Chapter 7), shown in Figure 5.11. This diagram looked for causes in three main areas: resources and priorities, equipment issues, and errors.

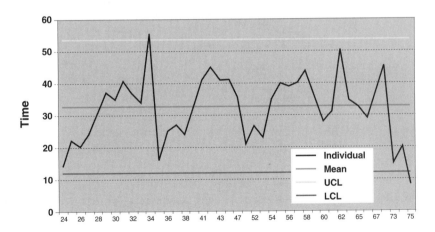

FIGURE 5.9   Control chart of Product A batch record review time.

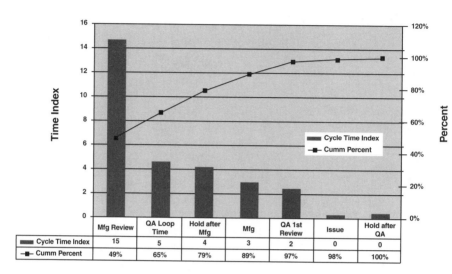

FIGURE 5.10   Pareto chart of Product A batch record review subprocess
cycle times.

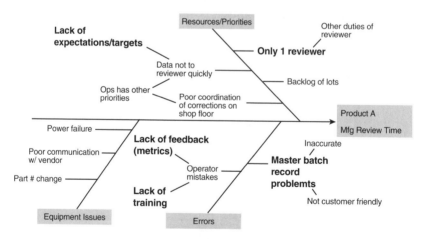

FIGURE 5.11   Cause-and-effect diagram for manufacturing review time
of Product A batch records.

After discussing these potential root causes in further detail, the team identified five primary issues that needed to be addressed:

- Lack of expectations and targets—overall and for subprocesses

- Having only one reviewer, with no backup

- Lack of feedback in the form of metrics

- Lack of training

- Problems with the batch records themselves

Improve

The team worked with management to develop target cycle times for substeps in the process. This enabled people to manage to a specific cycle time for their steps in the process and identify any issues early. This also enabled the overall review process to be tracked and problems to be identified as the batch records were being reviewed. The team also set up a system to collect and report data on performance relative to the targets. This brought a lot of attention to the problem. Training was initiated where needed, and backups were created to fill in during vacations or illness. The training included helping operations better understand the needs of the QA organization, and helping QA better understand the manufacturing process.

In terms of the batch record review process itself, the team made several fundamental changes. They completely restructured the regular tracking meeting to focus more on exception reporting and issue resolution, and less on routine data gathering and review. Another innovation was to submit individual records for review as they became available, instead of waiting until all records were complete. The team found that individual records could be reviewed while waiting for the rest of the records, thus speeding up the review process. They decided to reallocate work across the facility to balance workloads and to revise the structure of various other meetings, including QA reviews.

So what impact did these changes have? Figure 5.12 shows a run chart of the overall cycle time for Product A, with the change in average cycle time noted. This reveals a 55% reduction in average cycle time, freeing up about $3.6 million in inventory, not to mention resulting in better order fulfillment and customer satisfaction. In addition, the variation around this average is lower, resulting in greater consistency and predictability. For Product B the results were also quite significant: a 36% reduction in cycle time, freeing up $1.6 million in inventory. The main reason that the Product B cycle time reduction was less on a percentage basis was that Product B began the project in better shape, in terms of a lower average cycle time. The total amount of inventory freed up was therefore $5.2 million. The inventory reductions were one-time cost reductions. There are also ongoing cost reductions of more than $200,000/year related to cost of capital reductions and additional savings resulting from reduced floor space and reduced handling costs.

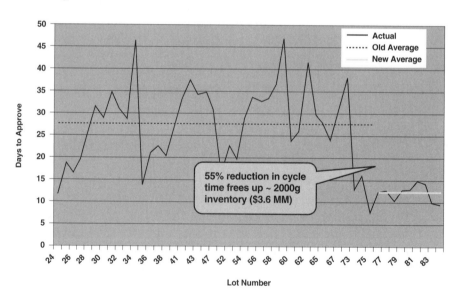

FIGURE 5.12   Product A batch record review time.

Control

To sustain the gains, the team initiated a continuous improvement process to manage and improve cycle time and errors over time. This system provided data on process performance and mechanisms for the right people to get together to review the data and make improvements as needed. The system scheduled regular management reviews to ensure that these data would receive appropriate attention and that the gains would be maintained and taken further. The DMAIC approach provided a standard means of attacking problems that arose.

This project also led to identification of a follow-on project to focus specifically on the Master Batch Record. Many who used it thought that it should be fundamentally redesigned to make it simpler and more effective (and to make it harder to make errors [error-proofing]). In addition, management planned future evaluations of subprocess cycle time targets to look for opportunities for further improvement. The identification of additional opportunities for improvement is a standard aspect of the control phase of the DMAIC process and typically uncovers additional improvement projects.

Conclusion

This project team had to deal with an additional constraint not present in most projects—detailed government regulations. Not only did the team have to reduce errors and improve cycle time, they also had to do it in a way that maintained compliance with government pharmaceutical regulations. The success of the project says much about the ability of Six Sigma to succeed in regulated environments.

Teamwork and the use of data are important aspects of the Six Sigma approach. By focusing on the entire process and having actual data to analyze, the team was able to overcome departmental "silos" and work collaboratively to improve the process. Every person could see how his or her work fit into the overall puzzle, and the downstream impact of his or her actions. When people started working as a team and focused on the big picture, ideas for improvement quickly appeared. This approach was also helpful in building commitment among team members to implement improvements because their input was used to create the improvements.

Although this project occurred in a production environment, the scope focused on development and maintenance of batch records rather than the manufacturing process. In many ways, the batch records process was more complex than the manufacturing process itself. This can be true in various functional arenas within a product manufacturing business, and is another reason why taking Six Sigma beyond the factory floor is so critical for all types of manufacturers.

Summary

Each of the projects reviewed in this chapter achieved significant success, although they were in very different areas: financial services, litigation, and compliance with manufacturing standards and government regulations in the pharmaceutical business. As we have seen elsewhere, the keys to success rarely change from one application area to another. To obtain project success, you generally need such things as these:

- Good selection of appropriate projects

- Assignment of top talent

- Proper use of the Six Sigma approach

- Project reviews with management

- Proper support from functional groups such as IT and finance

Each of these projects benefited from these success criteria.

This chapter also presented some projects from a real economy business (GE Capital) and some from real economy functions within a manufacturing business (DuPont legal and Ajax Pharmaceuticals batch records compliance). Obviously, there are many other application areas for which we could have selected project case studies. Hopefully, seeing some closely associated with manufacturing (batch records) and some not at all associated with manufacturing (default prediction) will stimulate readers to identify potential projects in both arenas. We will now elaborate further on how to ensure project success in Chapter 6.

References

Black, F., and M. Scholes. 1973. The pricing of options and corporate liabilities. *Journal of Political Economy* 81: 637–654.

Hoerl, R. W., and R. D. Snee. 2002. *Statistical thinking: improving business performance*. Pacific Grove, CA: Duxbury Press.

Mazza, J. 2000. *Cost reduction for document processing in major litigations*. Presented at 54th Annual Quality Congress. Charlotte, NC (May).

Merton, R. C. 1996. *Continuous-time finance*, revised edition. Oxford, UK: Blackwell.

Neagu, R., and R. W. Hoerl. 2004. A Six Sigma approach to predicting corporate defaults. To be published in *Quality and Reliability Engineering International*.

Ramaswamy, R. 1996. *Design and management of service processes*. Reading, MA: Addison-Wesley.

Snee, R. D., and R. W. Hoerl. 2003. *Leading Six Sigma: a step-by-step guide based on experience with GE and other Six Sigma companies*. Upper Saddle River, NJ: FT Prentice Hall.

Silverman, R. E. 2002. GE reports 14% increase in earnings. *Wall Street Journal*, July 15.

6

IMPROVEMENT HAPPENS PROJECT BY PROJECT

> Improvement happens project by project and in no other way.
> —Joseph M. Juran

The first two parts of this book introduced Six Sigma and discussed what it is, how its deployment differs beyond manufacturing, its benefits, and how to deploy it in the *real economy*. Our focus was on providing practical advice leading to successful deployment of the Six Sigma initiative. This part of the book focuses on the next level of detail in Six Sigma, ensuring project success. Project success is a critical element of overall deployment because rapid successful completion of improvement projects is at the heart of Six Sigma. Chapter 5 discussed some project case studies to illustrate what is involved in Six Sigma projects beyond manufacturing, just as Chapter 3 discussed some deployment case studies to illustrate what is involved in deploying Six Sigma beyond manufacturing.

Six Sigma, whether in manufacturing or not, is about improvement—obtaining and sustaining tangible improvements over time. Improvement is needed for businesses to succeed both short term and long term. Improvement processes and projects are most effective when tied to business goals, the bottom line, and reducing the pain the organization is feeling in the market place. In short, improvement must be part of strategic and annual plans and the associated budgets. This is even true for organizations not deploying Six Sigma.

We need a way to do this. The best answer that we are aware of is project-by-project improvement. Improvement pioneer Joseph M. Juran (1989, 35) admonished us that "improvement happens project by project and in no other way." Juran further stated, "A project is a problem scheduled for solution." As noted in Chapter 1, there are three types of improvement: design of new processes, enhancements of existing processes, and control of processes. Each of these types of improvement is accomplished by completing projects.

This chapter is about how to successfully identify and complete Six Sigma improvement projects in the real economy, both in non-manufacturing functions within a manufacturing business, as in the DuPont legal case, and service businesses, such as in the GE Capital default-prediction case. The following sections discuss keys to success, how projects can fail, a holistic model for improvement, guidance for application of improvement models, and training for project-by-project improvement. The focus is on those practical ideas that can spell the difference between project success and failure. Although much of this advice holds for both manufacturing and real economy projects, we highlight areas of unique challenge when completing projects beyond the factory floor.

Keys to Completing Successful Projects

Because the completion of improvement projects is the heart of Six Sigma, it is important to know and understand project success factors—those key things that must be in place for Six

Sigma projects to be successful. The key project success factors include the following:

- Selection of good Six Sigma projects

- Knowing process entitlement—the best possible process performance

- Keeping the project hopper full

- Assignment of a top talent *Black Belt* (BB) and Champion to the project

- Use of the right methodology

- Regular, well-structured project reviews

- Guidance from *Master Black Belts* (MBBs)

- Proper support, such as from functional support groups (IT, finance, HR)

- Clear project closeout criteria

This section discusses each of these success factors. Note that these are the same success factors one would likely find in manufacturing projects, but satisfying them beyond the factory floor requires some unique aspects. For example, there are often additional challenges to selection of good projects beyond manufacturing because of the typical lack of an improvement culture and potential scarcity of data available. Project selection is arguably the most important and the most difficult part of improvement (Snee 2001a, Snee and Rodebaugh 2002).

The first question to answer is, "What is a Six Sigma project?" Six Sigma is about solving business problems by improving processes. Typical problems fall into two major categories: solution known, and solution unknown. Six Sigma is aimed at solving problems in which the solution is not known, although as discussed later in this chapter the tools may also prove helpful in solution-known projects.

Such problems include decreasing errors in delivering health care, decreasing the time to fill orders and deliver products, and decreasing the days outstanding in accounts receivables. As noted earlier, Juran pointed out that "a project is a problem scheduled for solution." We define a Six Sigma project as a problem scheduled for solution that uses a set of metrics to set project goals and monitor progress, and applies statistical and other methods to scientifically study and improve the process.

The second category of problems frequently encountered is that in which the solution is known at the outset. Implementing a new computer network to conform to corporate guidelines, repaving the hospital parking lot, or opening a new bank branch are examples of known-solution projects. Most capital projects also fall into this category. In each of these situations, it is known what has to be done. The project is completed by assigning a project manager to the project, providing the needed resources, and using good project management techniques. Six Sigma techniques are usually not needed here, although project management can benefit from the process thinking, measurement, and monitoring techniques used by Six Sigma. Obviously, both types of projects are important to the organization.

Conducting successful Six Sigma projects requires that you carefully identify and document the process that contains the problem. The process provides the focus and context for the Six Sigma improvement work. Without identification of the process, projects may become vague, such as "improving customer service," leading to confusion and ultimately project failure. Process identification often presents a particular challenge beyond manufacturing because the processes are less visible, usually have less equipment involved, and frequently involve a lot of human intervention. Flowcharting and interviewing those who work in the process are tools that you can use to overcome this barrier.

To succeed at Six Sigma, you also need one or more measurements that quantify the magnitude of the problem and that can be used to set project goals and monitor progress. These measurements are usually called *critical-to-quality* (CTQ) measures. Defining the right measurements, and obtaining appropriate data on them, often presents a challenge in real economy projects. The application of *quality function deployment* (QFD) is helpful in defining meaningful metrics, and assistance from function groups can be invaluable in obtaining relevant data.

Selecting Good Six Sigma Projects

Now we turn our attention to the critical task of selecting Six Sigma projects. The characteristics of a good Six Sigma project are summarized in Table 6.1. Again, these characteristics are appropriate in any application area. Projects should be clearly linked to business priorities, as reflected by the strategic and annual operating plans. It is also appropriate to include projects addressing critical problems that must be solved for the organization to be successful in the next year, such as the need to respond to legal requests, as in the DuPont case.

TABLE 6.1   Characteristics of a Good Six Sigma Project

Clearly connected to business priorities:

- Linked to strategic and annual operating plans.

Problem of a major importance to the organization:

- Major improvement in process performance (e.g., > 50%).
- Major financial improvement (e.g., > $250K/yr).

Reasonable scope (doable in 4 to 6 months):

- Support for project often decreases after 6 months.
- Project scope too large is a common problem.

Clear quantitative measures of success:

- Baseline, goals, and entitlement well defined.

Importance is clear to the organization:

- People will support a project that they understand and see as important.

Project has the support and approval of management:

- Needed to get resources, remove barriers and sustain over time.

A project should represent a breakthrough in terms of major improvements in both process performance (e.g., greater than 50%) and significant bottom-line results (e.g., greater than $250,000). The determination of project impact is the responsibility of the financial organization working in cooperation with the BB and Champion.

This approach to measuring project impact sets Six Sigma apart from most other improvement approaches, because the financial impact is identified for each Six Sigma project by the finance department. Finance should estimate what the project may be worth to the bottom line before work begins. This makes finance an active participant in the improvement of the organization. This will be a new role for finance in many organizations. Of course, finance and other functions will still have their own projects to improve their own processes.

The projects should be doable in 4 to 6 months. As pointed out by Bill Gates (1999), it is critical that projects be completed in this timeframe to keep the organization and resources focused on the project. Organizations typically lose interest in projects that run longer than 6 months. This is even more of a concern in real economy applications, where management may not have significant experience in improvement projects, and may therefore be even less patient. Proper project selection and scoping can help here. Projects requiring more than 6 months of effort can usually be divided into subprojects of shorter duration, with the projects being conducted sequentially or in parallel. For this approach to work, there needs to be strong project management to coordinate the set of projects as a whole.

There should also be clear quantitative measures of success, the importance of the project to the organization should be clear, and the project should have the full support and approval of management. These three characteristics are needed so that the organization sees the importance of the project, provides the needed support and resources, and removes barriers to the success of the project. People are more likely to support a project that they can see is clearly important to the organization.

Of course, these are generic attributes of a good project. Organizations still need to develop their own specific project selection criteria. Compare the generic attributes in Table 6.1 to the more specific project selection criteria from one organization, Commonwealth Health Corporation, listed in Table 6.2. The criteria in Table 6.2 defined important areas to improve for this organization, and projects based on these criteria did, in turn, produce significant results. Note also that the areas to improve include customer satisfaction measurements. Different functional areas and types of businesses will likely have unique selection criteria.

TABLE 6.2   Project Selection Criteria Used by Commonwealth Health Corporation

Priority metrics to improve:
■ Customer satisfaction
■ Quality of care/service
■ Timeliness/speed/convenience
■ Cost
Initial application area:
■ Radiology
Doable within a reasonable timeframe (quick hits)
Methodology:
■ Identify key indicators
■ Develop high-level system maps
■ Define high-level CTQs

Project ideas can come from any source such as process assessments, customer and employee surveys and suggestions, benchmarking studies, extensions of existing projects, and so on. Some organizations struggle with how to find high-impact projects. Some sources that we recommend include the following:

■ Rework, overtime, warranty, and other sources of waste

■ Products with major backlogs—need for more capacity

■ High-volume products (small improvements can have huge impact)

■ Problems needing solutions to meet annual operating plan

- Major problems with financial impact (customer or regulatory crises)

- Large budget items, receivables, payables, treasury, taxes (follow the money)

Collectively these ideas are focused on major sources of waste, major problems (customer and regulatory), major opportunities (capacity limitations in growth markets), and places where the money is going. Budget statements and cost-of-quality studies are also good sources for identifying opportunities (Conway 1992, 1994).

Experience has also identified some characteristics of projects to avoid, or at least to further refine. Briefly stated, you should avoid, or redefine, projects that fall into these classifications:

- Fuzzy objectives

- Poor metrics

- Not tied to financials

- Too broad a scope

- No connection to strategic or annual plans

- Solution already identified

- Too many objectives

For the project to succeed, for example, the objectives need to be very clear. Such clarity is usually reflected in the process performance metrics and goals associated with the project. For example, provide at least 6 months warning of impending defaults, as in the default-prediction case. The process metrics should be clearly defined and have identified baseline and entitlement values, as discussed in the next section. The most useful process performance metrics in real economy projects are typically some form of accuracy, cycle time, or cost. Cost is often directly related to accuracy and cycle time metrics. In Table 6.2 you can see that these are the priority metrics used by Commonwealth Health Corporation.

With the exception of projects solely focused on customer satisfaction issues, the project should be tied to the bottom line in some way. The project scope should enable improvements to be attainable in the 4- to 6-month timeframe. An unrealistically large scope (often referred to as a "boiling the ocean" project) is probably the most commonly encountered cause of project failure. Projects that are not connected to business priorities or that have too many objectives also need further refinement. Projects with an identified solution should be handled by a project manager instead of Six Sigma, or as mentioned earlier be redefined to omit the specified solution in favor of allowing the Six Sigma methodology to identify the best solution.

Process Entitlement—The Best Possible Process Performance

Entitlement is one of the most important concepts in process improvement, and is particularly useful in project selection. It is defined as the best performance that you can reasonably expect from a process (Harry and Schroeder 2000). As the term implies, leadership is essentially entitled to this level of performance based on the investments they have already made. However, experience has shown that very few processes, on the factory floor or beyond, operate at process entitlement.

Knowing the process entitlement defines what's possible. If entitlement is 5,000 invoices per day and the baseline performance is 2,500 invoices per day, you can easily see that there is a lot of room for improving this process. On the other hand, if current baseline performance is 4,800 invoices per day, there is little room for improvement. If higher rates are needed, a search for a totally new process may be in order (for example, reengineering or design for Six Sigma).

As an analogy, the concept of par for a golf hole is intended to represent the entitlement for a very good golfer. That is, for such a golfer par represents what score is possible and reasonable to expect. On one hole, a golfer may score less than par, but it is unrealistic to expect such performance on every hole, or even on average. Of course, all golfers have their own unique capability, so the official par doesn't represent process entitlement for the average duffer. Proper analysis and/or calculations would reveal the appropriate individual entitlement, which for professionals would be better than par, and for most golfers much worse. Note that standard golfing handicaps are usually based on average performance, which is not the same concept as entitlement.

It is not uncommon to learn in situations where capital is being requested to increase operating capacity (e.g., to approve credit card applications) that the current operation is not near entitlement, once it is carefully calculated. Six Sigma projects are subsequently instituted to increase the capacity of the current process with solutions that don't require capital. Most companies deploying Six Sigma have been able to cancel existing capital expansion plans because of capacity that has been freed up through Six Sigma without capital expenditures.

In a highly computerized order-fulfillment process, for example, a $2 million capital project had been approved to enhance the computer system to handle the large number of orders that were "falling out" of the main system because of order errors. Baseline data indicated that only 67% of the orders were passing through the system without any problems. The first improvement project identified the root causes of many of the order problems. The process improvements put in place resulted in 94% of the orders passing through the system without any problems. This eliminated the need for the enhanced computer system and the associated capital expenditure. It reduced operating costs by $11 million and increased sales revenues via the higher throughput.

Entitlement should be determined for all key process performance measures (cycle time, cost, capacity, downtime, etc.). It may be the performance predicted by the design characteristics of the process, or just the best, prolonged performance observed to date. For example, if you intend to pay invoices in 30 days to receive net 30-day discounts, process entitlement is likely 30 days minus perhaps 5 days for mailing time (that is, entitlement = 25 days), unless electronic payment is being used. Assuming that your payment system is designed to handle the volume of invoices coming in, there is no reason why you shouldn't be able to meet the 25-day objective.

Entitlement can also be predicted from empirical relationships. For example, suppose you have observed that the process of approving mortgage applications is averaging 36 person-hours, but had at one time operated at a 16-hour average. This would suggest that the process entitlement (as determined by best prolonged performance) should be 16 hours. On further investigation, it might be observed that there is a linear relationship between defects (incorrect or missing information) and cycle time of the following form:

$$\text{Cycle time} = 12 + 3(\text{defects})$$

Therefore, if defects could be reduced to very low levels (essentially zero), the true process entitlement may be as low as 12 hours.

Entitlement is used in project selection as follows:

- Look at the gap between baseline performance (current state) and entitlement (desired state)

- Identify a project scope that will help close the gap and can be completed in 4-6 months

- Assess the bottom line impact of the project and compare it to other potential projects

- Assign a *Black Belt* (BB) or *Green Belt* (GB) when available

The gap between baseline and entitlement is rarely closed in the course of a single project. It is not uncommon for several projects to be required. In each instance, the business case for the project is determined, the project is prioritized relative to the other potential projects, and a BB or GB is assigned as business priorities dictate.

Keep in mind that process entitlement can, and often does, change as you learn more about the process. In most cases, the process entitlement calculations are just estimates of the true entitlement, and you can update and enhance them over time. After a few Six Sigma projects, it is not uncommon for a process to be performing beyond the entitlement level initially determined for the process. Changing the value of process entitlement as you better understand the process is a natural result of Six Sigma projects, and the need to do so should not come as a surprise. This is particularly true of projects beyond manufacturing, when data are often initially scarce.

Keep the Project Hopper Full

When the BBs have completed their first project, they are ready to take on another project. You don't want to lose any momentum. After this new project has gotten under way, full-time BBs will be ready to take on another project simultaneously. This ramp-up will continue until fully operational BBs are handling three or four projects at a time.

Clearly, with a lot of BBs working in an organization, you need to plan carefully to ensure that you have important, high-impact projects identified and ready to go when the BBs are ready. A frequent mistake companies make is waiting for the BB to finish a project before looking for another one. Such a strategy wastes the time of the BBs, a valuable resource. A BB without a project is a sin in the Six Sigma world. Lack of planning also often results in mediocre projects being selected, because sufficient thought had not been put into the selection process. Good project selection is a key to success.

Now that you have numerous projects and BBs, you cannot rely on ad-hoc project selection, but must implement a formal selection and prioritization system. A schematic of an ongoing project selection process and its associated project hopper is shown in Figure 6.1 (Rodebaugh 2001). Project selection should be an ongoing process that ensures you always have a collection of appropriate projects ready for BBs to tackle. One strategy for keeping the project hopper "evergreen" is to require that a new project be added to the hopper each time a project is removed and assigned to a BB or GB.

The project hopper can be thought of as an organizational to-do list and should be managed in much the same way. Projects are continually being put into the hopper, the list is continually being prioritized, and prioritized projects are assigned to BBs or GBs as these resources become available. By continually searching for projects, and reprioritizing the list of projects in the project hopper, you ensure that problems most important to the organization are being addressed by Six Sigma.

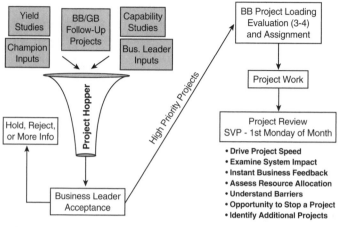

FIGURE 6.1 Project selection and management process.

Process baseline and entitlement data should be maintained and updated for all key process performance metrics associated with all key manufacturing and non-manufacturing processes used to run the organization. The job of creating and maintaining this database is typically assigned to an MBB or experienced BB. This database should be updated every 6 months or so and be an item for at least every other quarterly Six Sigma Initiative Review (see Chapter 4). Although development and maintenance of such databases is simply good management practice, our experience is that typically they either don't exist at all, or are solely focused on accounting information, and therefore are inadequate for improvement purposes. Lack of good data is probably the greatest issue faced by BB teams. This is one reason why evaluation of the measurement system is a key element of the measure phase of *define, measure, analyze, improve, control* (DMAIC) projects.

Selecting the Right People

Use of top talent in Six Sigma is a theme running throughout the initiative, but is perhaps most critical in the BBs leading the individual projects. We have seen huge variation in success rates between projects that were led by true top talent and projects that weren't. For example, one management group we know of ranked

25 persons to identify candidates for 3 BB positions. The 3 persons selected were ranked 5, 15, and 16 on the list. The fifth-ranked BB did well and was a strong leader. The projects completed by the fifteenth- and sixteenth-ranked persons were less successful. Many interpreted the fact that none of the candidates ranked 1 through 4 were selected as BBs for Six Sigma as a lack of strong support by the management team. Although, of course, the rankings were not made public, people generally know who their most talented peers are.

Finding the most appropriate BBs beyond manufacturing deployments can be a challenge, because without engineers in large numbers it is difficult to find people with skills in scientifically based improvement methodologies. As noted in Chapter 2, some organizations, such as banks and hospitals, have therefore searched out experienced BBs with manufacturing experience and attempted to teach them their business. Bank of America is one such example. This approach can work, although in many cases such BBs will lack needed subject-matter knowledge. Many real economy organizations do have scientifically or at least statistically trained workers already. Examples include actuaries in insurance, nurses in hospitals, and computer scientists in e-commerce.

Of course, technical skills are only one relevant criterion. BBs, as well as other key Six Sigma roles, should possess strong leadership skills, demonstrated ability to deliver tangible results, and effective teamwork and communication ability. These other skills are just as prevalent beyond manufacturing as they are on the factory floor.

Using the Right Methodology

Using the right methods and tools is another success factor for Six Sigma projects. This means following the DMAIC improvement process and using the tools in the proper way and sequence. Not all the tools are used in every project, but in each project each tool should be considered, and a conscious decision made as to whether the tool is needed. For example, we know a bright young professional who used bits and pieces of the DMAIC approach along with his process knowledge to complete his project. The project was successful, but no one could understand how he got his results. As a result it was difficult for the organization to build on or leverage his results. The Six Sigma methodology, properly used, is a very effective communication tool regarding processes and their design, improvement, and control.

We have seen many projects fail because BBs decided to skip a step, or not follow the Six Sigma methodology at all. Often this is due to the best of intentions, but typically it results in missed opportunities. Similarly, in real economy projects, there is often a tendency to bypass the statistical tools and focus on the knowledge-based tools such as flowcharts and cause-and-effect diagrams. This is particularly true when the BB does not have a technical background. Although we encourage BBs to utilize the simplest tools that will work in a given situation, and although we have seen tremendous improvement achieved with basic tools, we must also emphasize that results will be maximized when BBs have the ability to apply all the tools in the Six Sigma toolkit, including the statistical tools. Therefore, training is particularly important when non-technical people are selected as BBs or GBs.

Management Project Reviews

Management review is a critical success factor for Six Sigma projects. Regular management review keeps the project focused and on track. We know of no successful Six Sigma implementation in which management project reviews were not a key part of the deployment process. Reviews of projects beyond the factory floor are even more imperative because of the unique challenges discussed throughout this book. Project reviews should be done weekly and monthly, whereas reviews of the overall initiative are preferably done quarterly, or at a minimum, annually, as discussed in Chapter 4.

Six Sigma projects are most successful when Champions review them weekly and the business unit and function leaders review them monthly. Such a drumbeat prevents projects from dragging on and provides leadership with early warning of any problems. A useful agenda for the Champion review is as follows:

- Activity this week

- Accomplishments this week

- Recommended management actions

- Help needed

- Plan for next week

This review is informal and need not be time-consuming—taking approximately 30 minutes. The idea is to have a quick check to keep the project on track by finding out what has been accomplished, what is planned, and what barriers need to be addressed. Typically, Champions guide only one or two BBs, so the time requirements are not overwhelming. These reviews help the Champions fulfill their role of guiding the project and addressing barriers. MBBs also attend these reviews as needed, and the MBB and BB also meet separately to resolve any technical issues that might have arisen.

Typically, all current projects are reviewed monthly as well. This monthly review with the business unit or functional leader is shorter than the weekly review, being no more than 10 to 15 minutes per project. The purpose is to keep the project on schedule with respect to time and results, and to identify any problems or roadblocks. This review helps the business unit and functional leaders stay involved in Six Sigma and directly informs them of any issues they need to address. A useful agenda for these reviews is as follows:

- Project purpose

- Process and financial metrics—progress versus goals

- Accomplishments since the last review

- Plans for future work

- Key lessons learned and findings

Notice that this agenda is similar to that for the weekly review with the Champion. In the monthly review, much more emphasis is placed on performance versus schedule, progress toward process and financial goals, and key lessons learned and findings. As Six Sigma grows, the number of projects may become large, requiring a lot of time for the reviews. Organizations can reduce the review time by rating projects as green (on schedule), yellow (in danger of falling behind schedule if something isn't done), or red (behind schedule and in need of help), and reviewing only those rated as red and yellow.

One way to increase the speed, clarity, and understanding of the review process is to use a common reporting format, such as the one shown in Figure 6.2. This format is similar to templates used by GE, AlliedSignal, DuPont, and other companies. An overall project summary is shown on one page using the four headings of project description, metrics, accomplishments, and needs. Additional backup slides to support the material in the summary can be added as needed.

Project Description

• Reduce Days Sales Outstanding (DSO) for Concrete Products U.S. from 55 to 45 days
• Team Members:
  – SAP Business Analysis
  – District Sales Manager
  – Project Champion
  – Senior Credit Specialists
  – Mgr. of Treasury Services
  – Customer Service & Logistics Mgr.
• Projected Savings: $500,000   Projected Completion 4-15-00

Accomplishments Since Last Review

• Requested Credit Dept. to verify customer address, identify customers with different bill to and payer address, and note date of invoice requested.
• Southeast region is the pilot for Point of Delivery project. This can reduce billing cycle from 5 days to 1.
• Developed a report that measures days to bill.
• Developed process and procedures for calling late paying customers 35 days after delivery.

Metrics

	BSL	Goal	ENT
DSO	55	45	35
Days to Bill	5	1	1

• Reasons for late payments
• Reasons for credits
• Reasons for billing errors

Issues/Needs

• Identify why some customers do not have an invoice (2-1-00)
• Call late paying customers on day 35 (2-1-00)
• Implement credit checks for bulk shipments (88% of business) prior to shipment
• Implement credit hold & credit block procedures
• Reduce billing cycle time (3-1-00)
• Reduce billing errors- pricing & sales tax (2-15-00)

Key Takeaway

Call customer early to modify their Accounts Payable policy and resolve any problems

FIGURE 6.2   Example project status reporting form.

We all need feedback. Feedback is required to know how we're doing and to improve. Former New York City Mayor Ed Koch used to ask at every opportunity "How am I doing?" The Beatles also needed feedback. The rock group's last outdoor concert was held in Candlestick Park (San Francisco) in 1966. The crowd noise was extremely loud, so they knew their music was appreciated; because of the noise, however, they couldn't hear themselves sing.

They had no direct feedback of their voices. Without this feedback the Beatles couldn't monitor their own performance and improve it where necessary. This led them to discontinue outdoor concerts.

Feedback provided during reviews is an important aid to improvement. BBs want and need feedback, and management reviews are one important form of providing it. In all project reviews, it is important to ask questions to identify the *methods, logic,* and *data* used to support decisions. It is also important to pay attention to both *social* and *technical* issues. Sometimes the social concerns such as interpersonal relationships and leadership skills are more important than the technical issues.

When Roger Hoerl became the Quality (Six Sigma) Leader for the GE corporate audit staff, a breakthrough occurred during a project review with the vice president of the audit staff. One particular GB who had resisted utilizing the full Six Sigma methodology on his project was presenting and noted that his team had identified a root cause of a problem in a financial system. The VP asked him, "What data or analysis revealed that this is the root cause?" When the GB was unable to give her anything concrete, the VP said, "We're going to end the review now. When you have the data, and have done the appropriate analysis, come back and let me know, so we can continue."

The GB stopped by Hoerl's office that afternoon for help and eventually ended up with a very successful Six Sigma project. More importantly, word spread rapidly throughout the audit staff that the VP expected people to have done their projects using the appropriate Six Sigma methodology and tools, and would accept nothing less. This one comment in one review was the turning point in Six Sigma deployment at the GE audit staff.

It is also important to do a lot of listening in these reviews. Open-ended questions, rather than those that can be answered yes or no, generally lead to more informative answers. Two helpful questions are "Could you explain that in more detail?" and "Could you help me understand how you arrived at that conclusion?" This latter question is equivalent to the audit staff VP's question just mentioned.

When you want to learn how the project—or any activity for that matter—is progressing, ask two questions: "What's working?" or "What are we doing well?" and "What do we need to do differently?" The answers will take you a long way toward understanding what is going on in the project or activity.

The BBs, Champions, or a combination of BBs and Champions can present the projects at the monthly reviews. Having the Champions give the reports involves them more deeply in the Six Sigma initiative and increases understanding and ownership. When appropriate, Champions can report on several projects, reducing the amount of time required for the reviews.

Guidance from MBBs

Another critical success factor for Six Sigma projects is guidance for BBs and GBs from MBBs. This is particularly true in the early stages of the BB and GB assignments when they are short on experience. They typically have questions regarding project scope and organization, how to use the tools, how to interface with the Project Champion, how to deal with team issues, and so on. In the GB story discussed in the previous section, Roger Hoerl was acting in the role of the MBB as he advised the GB. The MBB typically works with the BB and GB in three key ways: providing formal training, coaching and mentoring, and reviewing project progress in cooperation with the Project Champion. Each of these roles is critical to the success of the BBs/GBs and their projects.

Right Involvement by Functional Groups

It is also important that projects have access as needed to resources from support groups, such as IT, finance, or purchasing. Functional groups provide expertise, data, and team members needed for Six Sigma projects to be successful. In particular, finance determines the financial impact of the project before the project is started to help decide whether the project is worth pursuing, and after the project is completed to determine the actual financial impact attained by the project.

Functional group support often is most critical in the improve phase of projects, when an identified improvement needs to be implemented. If the improvement calls for a process step to be digitized, for example, the prompt support of the IT organization is necessary. We have seen situations in which the improvements recommended by the BB or GB couldn't be implemented because the functional support groups didn't agree with the project recommendations. In other cases, sufficient resources weren't available from the functional groups to implement the process changes. Careful upfront planning and clear communication during the life of the project can certainly reduce, if not eliminate, the occurrence of these barriers to success.

Project Closure—Moving On to the Next Project

Project closure is an important event. It is the signal that the project is done, that the BB can move on to the next project, and that you can ring the cash register with money flowing to the bottom line. Project closure criteria form an important part of the project identification/prioritization system, because they help BBs and others move on to their next projects promptly. They should neither linger on projects too long nor leave prematurely before critical controls are in place.

Some perfectionists will not want to move on until they have reached entitlement, even though they have met their original objectives and there are now bigger issues elsewhere. Other BBs or GBs may be anxious to tackle the next problem and want to leave before critical controls are in place. The key players in this event are the BB or GB, Champion, finance representative, and the person who owns the process. The process owner is needed because the process improvements developed by the BB or GB will become standard operating procedure for the process in the future.

Key to project closure is the verification of the process improvements and associated financial impact (determined by finance), the completion of the process control plan, completion of the training associated with the new way of operating, and completion of the project report that summarizes the work done and the key findings. When this work is done, the BB or GB will often make a presentation to management, and the rest of the organization is informed through the project reporting system or other methods of communication used by the organization (e.g., newsletters, Web sites, storyboards).

You can manage project closure by having a standard set of steps to close out a project, a project closure form that is an integral part of the project tracking system, and a method for electronically archiving the project in the reporting system so the results will be available to the whole organization. This last item is important because BBs working in unique areas, such as risk management, find documentation of previous projects in this same area extremely helpful. The specific closure steps and form should be tailored to each organization, but we recommend that the following steps be required:

1. Successful completion of each phase of the DMAIC (or DFSS) process

2. Finance signoff on the savings claimed

3. Control plan in place and being used by process owner

4. Any needed training implemented

5. Final Champion and management reviews

The existence of a project closure form helps a BB or GB see what's required to close out a project.

How Projects Can Fail

For Six Sigma to be successful, you must understand how Six Sigma projects can fail. In our experience, there are two main sources of project failure: project selection and management, and support for the project (Snee et al. 1998). We have found these to be the most common root causes of project failure both on the factory floor and beyond. Key contributors in each of these areas are summarized in Table 6.3. Projects are often literally set up for failure with an unrealistic scope of work, no statement of project metrics and goals, and the wrong Champion or BB assigned to the project.

TABLE 6.3   Six Sigma Project Failure Modes

Poor Project Selection and Management	Poor Project Support
Projects not tied to financial results.	BBs have little time to work on projects.
Poorly defined project scope, metrics, and goals.	Technical support from MBB not available.
Many projects lasting more than 6 months.	Poor or infrequent management reviews.
Wrong people assigned to projects.	Poor support from finance, IT, HR, maintenance, quality-control lab.
Large project teams.	Focus is on training not improvement.
Infrequent team meetings.	Poor communication of initiative and progress.
	Lack of appropriate recognition and reward.

In our experience, having too large a scope and the wrong people assigned to the project are the biggest reasons for project failure, by far. One way to ensure an appropriate scope is to ask those most knowledgeable about the problem if they feel it can be solved in 4 to 6 months. If the answer is a clear no, reduce the scope. Assigning the wrong Champion or BB or GB to the project is probably the second biggest source of project failure. Both the Champion and BB should have a keen interest in the project. In his or her first project, the BB/GB should have some subject-matter knowledge of the process being improved. This is less of a concern after he or she has learned the Six Sigma methodology well, because BBs become skilled in applying the generic DMAIC approach to improve a wide variety of projects. Of course, project success requires that good subject-matter knowledge exists on the team, but it does not always have to belong to the BB.

Large teams and infrequent team meetings are also sources of project failure. BB teams should typically be no larger than four to six persons. Larger teams have difficulty arranging team meetings due to conflicting schedules and may have difficulty reaching decisions due to conflicting agendas. Large teams are often a sign of lack of trust in the organization—everyone has to be represented to protect their interests. Infrequent team meetings may be due to the size of the team or the leadership style of the BB (who may prefer to work alone). Project Champions should be on the lookout for such behavior and ensure that the whole team plays an integral role in the project.

Other common sources of project failure include not giving the BB or GB sufficient time to work on the project, lack of technical guidance from a competent MBB, infrequent reviews by management, and inadequate support from functional groups. Each of these items is critical to keeping the project on schedule with a keen focus on the desired end result.

Failures in Specific Project Phases

Specific project failures can also take place in the different phases of the DMAIC process. As noted previously, projects can fail in the design phase due to unrealistic scope of work, no statement of project metrics and goals, the wrong Champion or BB assigned to the project, and projects not tied to financial goals. In addition, if projects are selected that are not important to the business, the typical result is that no one cares about the project, and support for the project is difficult to develop. Projects related to processes with long cycle times (for example, process output measurements result only once per month or once per quarter) can also be a problem. The result is that it "seems to take forever" to complete the project because it takes a long time to collect the data to identify the problem and to verify that the improvements actually had the intended benefits.

In these situations, the expectation should be set properly up front so that management impatience does not hinder the success of the project. The problem can also be offset if there are significant historical data that are relevant, such as for projects intended to reduce the time it takes to close the monthly books. Obviously, you can only obtain one data point a month in this case, but hopefully there are historical data that can be used in the measure and analyze steps.

Projects can fail in the measure phase due to lack of process measurements, wrong measurements being used, poor data quality, and small samples of attribute data. You can handle the lack of process measurements by designing and implementing a measurement collection system that focuses on the data needed to support the project. You can implement the measurement system needed to monitor process performance over time after the project has been completed. Output measurement systems typically include measurements of process quality (for example, defects, errors, inaccuracies), cycle times, costs, and customer satisfaction. Conducting surveys is another good way to collect data in a timely fashion. The Motorola finance project discussed in Chapter 3 made effective use of surveys.

Attribute data, in which the data are discrete characteristics of the process output (e.g., accurate/inaccurate, error/no error, favor/don't favor) and not quantitative measurements can be a problem because of less information in this type of data. An attribute Gauge R&R study can be used to assess the quality of the attribute data (Windsor 2003). Sample sizes of 100 or better are typically recommended for attribute data. The guiding consideration is how large a difference you need to detect for this project. We recall that political opinion polls in which the response is favor/don't favor typically involve samples of 1,200 or larger and report a sampling error of +/-3% to 4%. A sample size of 100 has a sampling error of approximately +/-10%. We discuss the issues of attribute data in more detail in Chapter 7, because this is a common problem in real economy applications.

The two typical problems in the analyze phase involve *failure modes and effects analysis* (FMEA) and multi-vari studies. We frequently see that after an FMEA is completed there is little pressure to implement the results. This attitude is often symptomatic of an organization that is adverse to change. Leaders of Six Sigma should be on the lookout for such situations and work quickly to remedy the situation. We also discuss FMEA and multi-vari studies in greater detail in Chapter 7.

Multi-vari studies are often designed and implemented poorly. Key variables may be missing. Measurement variation may be large due to the *measurement system analysis* (MSA) not being done or the improvements of the MSA not being implemented prior to the multi-vari study. Data errors may be present, and data records are often incomplete. The sampling procedures may be making it difficult to get good estimates of the effects of variables and their interactions (see Hoerl and Snee 2002, Chapter 6). Table 6.4 describes some keys to the success of multi-vari studies (also see Snee 2001b).

TABLE 6.4   Multi-Vari Studies: Keys to Success

- Collect data over a period sufficient to see the total variation in the process.
- Collect data frequently enough to see important sources of variation.
- Include all the important variables in the sampling plan, including process inputs, controlled and uncontrolled variables, and output variables.
- Ensure the measurement systems are adequate for all the variables sampled.
- Pay attention to administration of the study; develop a plan and be sure all involved understand their roles.
- Be sure to consider the effects of rotating shifts when developing sampling plans.
- Focus analysis on identifying the important sources of variation (key drivers).
- Use graphical as well as analytical techniques.
- Pay attention to the limitations of studies in which data are collected without a statistical design.

In the improve phase, problems often revolve around the use of *design of experiments* (DOE). DOEs are often run too soon before the measure and analyze phases are completed. As a result, the process is not well understood, the process measurements may be of poor quality, and key variables may not be studied. Project Champions should make sure that DOEs are run in the improve phase or possibly in the analyze phase when the number of candidate variables is large and it is necessary to run a screening experiment to identify the key drivers of the process (Snee 2003).

Another frequently occurring problem is that there is no time or resources to do the DOE. Other priorities are "more important." A discussion of the importance of the project and the role of the DOE usually breaks down this barrier. Six Sigma projects are by definition high priority and have a sense of urgency associated with them. All data collection studies and experiments should be given high priority to get the project completed quickly and get the resulting financial benefits to the bottom line as quickly as possible. However, sometimes stated issues are simply convenient excuses, whereas the real barrier is a lack of confidence in conducting DOEs by the BB or GB. DOE is applied commonly in most manufacturing environments. The method is often new in areas outside manufacturing such as banking, accounting, and legal, but its use is growing (Koselka 1996). Additional help, typically from a strong MBB, can resolve this barrier when it exists.

The control phase may go poorly due to the project being improperly brought to closure. Examples of poor project completion include a poor handoff between the project team and the persons who own and operate the process, control plan not being constructed—or worse yet, the control plan not being used—or a long-term capability study not being completed to verify the results of the process improvements. A key role of the project Champion is to see that the control phase of the project is completed and that the project is closed out properly.

A Holistic Model for Improvement

Chapter 1 pointed out that to reap maximum long-term benefits from Six Sigma, organizations must use Six Sigma holistically as a key element of their improvement strategy and eventually integrate it into their overall process management system. This section discusses process management from a systems perspective, defining its elements and explaining how the pieces fit together. We present this information now because properly positioning Six Sigma as part of your overall improvement system will help ensure that you select proper Six Sigma projects and avoid the pitfalls noted previously. As shown at a conceptual level in Figure 6.3, the process management system takes data and information from the process, customers, and the market and uses it to initiate actions that manage and improve the process as needed to serve customers more efficiently and stay ahead of the competition.

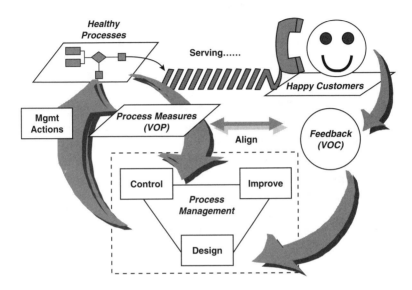

FIGURE 6.3   Process management.

The system needs to integrate and align information from customers, which we refer to as the *voice of the customer* (VOC), with information from the process, which we refer to as the *voice of the process* (VOP). Long term, you need to both provide services and outputs that satisfy or even delight your customers, while at the same time operating the process effectively and efficiently. Some organizations focus solely at optimizing their internal processes, to the detriment of customers. These organizations tend not to last very long. Others may focus solely on customer satisfaction, ignoring the business needs for efficiency. Although these organizations may be supported by their customers, they are unlikely to be profitable (and hence likely to fade away). Organizations successful over the long term find the appropriate balance of delighting customers while at the same time operating internal processes efficiently.

There are three major aspects of a process management system: process design/redesign, process improvement, and process control. Process design/redesign focuses on the design of new processes and the redesign (reengineering) of existing processes. This model is similar to the Juran trilogy for quality management, which has three elements: quality planning, quality improvement, and quality control (Juran 1988). Both models contain the three key types of activities needed for success: strategic (planning, process design/redesign), tactical (improvement), and operational (control).

Six Sigma can contribute significantly to design efforts through *design for Six Sigma* (DFSS), which utilizes the *define, measure, analyze, design, verify* (DMADV) framework. DFSS is used when there is a need to develop a new process or product for new markets, or it is clear that the existing process will no longer meet the required levels of performance. One example would be a manual order-processing system that is performing at entitlement (the best performance that can be expected from this process), and yet higher levels of performance are needed to be successful in the market place. The company may need to move to a totally new Internet-based processing system, instead of attempting to improve their existing manual system.

Process improvement focuses on the improvement of existing processes without changing the fundamental design of the process. The DMAIC—*define, measure, analyze, improve, and control*—improvement model is typically used. It is not unusual for DFSS projects to utilize DMAIC to improve the process after it has been launched. DFSS is effective, but not perfect. There is often need to improve the newly designed process after it has been launched. In addition, there will often be improvement projects for which the solution is known, such as an upgrade to the corporate intranet, for which other methods besides Six Sigma are more appropriate.

Process control focuses on keeping the process operating on target and within requirements so that it produces products and services that consistently satisfy customers profitably. Process measurements are routinely collected and analyzed by management to determine whether the process is operating on target and whether process corrections/adjustments are needed to bring the process back to operating on target. Six Sigma utilizes the control phase, typically employing a control plan to improve the control of the process. We should emphasize that there is much more to process control than Six Sigma control plans, such as *standard operating procedures* (SOPs), maintenance procedures, safety regulations, etc. The Six Sigma control plan works with these other elements of process control to effectively operate and control the process.

As noted earlier, the key distinction between process improvement and process control is that process improvement attempts to drive the process to new levels of performance. Process control, on the other hand, identifies root causes for why the process performance has deteriorated, so that performance can be brought back to normal levels. For example, better process control will result if a multi-vari study identifies employee differences that are increasing the variation in the cycle times required to produce bills for hospital stays. The root cause of these differences may then be identified as lack of knowledge of the billing system by two new employees. Providing better training to these employees is likely to resolve the problem and bring the overall system performance back to normal.

However, resolving this problem will not likely drive new levels of performance in cycle time. Modifying the procedures used by all employees in billing to reduce the cycle time to levels not experienced previously is an example of process improvement. Purchasing a new computer billing system that automatically produces bills when patients are discharged would be an example of process redesign. Note that although process redesign often involves the introduction of new technology, this is not always the case. In some cases, such as the DuPont legal case in Chapter 5, the line between process improvement and process redesign can become blurred.

Integrating Process Improvement and Control

The effectiveness of process improvement and control is maximized when the two components are integrated and used on a routine basis. On a daily or more frequent basis, process control makes adjustments to the process, often in real time, to maintain the performance level. It also fixes problems that have caused deterioration in performance and returns the process to standard conditions. These are the routine actions taken by conscientious employees in banks, hospitals, retails stores, and other workplaces to keep the place running.

As a simplistic example of a textbook case of process control in action, consider this example: Long customer lines at a grocery store (a count of customers in the aisle) trigger a call over the intercom asking for more employees to come to the registers. There is a problem—long lines—that makes it difficult to serve customers promptly. Noticing this problem, someone in the organization, perhaps a manager, perhaps not, identifies a potential solution and takes action to address the problem. Hopefully, the additional registers that are now open resolve the problem and customers are checked out promptly, returning the checkout process to normal.

In contrast, process improvement makes fundamental changes to the process itself, or the way it is operated, to achieve higher levels of performance. For example, someone might study customer traffic loads during the day and revise work schedules to ensure that the right number of employees are always available during peak loads, resulting in a significant and permanent reduction in checkout times at this store. Process improvement works best on a solid platform of good process control, which is required to sustain the gains of the improvement projects. It is difficult even to study the process when process control is poor, resulting in a chaotic process. In addition, some people unfortunately believe that process control actions are process improvement, with the expected result that they never take longer-term actions to take the process to new levels of performance.

There are many ways to integrate Six Sigma into process management systems and processes. A few guiding principles are helpful:

- Focus on key processes.

- Routinely monitor key processes using data generated by the process.

- Have people at various levels in the organization routinely analyze process data using relevant tools and take appropriate actions.

- Utilize two types of routine actions: controlling (adjusting) the process to maintain performance, and making improvements to the process to achieve even higher performance.

Figure 6.4 (adapted from Snee 1999) depicts a high-level schematic of a typical process management system based on these principles. The organization collects data from the process on a routine basis. Various levels of management review these data on a regular basis to decide what process actions should be taken. Typical review groups for high-throughput environments (billing, logistics, etc.) are as follows:

Review Team	Review Timing
Process workers	Continuously and daily
Process managers and staff	Weekly
Site manager and staff	Monthly
Business manager and staff	Quarterly

Process operators, such as customer service reps, accountants, and salespeople, review the process performance data continuously to look for out-of-control situations, and review daily summaries to detect other sources of problems. Analysis tools often present the data in a statistical control chart format or other graphical presentations.

The process control plan, developed in the control phase of the Six Sigma improvement project, documents for the workers what to look for, what actions to take, and whom to inform when additional assistance is needed. The control plan typically details the process adjustments needed to bring the outputs back to the desired target and range. The Six Sigma tools used by the operators for troubleshooting typically include process maps, control charts, histograms, and Pareto charts.

Examples of such process adjustments are calling in additional accountants to close the books on time or having a salesperson work overtime to meet a sales quota. However, such efforts are primarily aimed at sustaining current performance levels rather than improving to new levels. Improvement to new performance levels often requires the involvement of additional people with specialized skills, such as engineers in manufacturing or experienced underwriters in insurance. Project teams that include process workers, technical specialists, and perhaps someone trained in improvement methodologies if needed are typically required to make true improvement.

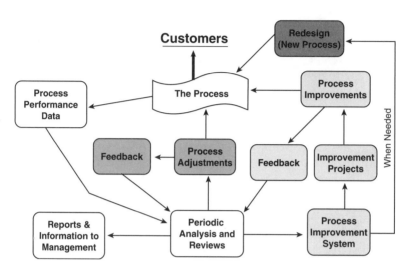

FIGURE 6.4 Typical process management system.

Note that in Figure 6.4 the reviews of the data also feed the process improvement system and, when needed, process redesign. This process improvement system has similarities to the project selection system in Six Sigma: The organization identifies good improvement opportunities, identifies specific projects, makes improvements, and provides feedback on how the overall system is working so that it can be improved. Utilizing Six Sigma projects, where appropriate, to make these improvements as part of the process management system will ensure that you continue to receive benefits from Six Sigma long into the future. The process management infrastructure, which has hopefully existed all along, gradually replaces the Six Sigma infrastructure. Fortunately, once it is properly set up, the process management infrastructure should be smaller than for Six Sigma because you are no longer ramping up a new initiative.

The following example from Ron Snee's consulting experience illustrates how this management system can work, especially in terms of integrating process control and process improvement. A monthly billing process was operating poorly, requiring 17 days on average to get the bills out versus an 8- to 9-day target. Not only did this delay payment, customers were also unhappy. Herculean efforts were routinely required to keep the process operating.

Process workers were meeting daily at 10 a.m. to review process operations and make needed adjustments, but the process performance did not improve.

A process review structure, following the model detailed above, was created to better manage the process. The 10 a.m. process worker meeting was continued. A process manager's meeting was held daily at 11:30 a.m. to review the process operations and the results of the 10 a.m. process worker's meeting. At the end of the month, the process owner and his staff met to review the data on the month's operation, the results of their improvement activities of the previous month, and to identify any needed additional improvement activities. In this process review structure, the process worker's and process manager's daily meetings focused on needed process adjustments, whereas the monthly process owner's meeting focused on process improvements.

Over the following 6-month period, the performance of the process improved dramatically. The billing process was consistently meeting the 8- to 9-day target to get the bills out, which resulted in happy customers, a great reduction in the Herculean efforts of the process workers operating the process, and a cost reduction of $2.5 million per year. The combination of daily process adjustments and longer-term process improvements worked. The amount of management review time required also decreased as the organization learned how to use the process. The 11:30 a.m. process managers meeting, which initially took 1.5 hours to complete, reduced over time to 15 minutes per day, and was then moved to a once per week frequency. This daily, weekly, and monthly management review schedule continued, and the process continued to operate on target, getting the bills out in 8 to 9 days on average, with reduced variation. In this case, a process redesign was not required.

Creating the Improvement System

Now that we have discussed integration of process improvement with process control, we will discuss creation of the improvement system. As you progress in your Six Sigma deployment, you will see that other improvement activities compete for resources and management attention, such as capital improvements. Your long-term goal should be to combine all your improvement initiatives into an overall improvement system, make Six Sigma an integral part of this system, and create the supporting management systems required to sustain it. This is the process improvement system indicated in Figure 6.4; it will make improvement a routine managerial process just like any other, such as the annual budgeting process, the internal audit process, and the recruiting process. Note that we include redesign projects as part of the overall improvement system.

Guiding principles for creating an overall improvement system that effectively incorporates Six Sigma include the following:

- Improvement and growth occur project by project.

- A project is a problem scheduled for solution.

- Improvement projects come from many different sources and should be managed by a common system.

- Projects should be linked to the strategic needs and priorities of the organization.

- Continual review, assessment, and evaluation of the combined list of projects will keep it up-to-date.

- Effective project management skills are needed for success.

- A joint focus on both control and improvement is essential; process performance deteriorates after improvement if there is insufficient focus on control. This is one reason why integration of control and improvement is so important.

The organization's improvement portfolio will generally include a mixture of projects in three main categories:

- Projects with known solutions, such as capital projects (repairing the roof, paving the parking lot, building a new facility).

- Six Sigma projects where the problem has no known solution. These may be either DMAIC improvement projects or DMADV design projects.

■ Other improvement initiatives, such as ISO 9000, digitization, new performance management system, and so on.

An organization's annual improvement plan should be a blend of these three types of initiatives, and include projects related to such diverse areas as productivity improvement, cash generation, revenue growth, and organization learning and improvement. Note that Six Sigma does not address all the improvement needs of the organization, although it is a critical component of the improvement system. Putting all improvement projects in a single list aids the budgeting process and focuses the organization on what needs to be done, given the available resources. The list will also raise necessary questions regarding capital projects and whether there are sufficient data to justify each one.

In some cases, planners charter a Six Sigma project to assess whether the solution proposed by the capital project is in fact the best solution, or whether the same level of improvement can be obtained without significant capital. For example, in the case of capacity improvement projects, such as purchasing additional CT scanners in a hospital radiology department to meet patient demand, planners want to make sure the process is at entitlement before they spend capital to upgrade it. Six Sigma projects can also result in capital expenditures. Our experience is that such capital projects are approved more quickly because of the data provided by the Six Sigma improvement process.

Using the DMADV and DMAIC Improvement Models

Developing new and better products and services are obviously key means to growing the top line. DFSS is the most common approach to accomplishing this objective within the redesign part of the process management system. We've seen that DFSS is typically started about 1 year after the organization has initiated the DMAIC methodology for improving existing processes and has gained confidence that Six Sigma will work. Conceptually, you can consider product design a process and apply Six Sigma in a straightforward manner to improve it. In most cases, however, organizations want to apply Six Sigma to the design of a specific new product or service. Although it applies equally well here, Six Sigma requires a different road map more tailored to design. If a team applies the DMAIC road map to designing a new product, it will likely stumble in the measure phase, because there is no existing process on which to take measurements.

GE developed the DMADV road map for DFSS, adopted by many others since then, to apply to design projects. The major phases of DMADV, and their fundamental purposes are shown here.

DMADV Phase	**Purpose**
Define	Set up the project for success
Measure	Determine CTQ characteristics and process measurements
Analyze	Develop conceptual design
Design	Create detailed design
Verify	Pilot test to verify design capability

The define stage is analogous to define in DMAIC, although typically more complicated because you are designing a new product or service, not improving an existing process. In the DMADV measure phase, you determine the CTQ characteristics and ensure that you have measurement capability, but you do not measure an existing process, unless the new design is an enhancement of a current design.

The analyze phase focuses on conceptual design, in which you use creative thinking to determine the most promising high-level design to satisfy your CTQs. For product designs, you may develop prototypes; for service designs, you may develop computer simulations. The details of this design are completed in the design phase, where you make calculations to predict final design capability. If these calculations are not promising, the team must repeat the analyze phase and design phase to improve the design capability. In the verify phase, you pilot the new design under realistic conditions to obtain real data verifying design capability. For example, if you are designing a Web-based insurance application and underwriting system, you would utilize people with computer skills similar to your targeted market to access the system and do so during normal business hours using standard platforms.

It is rare that the results of the verify phase indicate that the newly designed process is exactly what is needed. Process refinements or improvements are often required to achieve desired performance levels. In such cases, you may go through one or more DMAIC projects to remove design flaws observed in the pilot. If there are major discrepancies in capability, you may have to loop back through the analyze or design phases again.

This approach to DFSS maintains the key technical elements of DMAIC:

- Disciplined approach

- Use of metrics throughout the process

- Use of analytical tools

- Emphasis on variation

- Data-based decision making

This similarity results in a consistent approach and language for the organization to use in their development of new processes and products.

DMAIC Process Improvement Model

DMAIC is used to improve the performance of existing processes. To successfully use the DMAIC improvement model, it is important to understand the purpose and objectives of the different phases of DMAIC.

DMAIC Phase	Purpose
Define	Set up the project for success
Measure	Understand your process and its measurements
Analyze	Identify root causes of gaps in process performance
Improve	Identify, implement, and test improvements
Control	Hold the gains

Much has been written on the use of the tools of Six Sigma, but precious little has been written on the DMAIC model itself. Hopefully the following paragraphs will help fill this void.

The purpose of the define phase is to set up the project for success. The problem is identified and defined. The financial impact of the project is determined, the Project Champion and BB or GB are selected. The Project Champion writes the project charter in collaboration with the BB or GB, and management approval is obtained. The project is now ready to go. As noted earlier, it is critical that the project objectives be clear and connected to the business goals, that the scope is doable in 4 to 6 months, and that the process performance metrics are identified and data are available.

In the measure phase, you get to know and understand your process and its measurements. The process is documented using a process map, including the identification of the process input (Xs) and output variables (Ys). The *cause-and-effect matrix* (C&E) may be used to summarize the current knowledge of the team regarding the key drivers of the process. The measurement quality is analyzed, and the baseline performance data are collected and analyzed to establish the baseline performance level, including process stability and capability.

The purpose of the analyze phase is to build on the results of the measure phase and identify root causes (key Xs) for the observed variation in the output variables (Ys), also known as CTQs. Often a risk analysis is created for the process to determine what can go wrong, using an FMEA. This analysis may be followed by a multi-vari study to identify important sources of uncontrolled variation, as well as important controlled and input variables. It is not unusual in this phase to identify "quick-fix" process improvements that result in significant bottom-line impact even before the project is completed.

Process improvements are identified, tested, and implemented in the improve phase. DOE techniques are often used to establish cause-and-effect relationships and identify optimum operational conditions. Key process variables are often "mistake-proofed" in this phase, and in the following control phase. The results of improvement efforts are carefully documented and the improvements verified prior to moving on to the control phase.

The purpose of the control phase is to "hold the gains" of the process improvement work done in the DMAI phases. In this phase, the team finalizes and implements the control plan, which explains how to operate the process so as to maintain improvements. Process workers receive training in the new way of operating the process, and you determine the long-term capability of the process. All relevant parties identify future improvement needs and add the associated projects to the project hopper, and you transfer the project to the process owner. Finally, you close out the project, and the BB or GB moves on to the next project.

Solution-Known Projects

At first thought, one might think that there is no place for the Six Sigma tools in projects for which the solution is known. In these projects, such as capital projects, a project manager is assigned, management allocates resources—funds and people—and the project manager manages the completion of the project. Upon closer evaluation, one can see that the DMAIC model may be a useful framework to guide the project. The define, measure, analyze, and control phases are the most useful phases in this situation. In theory, there is no creativity or analysis needed for the improvement because we already know what the solution is. However, as shown below, in the course of the analysis phase, unforeseen improvements may be identified, resulting in all five phases of DMAIC being used.

Here is how it works. The process of completing solution-known projects can be more effective through the use of the Six Sigma tools. In the define phase, project managers can use VOC methods to make sure that critical requirements for performance of the project (CTQs) are being considered. For example, in the case of a new computer system installation, customer requirements might include system uptime, installation time, and ongoing maintenance costs. In the measure phase, the project manager would identify measurements to monitor the success of the project, including installation time and cost mentioned above, as well as measurements to minimize disruption to the operations in which the installation is conducted. The C&E matrix might be helpful to prioritize the functional requirements. Analysis of the high-priority functional requirements using FMEA would help identify critical failure modes and areas where mistake-proofing is necessary. The project manager would address any improvements needed in the improve phase of DMAIC. Finally, a control plan would ensure that the system has been installed as designed and that over time maintenance, training, SOPs, and so on are in use.

Training for Project Improvement

Six Sigma requires people to think and work in new and different ways. This requires that they be trained in the new way of thinking and working. There is a lot of training to be done, as spelled out in the deployment plan. We discuss training needs in this chapter because proper training is required to enable leaders to select good Six Sigma projects, and for BBs and GBs to successfully complete them. The key groups to be trained are executives, business teams, site management teams, functional management teams, Champions, MBBs, BBs, and GBs. From an improvement project perspective, the executives, business teams, site management teams, functional management teams, Champions, and MBBs should be trained in how to select projects, how to review projects, and how to manage the project hopper. The MBBs, BBs, and GBs should be trained in how to lead and manage improvement projects. Specific recommendations for BB and GB training are discussed below.

BB training typically lasts 4 weeks, with each week focused on a specific phase of the DMAIC process. The usual sequence is Week 1 (define and measure), Week 2 (analyze), Week 3 (improve), and Week 4 (control). We show recommended outlines for finance and general real economy BB courses, based on Hoerl (2001), in Tables 6.5 and 6.6. Note that these outlines include both DMAIC methodology and DFSS tools. Some companies teach DFSS separately, whereas others prefer to integrate it with DMAIC training. Both approaches can work.

TABLE 6.5   Finance-Oriented Black Belt Course Outline (Hoerl 2001)

(Week 3 Comprises the "Black Belt Adder" to a Green Belt Course)

Week 1:

- The DMAIC and DFSS (Design for Six Sigma) improvement strategies
- Project selection and scoping (define)
- QFD
- Sampling principles (quality and quantity)
- Measurement system analysis (also called Gauge R&R)
- Process capability
- Basic graphs
- Hypothesis testing
- Regression

Week 2:

- DOE (focus on two-level factorials)
- Design for Six Sigma tools
  - Requirements flowdown
  - Capability flowup (prediction)
  - Piloting
  - Simulation
- FMEA
- Developing control plans
- Control charts

Week 3:

- Power (impact of sample size)
- Impact of process instability on capability analysis
- Confidence Intervals (versus hypothesis tests)
- Implications of the Central Limit Theorem
- Transformations
- How to detect "Lying With Statistics"
- General linear models
- Fractional factorial DOEs

TABLE 6.6   General *Real Economy* Black Belt Course Outline (Adapted from Hoerl 2001)

(The week in which the material appears is noted as a superscript)

Context:[1]

- Why Six Sigma
- DMAIC & DFSS processes (sequential case studies)
- Project management fundamentals
- Team effectiveness fundamentals

Define:[1]

- Project selection
- Scoping projects
- Developing a project plan
- Multigenerational projects
- Process identification (SIPOC)

Measure:[1]

- QFD
- Identifying customer needs
- Developing measurable critical-to-quality metrics (CTQs)
- Sampling (data quantity and data quality)
- Survey design
- Measurement system analysis and development
- SPC Part I
    - The concept of statistical control (process stability)
    - The implications of instability on capability measures
- Capability analysis

Analyze:[2]

- Basic graphical improvement tools ("Magnificent 7")
- Management and planning tools (affinity, ID, and so on)
- FMEA

(The week in which the material appears is noted as a superscript)

- Confidence intervals (emphasized) and Hypothesis testing (de-emphasized)
- ANOVA (de-emphasized)
- Analysis of survey data
- Regression
- Multi-vari studies and general linear model
- Transformations
- Contingency table analysis
- Developing conceptual designs in DFSS

Improve:[3-4]

- DOE (focus on two level factorials and screening designs)
- Piloting (of DMAIC improvements)
- Stakeholder building
- Mistake-proofing
- DFSS design tools
  - CTQ flowdown
  - Capability flowup
  - Simulation

Control:[4]

- Developing control plans
- SPC Part II
  - Using control charts
- Piloting new designs in DFSS

GB training typically lasts 2 weeks, with Week 1 focused on the define, measure, and analyze phases of DMAIC, and the second week focused on the improve and control phases. A recommended outline of topics for a general real economy GB training is shown in Table 6.7. Note that this is very similar to what would be recommended in manufacturing, although case studies and examples should be relevant to the audience. We discuss some specific differences of training beyond the factory floor in the next section.

TABLE 6.7   General *Real Economy* Green Belt Course Outline (Adapted from Hoerl 2001)

(The week in which the material appears is noted as a superscript)

Context:[1]

- Why Six Sigma
- DMAIC (sequential case studies)
- Project management fundamentals
- Team effectiveness fundamentals

Define:[1]

- Project selection
- Scoping projects
- Developing a project plan
- Process identification (SIPOC)

Measure:[1]

- QFD
- Identifying customer needs
- Developing measurable critical-to-quality metrics (CTQs)
- Sampling (data quantity and data quality)
- Survey design
- Measurement system analysis and development
- SPC Part I
  - The concept of statistical control (process stability)
  - The implications of instability on capability measures
- Capability analysis

Analyze:[1,2]

- FMEA
- Basic graphical improvement tools ("Magnificent 7")
- Confidence intervals (emphasized)
- Hypothesis testing (de-emphasized)
- ANOVA (de-emphasized)

(The week in which the material appears is noted as a superscript)

- Analysis of Survey Data
- Regression
- Multi-vari studies
- Contingency table analysis

Improve:[2]

- DOE (focus on two-level factorials)
- Piloting (of DMAIC improvements)
- Stakeholder building
- Mistake-proofing

Control:[2]

- Developing control plans
- SPC Part II
  - Using control charts

We recommend that you base the BB and GB training topics and areas of emphasis on the specific needs and targeted applications of the organization. We do *not* recommend "one-size-fits-all" Six Sigma training. The sample curricula presented here form a base of reference or starting point and should not be viewed as the final answer for all organizations. Alternative curricula, as well as guidelines for conducting effective training, can be found in Hoerl (2001) and its associated discussion.

We have found that the practice of working on real projects during the training is key to the success of BB and GB training. It is our firm belief that a real, significant project should be the admission ticket for the training: "No project, no training." As noted earlier, if the projects are successfully completed, the resulting benefits should more than pay for the training.

Organizing and conducting Six Sigma training needs careful planning, coordination, and execution. It is so important for the training leaders to have experience in the deployment of similar efforts that most companies hire outside Six Sigma consultants to provide this service initially. Experienced providers have the knowledge, experience, capability, and capacity to do what is needed to create a successful deployment. The organization may hire these external resources as permanent employees or utilize them on a consulting basis. After the initiative has been successfully launched and the internal MBBs obtain sufficient experience, they should begin to assume leadership of this effort.

Training Beyond the Factory Floor

Doing Six Sigma training beyond the factory floor is often different because of the nature of the processes, people, and data involved. The result is that a slight variation on the tools is needed to be most effective. You must first recognize how the work is unique; we recall some of the unique aspects of real economy processes discussed in Chapter 2. For example, real economy processes typically involve more human intervention and are often not well defined, at least initially. It is not unusual for there to be no standard process. Further, measurements are often non-existent or ill defined at best. The employees working in these processes tend not to think in terms of processes, variation, and data. They may be more "right-brained" in their thinking—that is, intuitive and conceptual rather than quantitative and detailed. Analytical problem solving may not be a well-developed skill.

These considerations provide guidance in how the Six Sigma tools should be presented. Because many processes are not well defined or agreed on, the process mapping material should include direction on how to identify both the current state ("as is") and desired future state ("to be") process maps, including the identification and elimination of non–value-added work. Also recall that there may be large differences between how people *think* the process operates today and how it actually operates. Process cycle time analysis should also be included. Because most real economy processes cannot be seen visually, process mapping becomes even more important than in manufacturing.

Because much of the process data can be attribute data, the measurement system analysis should include how to do attribute Gauge R&R studies to assess attribute measurement quality (Windsor 2003). In cases where little or no data exist, the discussion should include the development of process measurement systems and the associated data collection strategies. Survey data are also more common, so curricula should include both design of surveys and analysis of survey data.

Process capability studies are often overlooked because it is thought that process specifications are not useful in this environment. To the contrary, process specifications (requirements) are widely used in real economy processes. In many cases, however, the specifications are not clearly identified. Some common examples are summarized in Table 6.8. Note that a lower spec on credit delinquencies might be appropriate if we think that zero delinquencies implies that we are not taking enough risk and thereby losing profitable business. Also contrary to popular opinion, you can calculate process capability for the attribute data that occur frequently beyond the factory floor, as well as for continuous data. We discuss this analysis further in Chapter 7.

TABLE 6.8   Examples of Specifications for Real Economy Processes

Process	Metric	Lower	Upper
Closing the books	Cycle time (days)		5
Customer call process	Rings to answer (number)		3
Customer call process	Length of call (minutes)		10
Accounts payable	Days to pay	20	30
Accounts receivable	Days to pay		30
On-time delivery	Percent of orders	80%	
Overtime	Percent		2%
Capital project return	Percent	25%	
Credit delinquencies	Percent	2%	10%

Multi-vari studies are very useful beyond the factory floor, particularly because of the high amount of human intervention in these processes. Without SOPs and closely adhered-to control plans, different teams or individual workers will almost always be working in different ways, increasing process variation. Six Sigma training should therefore focus considerable attention on these studies, including design, analysis, and reporting techniques (see Snee 2001b). For multi-vari studies, we generally promote more graphical tools, such as scatter plots and box plots, with some decrease in formal statistical methods, such as hypothesis tests.

This is a general principle in real economy training; we recommend the simplest procedures that will suffice. For example, Table 6.6 does not include response surface methodology, which is a specialized area of DOE that is very applicable in manufacturing settings, because it is less applicable outside manufacturing and engineering. Note, however, that we do not advocate "taking a pass" on formal statistical methods! This "statistics phobia" is a common problem in real economy deployments. Rigorous tools such as DOE and regression have widespread application beyond the factory floor and should be included in training. BBs and GBs can learn these tools, even in non-technical functions and businesses.

Speaking of DOE, there is much debate regarding the use of DOE beyond manufacturing. It is our experience that there is a lot of opportunity for experimentation outside the factory floor, and that the lack of broad use of DOE in real economy environments to date is due to lack of experience, not lack of applicability. Several examples are discussed by Koselka (1996). Roger Hoerl reported on a Six Sigma collections process improvement project that utilized a DOE and resulted in $2.9 million per year savings produced by a 50/50 blend of increased cash flow and reduced write-offs (Bisgaard, Hoerl, and Snee 2003). We believe that the use of DOE is growing in areas such as financial services, sales, and e-commerce, and will continue to grow in the coming years. Interestingly, DOE has a long history in areas such as medical studies and marketing research, and should be part of BB and GB training programs.

Summary

Project-by-project improvement is at the heart of Six Sigma. Therefore, you need a methodology for conducting Six Sigma projects, as well as a management system for making sure that you are completing a steady flow of projects. This will enable you to meet the improvement goals in the organization's strategic and annual plans. Central to this approach is a keen focus on improving the processes your organization uses to run its business, as well as the development of an improvement management system. This improvement system must have characteristics and priority similar to the other organizational management systems, such as finance, performance management, and IT.

We have described such a methodology in this chapter. We pointed out that process management is made up of three related activities: process design/redesign, process improvement, and process control. We also pointed out that completion of projects is central to each of these activities. We recommend the DMADV model for design for Six Sigma for product and process design. We recommend DMAIC be used for process improvement and process control, especially for solution-unknown projects.

We also discussed the key success factors for Six Sigma projects, those things that can lead to project failure, and the training needed for successful Six Sigma projects. A deep understanding of the following key elements of project-by-project improvement will take an organization a long way toward success in its improvement efforts:

- Six Sigma DMADV and DMAIC models

- Management systems for the selection, review, and closure of projects

- Holistic model for the design, improvement, and control of processes, and associated management systems

- Project success factors and failure modes

- Training for BBs and GBs

References

Bisgaard, S., R. W. Hoerl, and R. D. Snee. 2003. *Improving business processes with Six Sigma.* Transactions of the American Society for Quality Six Sigma Conference. Palm Springs, CA (January).

Conway, W. E. 1992. *The quality secret: the right way to manage.* Nashua, NH: Conway Quality, Inc.

Conway, W. E. 1994. *Winning the war on waste.* Nashua, NH: Conway Quality, Inc.

Gates, William H., III. 1999. *Business @ the speed of thought.* New York: Warner Books.

Harry, M., and R. Schroeder. 2000. *Six Sigma: the breakthrough management strategy revolutionizing the world's top corporations.* New York: Currency Doubleday.

Hoerl, R. W. 2001. Six Sigma Black Belts: what do they need to know? (with discussion). *Journal of Quality Technology* 33 4: 391–435.

Hoerl, R. W., and R. D. Snee. 2002. *Statistical thinking: improving business performance.* Pacific Grove, CA: Duxbury Press.

Juran, J. M. 1988. *Juran on planning for quality.* New York: Free Press.

Juran, J. M. 1989. *Leadership for quality: an executive handbook.* New York: Free Press.

Koselka, R. 1996. The new mantra: MVT (multivariable testing). *Forbes* (11 March) 114–118.

Rodebaugh, W. R. 2001. *Six Sigma in measurement systems: evaluating the hidden factory.* Presented at the Penn State Great Valley Symposium on Statistical Methods for Quality Practitioners (October).

Snee, R. D. 1999. Statisticians must develop data-based management and improvement systems as well as create measurement systems. *International Statistical Review* 67 2:139–144.

Snee, R.D. 2001a. Dealing with the Achilles' heel of Six Sigma initiatives: project selection is key to success, *Quality Progress* (March) 66-72.

Snee, R. D. 2001b. My process is too variable, now what do I do? *Quality Progress* (December) 65-68.

Snee, R. D. 2003. Eight essential tools. *Quality Press* (December) 86-88.

Snee, R. D., K. H. Kelleher, and S. Reynard. 1998. Improving team effectiveness. *Quality Progress* (May) 43-48.

Snee, R. D., and W. F Rodebaugh. 2002. Project selection process: every company should focus on managing its project portfolio and creating an overall organizational improvement system. *Quality Progress* (September) 78-80.

Windsor, S. E. 2003. Attribute Gauge R&R. *Six Sigma Forum Magazine* (August) 23-28.

PART IV

OVERCOMING METHODS AND TOOLS CHALLENGES

7

UNIQUE TECHNICAL CHALLENGES IN APPLYING THE METHODS AND TOOLS

All physical theories, their mathematical expressions not withstanding, ought to lend themselves to so simple a description that even a child could understand them.
—Albert Einstein

Part III of this book, which consisted of Chapters 5 (project case studies) and Chapter 6 (keys to project success), focused on how to ensure success of individual projects in the real economy. Now this chapter goes to the next level of detail and discusses how to successfully address some technical challenges involving the methods and tools of Six Sigma that are frequently seen in real economy applications. We noted this concern in Chapter 2 and address it in more detail here. These challenges include the typical non-normal distributions encountered with cycle time and other common *critical-to-quality* (CTQ) measures in projects beyond the factory floor, the prevalence of discrete data (such as with accuracy CTQs) and the mix of tools typically applied in these applications.

This chapter begins with a discussion of Six Sigma tools, in particular how to think about the tools and their use. We have found widespread misunderstanding about the tools and their appropriate use, not only among Six Sigma practitioners but also among Master Black Belts and even consultants offering training in the tools. Our objective is to dispel these common misunderstandings. After we discuss how to think about the tools, we review the major methods and tools typically used in projects in the real economy and how their use may differ from typical manufacturing applications. We make no attempt to offer complete instruction in all the Six Sigma tools—this would require an entire book in itself. Instead, we focus on conceptual understanding of the key methods and tools and how they should be used.

We also provide information about additional tools that are often employed in *design for Six Sigma* (DFSS) projects, but which are not typically taught as part of *Black Belt* (BB) or *Master Black Belt* (MBB) training, such as discrete-event simulation. Following this discussion of the tools themselves, we present common technical challenges to their appropriate application beyond the factory floor and examine how these challenges should be addressed. This discussion is naturally of a technical nature more geared toward BBs and MBBs than Quality Leaders and Champions. Finally, we discuss how some Lean manufacturing concepts can be successfully integrated with Six Sigma, even outside manufacturing.

How to Think About the Tools

We begin this discussion by noting that a more detailed treatment of this topic, as it applies to leaders, can be found in Chapter 8 of Snee and Hoerl (2003). The statistical and process improvement tools are clearly an integral part of the Six Sigma approach. As illustrated in the case studies in Chapter 5, without these powerful technical tools, Six Sigma would regress into a collection of vague concepts, slogans, and other fluff. It is the technical toolset that brings rigor to Six Sigma. This is equally true in applications beyond the factory floor as it is on the factory floor. However, there are some important differences in the way the tools tend to be applied, and in the mix of tools that are typically applied. It is therefore important that we discuss this topic specifically related to real economy applications.

First of all, the key points made in Snee and Hoerl (2003) regarding how to think about the tools are as follows:

1. The statistical and process-improvement tools provide the rigor in Six Sigma, but BBs and even MBBs do not have to be professional statisticians.

2. The tools themselves don't make improvements; rather it is the action taken by people based on application of the tools that generates improvement.

3. The tools must be properly sequenced and integrated in a disciplined fashion to be effective.

4. If the leadership aspects of Six Sigma are not in place, the tools will not have any lasting effect.

5. The tools should be combined with subject-matter knowledge in an iterative fashion of generating, testing, and revising hypotheses.

These points remain valid in real economy applications. The good news about Point 1, and a major reason why Six Sigma has been so successful beyond the factory floor, is that you don't need an army of professional statisticians to make Six Sigma work. "Ordinary people" can be trained to conduct Six Sigma projects successfully. Of course, it does help to have people with advanced knowledge in the tools to provide technical backup for difficult problems. This is a key role for MBBs.

Point 2 reminds us that a tool is only as valuable as the action that people take based on the tool. For example, the default-prediction case study in Chapter 5 was motivated by huge losses that many investment organizations experienced on Enron, WorldCom, and other large companies that defaulted in 2002. Sadly, many of these investment organizations had default-prediction tools, of varying accuracy, at the time. The real reason they lost large sums of money was not lack of tools, but rather because people did not take appropriate action based on the tools, for whatever reason. This fact reminds us to not "worship" the tools, and to keep in mind the criticality of the human aspects of Six Sigma.

Point 3 relates to a key shortcoming of most training in statistics. Often tools are taught individually, with little discussion of how to integrate them into an overall approach to problem solving, or process improvement. The result is that students feel that although they understand the basics of each individual tool, they have no idea how to utilize them together to solve a real problem. An analogy would be teaching someone how to use a table saw, a plane, a level, and so on and then asking that person to build a house. This would be an impossible task if the student had never been taught the proper steps to building a house. Understanding individual tools and understanding how to properly integrate them to solve a real problem are two different things.

Figure 7.1 illustrates how the most commonly used tools are typically sequenced and integrated by the *define, measure, analyze, improve, control* (DMAIC) process during the course of BB and *Green Belt* (GB) projects. There is a logical progression, with the input of one tool often being the output from a previously used tool. We return to this model later in the chapter.

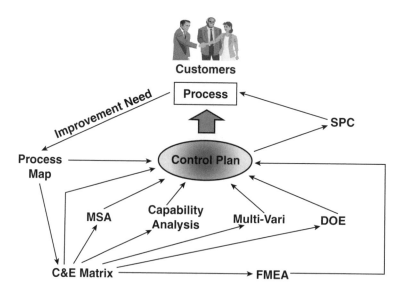

FIGURE 7.1   Six Sigma tool linkage.

Point 4 emphasizes the fact that if the leadership component is lacking, no amount of tool usage can overcome this deficiency. For example, when the default-prediction project was completed, if investors did not actually use the system to evaluate new
deals, and existing portfolios, no real benefits could be expected to
result from the tools used on this project. Fortunately, in this case
senior management incorporated this methodology into the standard risk management procedures required for any major new
investments. This is a positive example of showing leadership;
without this component, tools are worthless. This is why it is so
important that people do not think of Six Sigma as a collection of
tools, or as a training initiative. There is no substitute for leadership.

Leaders should be continuously looking for similar situations in their own organizations where effectiveness of tool applications is hampered by leadership issues (bureaucracy, politics,
lack of clear direction, etc.). These issues tend to be those that the
BBs and even MBBs are unable to address on their own, and they
are reasons for having a formal Champion role. Effective use of
tools should be a focus during both project and overall initiative
reviews; this is one means of integrating effective use of tools with
leadership.

As noted in Point 5, keep in mind that the tools work best
when they are combined with good subject-matter knowledge in
the technical area of the project, whether it is engineering, finance,
or marketing. This is why it is helpful to have BBs who are knowledgeable in the areas in which they are doing projects. Subject-
matter knowledge provides the theory to guide initial use of the
tools. The information gained from the tools then helps refine,
augment, or revise your original theories. This sequence continues
from phase to phase, and tool to tool, resulting in greater and
greater process knowledge. This is essentially application of the
scientific method to business problems. A more detailed discussion
of the proper integration of data-based tools and subject-matter
knowledge can be found in Hoerl and Snee (2002).

Clearly, it would have been virtually impossible to be successful in the default-prediction project without a solid understanding of finance. In this arena there are extreme positions that
can inhibit project success. For example, some BBs may become

enamored of the statistical tools and think that lots of data and analyses are a substitute for process knowledge. Such BBs will tend to skip over the step of interpreting the data in light of subject-matter theory, resulting in invalid, perhaps even ludicrous, conclusions.

Conversely, some purists may believe that all problems can be solved based on first principles (fundamental laws) of engineering, physics, or finance, and resist any data collection and analysis. Leaders must push back on both extremes and insist on proper integration of subject-matter knowledge and data analysis. You should always have data to back up your theories, and theories to explain your data.

Additional Guidance for Real Economy Applications

Although all the points noted above apply equally well beyond the factory floor, there are some additional points about the tools that become particularly relevant with real economy applications, including the following:

- The tools apply beyond the factory floor—all of them!

- The mix of tools most often used is likely to be different in the real economy than on the factory floor.

- Because the mix of tools, and certainly the applications themselves, is likely to be different than in manufacturing, the training should be different as well.

The first point is perhaps the most important here. A common form of resistance is to state that *statistical process control* (SPC) (or *design of experiments* [DOE], measurement system analysis, etc.) doesn't apply here, because we are not a factory. This may be due to ignorance as well as resistance. In reality, the tools are generic improvement tools; they don't care whether you are a factory, a bank, or a hospital. As noted in Chapter 2, when you begin to think of your organization's work as a system of processes—with inputs, processing steps, and outputs—it makes perfect sense to better understand how the inputs and process variables impact the outputs, so that you can improve them. The tools help you do this, so they apply anywhere. We have seen DOE applications in finance, SPC applications in HR, flowcharting applications in legal, and so on. The more critical question is *how* DOE, SPC, or other tools are applied in these types of applications. We discuss this further later in this chapter.

Although noting that the same tools apply everywhere, it must be admitted that the mix of tools is likely to change from one application to another. This is the emphasis of the second point. For example, DOE definitely applies to finance, but BBs in manufacturing will generally use DOE more often than those in finance. Similarly, BBs in finance will likely use both discrete measurement systems analysis and surveys more often than BBs in manufacturing. So although the toolkit is basically the same, the relative importance of the tools does change. For this reason, BBs, MBBs, and GBs in these application areas have a somewhat different set of expertise requirements than their manufacturing counterparts. It is certainly possible, and often a good idea, to move BBs from manufacturing to real economy application areas, and vice versa, but some "retooling" will likely be necessary for them to succeed. We provide more specifics on which tools are most frequently used beyond the factory floor later in this chapter.

The third point is a logical consequence of the second point. Because the mix of tools usage is likely to differ, it is important that BBs and others are properly trained to attack the types of problems they are likely to face. We are not proponents of the "one-size-fits-all" approach to training. On the contrary, we are proponents of training tailored to the types of applications each group is likely to face. Some organizations have attempted to include a variety of application areas in the course examples, and then train everyone the same. We have found this to be a low-yield strategy. We have found a strategy of tailoring training to the background of the students and the typical applications they are likely to see, focusing on the tools they are most likely to apply, to be most effective.

For example, while Roger Hoerl was Quality Leader at the GE *corporate audit staff* (CAS), all training classes after the first one used examples that were actual CAS applications (that is, taken from the applications of the first group). In this way, when any subject was discussed (DOE, for example), a real DOE application from CAS, their own organization, was presented as the example. After the first class, which admittedly used generic examples, no one ever again asked the question "But how does this tool apply in finance?" The students always saw a real example of how it had already been applied in finance by one of their peers.

Generic training, particularly training that has a manufacturing emphasis, is one of the failure mechanisms of deployments beyond the factory floor. It is critical that the training be tailored to the audience and contain real examples relevant to the students. Phony examples, such as typical textbook statistics problems, are very easy for bright students to see through and reinforce the perception that Six Sigma really doesn't apply here.

Key Tools Beyond the Factory Floor

This section covers the tools that BBs and GBs are most likely to actually use on their projects, with a specific emphasis on key differences relative to manufacturing projects. More detailed discussion of Six Sigma tools, and how they should be integrated, can be found in technical books such as Hoerl and Snee (2002) and Breyfogle (2003). We begin by revisiting Figure 7.1, because this model depicts not only the tools themselves, but also one way that they can be properly integrated. We shall discuss the big picture of tool integration first, and then discuss the individual tools.

We use this order because our experience suggests that BBs and GBs are more likely to struggle with the transition from tool to tool, and from DMAIC phase to DMAIC phase, than they are to struggle with the tools themselves. This is particularly true beyond the factory floor, where most people are not accustomed to following disciplined process-improvement methodologies. Fortunately, when you understand their linkages, the tool and phase flows make more sense, and are easier to follow.

Tool Integration

As shown in Figure 7.1, the process map, or flowchart, is typically the first tool used after you have defined an improvement need. The process map sets the stage for subsequent tools by carefully documenting a common view of the process. This map enables people to see their piece of the process in the context of the bigger picture. Such maps are particularly important in real economy applications because it is often hard to visualize processes such as acquisitions, financial closings, or patent filing. The *cause-and-effect* (C&E) matrix naturally follows the process map. After the team agrees on the major steps in the process, it is logical to determine which steps and process variables are most critical to achieving your CTQs. The C&E matrix does just this, by noting how strongly each process step and variable impacts each CTQ. The process map and C&E matrix also provide input to the control plan by documenting the process steps and variables that need to be included in it.

After the C&E matrix identifies the priority steps, the team needs to ensure that it can accurately measure the key variables at these steps, utilizing a *measurement system analysis* (MSA). For manufacturing applications, this MSA will likely consist of a *gauge reproducibility and repeatability* (GR&R) study, whereas beyond the factory floor it will more likely be an attribute measurement study for discrete measurements, such as accuracy of *identification numbers* (IDs) in consumer credit.

The team may also begin a formal *failure modes and effects analysis* (FMEA) to identify potential failures in the prioritized steps and variables, and begin proactive countermeasures to prevent them. When the team is convinced that it can accurately measure the key variables, it will likely evaluate process capability using capability-analysis tools. Again, this often requires attribute-capability analysis beyond the factory floor. Assuming the capability is insufficient, the team can use a multi-vari analysis to identify the key process variables that are causing the bulk of the variation in the process outputs (CTQs). Formal DOE provides additional power to resolve ambiguities and quantify cause-and-effect relationships. Although DOE remains an important tool in real economy projects, it is admittedly applied less frequently than in manufacturing. DOE therefore becomes somewhat less important, whereas multi-vari analysis becomes even more critical, because it is often used in place of DOE.

A key characteristic of the Six Sigma methodology is that the output of each of these tools provides input to the control plan, by determining the most important aspects of the process that need to be controlled to maintain improvements. This approach greatly simplifies development of the control plan because much of the hard work has already been done. SPC, the other commonly used tool depicted in Figure 7.1, is then utilized by the control plan to quickly identify abnormal behavior in the process so that root causes can be found. SPC uses control charts to document the range of normal behavior in the process, allowing early detection of potential problems before they become major issues.

Both SPC and control plans are equally as applicable beyond the factory floor as they are on it. However, although the need for control plans is generally recognized when operating complex machinery, it is less recognized when improving the release process at a hospital, or the fulfillment process in e-commerce. The purpose of the control plan is to ensure improvements are maintained over time, even when the Six Sigma resources (e.g., BBs, MBBs) move on to other projects. The control plan also simplifies the job of those working in the process because it documents what variables to keep a close eye on, and what actions to take when the unexpected occurs. It should be obvious that such documentation is equally as valuable in banking, health care, or marketing as it is in manufacturing.

Note that the preceding is intended to show how the tools are interrelated; it is not intended to depict the DMAIC process in its entirety. Therefore, Figure 7.1 should not be viewed as a competitor to the DMAIC process; it is only highlighting one aspect of DMAIC: tool linkages.

Individual Tools

As noted earlier, process maps or flowcharts become even more important in real economy projects than in manufacturing projects. They allow BB teams to come to a common understanding of the overall process flow, and provide a "line of sight" to a potentially invisible process. Figure 7.2 shows a process map of an off-list pricing process (that is, the process for allowing sales people to offer pricing to customers below listed or published prices). This is a particular type of process map called a top-down flowchart, because it shows the overall macro process at the top, and then shows details of each individual step in the macro process going down the chart.

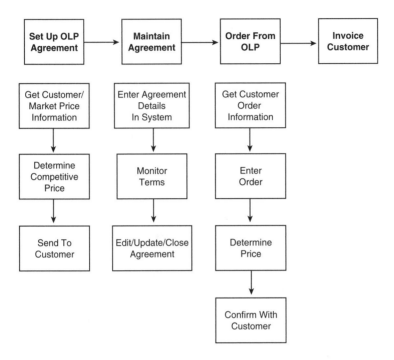

FIGURE 7.2   Flowchart of off-list pricing.

Although each process map is different, a common framework is typically employed. This is the SIPOC model, introduced in Chapter 2, which stands for suppliers, inputs, process, outputs, and customers. In other words, each process, whether in manufacturing or gardening, takes inputs from customers, adds value to them in some manner through various processing steps, and then delivers outputs to customers. Figure 7.3 depicts the SIPOC model.

Terms such as *supplier*, *processing step*, and *customer* are generic terms; in many cases beyond the factory floor the supplier and customer are people who work just down the hall. Consider the example of closing the monthly books in finance. Initially, many people do not see this as a process. In such cases, it is usually easiest to begin with outputs, by asking the question "What do you produce through your work?" Very few people will answer by saying "nothing," so you will usually get off to a good start with this question. In this case, the answer might be a completed monthly financial statement; this is an output from the monthly closing process.

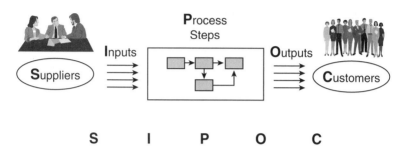

FIGURE 7.3   SIPOC model of processes.

The next logical question to ask is "Who needs or utilizes this output?" (That is, who are the customers?) There may be many customers. In this example, you might say that management at various levels, the external investment community, and perhaps government agencies are key customers who need this output. You would next ask about what work is needed to produce the outputs; a list of actions taken to produce the outputs provides the steps of the process. To close the monthly books requires a number of standard accounting steps, such as manual account reconciliation, running of various computer applications, approvals, and so on.

Next you ask about what inputs are required for these processing steps. Closing the books is totally dependent on data: No data, no closing process. The closing process needs various streams of data and information. In fact, organizations that have most dramatically improved the closing process often focus on improving the inputs rather than the steps in the closing process itself. Finally, you ask from whom they obtain the inputs. Whoever provides the inputs is the supplier, whether they work for the same company as those working in the process or not. Local and central finance departments generally supply the needed data for the closing process, hence in this case the suppliers reside in the same overall organization as those working in the process.

The C&E matrix is often developed soon after the process map, to identify the key process steps that impact the CTQs most significantly. The main purpose of the tool is to provide focus on the key process steps and variables on which the team must concentrate improvement efforts to see major improvements in the

CTQs. Focusing on the critical few steps and variables is one key to Six Sigma success. Figure 7.4 shows the C&E matrix for an accounts payable process that had 5 key steps, 17 process variables (*X*s), and 5 output variables (*Y*s). The top 10 variables are shown in Figure 7.4. The four variables at the top of the list are the highest priority (potentially most important) *X*s. As can be seen in this figure, the C&E matrix is similar to a *quality function deployment* (QFD) matrix (discussed later in this chapter), in this case showing how strongly the various process steps and variables impact the various CTQs. This information aids the team in prioritizing process steps for subsequent improvement efforts, and when searching for important variables. A good strategy for doing the FMEA (to be discussed later) is to focus the FMEA on the highest-priority variable identified by the C&E matrix.

		Rating of Importance to Customer	8	2	10	7	4	
		Output Variable	1	2	3	4	5	
			Discounts	Overtime	Timely Payment	Processing Time	Wait Time	Total
	Process Step	Process Input						
7	Invoice Posted	Match Invoice with Purchase Order	9	9	9	9	9	279
9	Invoice Posted	Check Vendor	9	3	9	9	3	243
1	Accts Payable Receives Invoice	Vendor Mails Invoice	9	0	9	3	9	183
8	Invoice Posted	Check Tax Code	9	0	3	9	3	177
10	Schedule Payment	Select Due Date	9	0	3	0	0	102
2	Invoice Posted	Enter Purchase Order Number	3	1	3	3	3	89
11	Match Invoice to Check	Invoice Copy	3	0	3	1	0	61
12	Match Invoice to Check	Check Copy	3	0	3	1	0	61
5	Invoice Posted	Invoice Number	0	0	0	3	0	21
14	File Invoice	Scanned Copy	0	3	0	0	0	6

FIGURE 7.4   Accounts payable cause-and-effect matrix.

Ideally, you would have data to indicate which process steps are impacting the overall CTQs. In such a case, the C&E matrix is just a convenient means of communicating the information in the data. In many other situations, however, particularly in real economy applications, the team simply doesn't have the appropriate process data to make this decision objectively. There may be no valid measurement system currently in place to obtain it.

In this situation, the team uses the C&E format as a means of reaching a consensus on which steps are most likely to influence the CTQs. In other words, the team decides subjectively, based on its collective knowledge and experience, how strongly each process step impacts each CTQ. When used in this manner, the C&E matrix is an example of a knowledge-based tool, such as QFD and process mapping. Knowledge-based tools utilize the data (knowledge) in people's heads, rather than objective, quantitative data collected from the process. It is helpful to think of the creation of the process map, C&E matrix, and FMEA as a process for capturing "tribal knowledge" (the collection of data, folklore, and opinion that has been accumulated by the "tribe" over the years as they operate the process).

There are obvious potential shortcomings of this usage of the C&E matrix, and knowledge-based tools in general. First of all, the result will only be as good as the knowledge in the room when the matrix was developed. For this reason, the team needs to have the right mix of skills and experience, which is usually accomplished through cross-functional teams. Second, if the team is not properly led and facilitated, decisions could be made on the basis of hierarchy or voting rather than on expertise. Although voting is certainly democratic, you do not want the most popular answer; you want the most correct answer. At times, teams should defer to those most knowledgeable about the current issue under discussion. Third, developing the C&E matrix subjectively could lead the team to a false sense of security, believing that they have found the correct answer because they have a matrix filled out. Therefore, when used in a subjective manner, teams should always go back to validate the C&E matrix later as they do obtain the necessary data.

As noted earlier, in most cases you begin the FMEA analysis by focusing on the highest-priority *X*s identified by the C&E matrix. FMEA is a well-established tool in engineering for identifying potential problems before they occur. It is often used in DFSS projects because you do not yet have process data to identify the most common problems, hence identifying potential problems makes particularly good sense. The output of an FMEA analysis also provides useful information to control plans. This tool, which is also a knowledge-based tool, requires teams to answer an integrated set of questions about potential failures. You first identify failure modes (how the process or product might actually fail), then failure effects (the practical consequences of failure), and then potential causes (why the failure mode might occur).

The team then further evaluates the degree to which the current process is likely to detect the cause of failure *prior to* an actual failure occurring, or at least prior to the failure effects occurring, allowing time to prevent them. For example, when tires fail by completely wearing out the tread, one can usually tell well ahead of time that the tread is getting low and can then replace the tires, preventing a failure. Of course, for other types of failures (other failure modes), such as a blowout due to hitting a sharp object, it would be virtually impossible to detect the cause prior to failure.

The team working on the FMEA numerically rates each of these elements. For the effect of the failure, they rate severity, typically on a 1 to 10 scale, where 10 would be "catastrophic." For the causes of failure, the team rates the likelihood of occurrence, with 10 typically being very likely. Detection is rated as to likelihood of detecting a cause or failure mode occurring with enough advance warning to prevent the effect. For reasons that will be obvious shortly, this scale is rated in reverse, with a 10 meaning a failure is virtually impossible to detect prior to the effect occurring.

These three numbers are multiplied for each effect-cause-detection combination (there may be several for each failure mode) to create a *risk priority number* (RPN). The higher numbers represent the potential failures of greatest concern, and are usually addressed first. As part of the FMEA process, corrective actions are often identified and assigned by the team, and the ratings repeated after the corrective action is completed. In this manner, the team can reduce the risk levels for the most critical items over time.

As noted, this technique has been applied in engineering for decades. However, it does not appear to be widely used in real economy applications. The most likely reason for this is that FMEA is closely associated with engineering, and hence many BBs may think that it only applies there. However, it is applicable whenever you want to document and analyze potential failures, including in financial, health care, and e-commerce processes. For example, Figure 7.5 shows excerpts from the FMEA completed on the DuPont litigation project discussed in Chapter 5, with some numbers modified for confidentiality.

Process Step	Potential Failure Mode	Potential Effects of Failure	Severity	Potential Causes of Failure	Occurrence	Current Controls	Detection	RPN
Pull Sheet Creation	Inaccurate Entries	Wrong Documents Pulled	9	Clerk Mistake, Inattention	8	QC	8	576
Priv. Log Check	Priv. Docs Not Identified	Wrong Documents Pulled	8	Clerk Mistake, Inattention	8	QC	8	512
Document Review	Miscounts, Wrong Documents	Wrong Documents Produced	8	Clerk Mistake, Inattention	7	QC	6	336
Tracking Form Creation	Inaccurate Entries	Wrong Documents Tracked	7	Clerk Mistake, Inattention	5	QC	6	210

FIGURE 7.5 Excerpts of FMEA for legal document process failures.

FMEA is frequently applied in both DMAIC and DFSS projects. Sometimes when the C&E matrix is completed, the team identifies potential problems not previously recognized, either because data have not been available or simply because the organization has been "lucky," such as finding potential security holes in a corporate computer network. In cases where the identified issues are beyond the project scope, the team may choose to take correction action prior to the completion of the Six Sigma project. In these cases, the information from the FMEA may go directly to the control plan, without going through any other DMAIC steps or other tools. Another potential use of FMEA in DMAIC projects is as a means of documenting the weak areas of the process and keeping track of the corrective actions taken along the way. Many projects attain bottom-line improvement prior to project closeout.

A measurement systems analysis is often the next logical step, where you evaluate your ability to measure the CTQs, and perhaps key process metrics. As with FMEA, MSA is a well-developed field that has been around for decades, if not centuries. Typically, people think of MSA in regard to evaluating mechanical measurement devices, such as gauges, through GR&R studies. Repeatability represents the ability for the same person to obtain similar results measuring the same item with the same measuring device, whereas reproducibility refers to the ability of different people and/or different measurement devices to obtain similar results. Again, it is often assumed that MSA is not relevant beyond the factory floor, because there are no gauges in accounting or marketing.

Although some Six Sigma practitioners assume that GR&R analysis is all that is required for a complete MSA, in actuality the problem is much deeper. Other measurement issues to consider are accuracy (obtaining the correct value on average), linearity (having the same degree of accuracy over the entire measurement range), and stability over time (the absence of drift). We refer you to books specializing in MSA, such as AIAG (1995) and Wheeler and Lyday (1989) for the specifics of how to perform such analyses.

In actuality, measurement is the act of assigning a value to something (including "yes/no" designations). Obviously, people assign values to things in areas such as accounting, HR, sales, and so on, so MSA is always relevant. In fact, one could suggest that the fundamental purpose of the accounting profession is to ensure standard, consistent financial measurements. Figure 7.6 shows why measurement system analysis is so important. The data you observe are always a result of at least two processes: the process of interest (such as checking patients into a hospital), and the measurement process. Often people initiate improvement projects because of problems observed in the data, but ultimately it turns out that the real issue was with the measurement system. Considering the measurement system as a source of variation prevents such "wild goose chases" and helps you understand the true variation in the process.

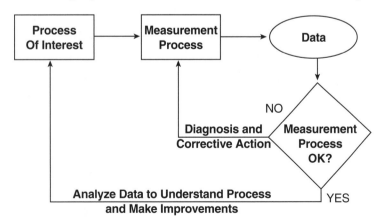

FIGURE 7.6   Impact of measurement process on improvement efforts.

Although the viewpoint that MSA only applies to manufacturing is obviously false, in many cases one has to take a unique approach to MSA outside manufacturing. In manufacturing, the majority of the measurements are continuous, such as weight, physical dimensions, or torque. In these cases, using GR&R studies to break down variation into percentages due to repeatability and reproducibility makes perfect sense, and is helpful. Measurement is the source of several challenges in real economy applications, including the following:

- Many measurements are discrete.

- Frequently data are collected by making surveys.

- It is often difficult to collect repeat measurements enabling you to estimate the short-term repeatability of the measurement system.

- Continuous measurements are often collected in a discrete fashion.

- There is often no absolute standard for what a "correct value" is.

Each of these challenges is discussed below.

First, in real economy applications many of the measurements are discrete measurements, such as determining that an insurance claim is, or is not, valid. With such data, it is not appropriate to try to break down total variation into percentages, because we are dealing with discrete versus continuous probability distributions. Instead, it is much simpler, and makes much more sense theoretically, to calculate the percent of time that different people agree on the correct measurement—for example, the percent of time that different adjusters agree that insurance claims should be paid. See Windsor (2003) for more detail on evaluating discrete measurement systems.

Another measurement challenge is the fact that surveys are used more frequently beyond the factory floor to obtain data from people. These may be customer surveys, employee surveys, vendor surveys, or just surveys to obtain ideas for improvement. Because most surveys are done anonymously, it is very difficult to perform traditional MSA on survey data. However, one can look at the variation in answers from respondent to respondent to get an idea of the degree of variation in opinion.

Even for continuous measurements, such as cycle time, there are complications beyond the factory floor. First, such distributions tend to be highly skewed, suggesting that a transformation might be appropriate prior to performing a GR&R study (see the discussion of normality later in this chapter). Second, it is much easier to take a repeat measurement of a sample on a scale than it is to obtain a repeat measure of cycle time. In many cases, obtaining a true measure of repeatability for cycle time is virtually impossible. In such situations, it is often still reasonable to look at variation in time measurement between people, however. For example, numerous insights have come out of delivery cycle time studies involving both customer and vendor. Often the two disagree on what delivery cycle times have been historically simply because they are measuring time differently.

Another common measurement issue beyond the factory floor is that in many cases people will record continuous measurements in a discrete fashion, thereby losing valuable information. Some examples are measuring time to pay invoices, or delivery times as either "on time" or "late." It should be obvious that in accounts payable, it matters whether we pay on the due date, or 10 days early, because we are losing interest. Also, paying a day late will not have the same impact on the customer as paying a year late. Therefore, data should always be recorded as continuous numbers, if the data are in fact continuous. One can always calculate percent on time from the continuous data if management needs this metric.

Unfortunately, some measurements common in real economy applications have no absolute standard, making it impossible to say for sure what the correct measurement is. For example, various underwriters may disagree as to whether a given loan application should be accepted or rejected. Note that this classification as to whether an application should be accepted is essentially a measurement—assigning a value to something. In such cases, the team must define a subjective standard, such as a panel of experts or a chief underwriter, so that a final determination of correct or incorrect measurement can be made.

When the team feels confident that it can accurately measure the key variables, the next logical tool in Figure 7.1 is capability analysis. This is where the sigma level of the process is calculated, and perhaps other capability metrics such as Cp or Cpk (see
Breyfogle 2003 for details). Calculation of the sigma level tells you
what performance you can expect from the process in the future,
and if performed over an extended time period can help diagnose
whether more variation is due to inherent process capability, also
known as process-variation "entitlement" (short-term capability), or
to process drift over time (long-term capability). Calculation of the
process capability is also important to ensure you are working on
the right problem; if the capability is acceptable, or if there are "bigger fish to fry" elsewhere, you may decide to postpone the project.
This information is obviously as valuable beyond the factory floor
as on it, if you have continuous data.

You can still calculate a sigma level of the process with the
discrete data common in real economy applications, but you need
continuous data to break down variation into components, such as
short term and long term. With sufficient data, however, control
chart techniques can be used to detect process drift over time,
even with discrete data. Another concern with applications
beyond the factory floor is that in many cases the process is so bad
at the beginning of the project that the calculated sigma level is
less than zero! For example, whenever the percent defective is
more than 50% with discrete data, the calculated long-term sigma
value will be less than zero, unless it is set to zero by default, a practice of several computer packages.

In such cases, the calculation of a sigma level adds no real
value to the project, and BBs will often focus on percent defective
as the key capability metric, rather than the sigma level. Having said
that, we would like to reemphasize that with continuous data collected over an extended time period (e.g., a month or more), it is
possible to obtain a great deal of diagnostic information about the
process through process capability analysis. This is another reason
why continuous data are in general preferred to discrete data. We
leave the details of calculating sigma levels to books focusing on
the technical aspects of Six Sigma, such as Breyfogle (2003).

After the process capability has been determined, and the team has verified that this is a problem worth solving, analysis of data collected passively from the process is often a logical next step. The purpose of this analysis, which in Six Sigma we call *multi-vari analysis*, is to identify the key input and process variables that appear to be driving variation and defects in the CTQs. In particular it is important to identify key uncontrolled (noise) variables such as day of week, season of year, work team member, and so on that may be affecting the performance of the process. There is no other way to collect data on uncontrolled variables than to observe the process as it operates.

These studies are called multi-vari studies because teams typically gather data on several variables at once. Multi-vari analysis includes a number of individual techniques for the analysis of data, including traditional statistical tools, such as the following:

- Hypothesis testing

- Confidence intervals

- Correlation and regression analysis

- Data mining

- Graphical techniques, such as box plots and scatter plots

Such techniques apply equally well beyond the factory floor, although there will be a tendency to use techniques appropriate for discrete data more often, such as Chi-square analysis for hypothesis testing, binomial or Poisson confidence intervals (versus normal distribution intervals), and logistic regression when using a discrete CTQ, such as accuracy. See Hoerl and Snee (2002) or Breyfogle (2003) for more information on these and other statistical methods used in multi-vari analysis. Data mining, the statistical analysis of massive data sets, is commonly applied in financial services and marketing, even outside Six Sigma projects. Some classical applications include mining databases on credit card purchases to better predict who is and isn't a good credit risk, or to determine who is most likely to respond to a targeted marketing campaign.

The key differentiator between multi-vari analysis, and the next tool in Figure 7.1, *design of experiments* (DOE), is how the data were collected. As noted, multi-vari uses data collected passively from the process. DOE, on the other hand, proactively intervenes with the process to determine cause-and-effect relationships and to obtain the most informative data. Passively collected data are known to have many potential limitations, such as when more than one variable changes at the same time. For example, if auto insurance sales declined dramatically exactly when a new sales manager arrived and two experienced salespeople retired, was the decline due to the arrival of the new sales manager, or to the retirement of the experienced sales staff? Statistically, it is impossible to say for sure. Situations such as this one lead to a general rule in statistics that says that analysts should never confuse correlation (things happening at the same time) with causation (one thing happening directly because of another thing happening).

Multi-vari techniques can determine that certain process variables are correlated with the CTQs, but for the reasons just mentioned, they cannot determine causation. For this we need DOE. Because DOE actively intervenes with the process, it can structure all the process variables so that it is easy to differentiate their effects on the CTQs. In addition, during a DOE the team attempts to keep all other potential variables (that is, those not being studied) strictly controlled, to avoid having them impact the results. Further, by running the experiments in random order, a technique known as *randomization*, DOE makes it virtually impossible for some unknown variable to change at exactly the same time as the variables in the DOE. The net result of all this effort is that teams are able to obtain high-quality data that allow them to infer with a great deal of confidence cause and effect relationships between the variables of interest.

Again, many assume that DOE can only be applied in factory or engineering settings. In reality, DOE can be applied whenever it is possible to proactively manipulate the variables of interest, which is often the case in real economy applications. Koselka (1996) showed that there is a growing trend in the use of DOE beyond the factory floor. Figure 7.7 shows a DOE from Hoerl and Snee (2002) used to understand drivers of sales for a retail product, including different locations of product display, different packaging, and different sizes of stores. A downside of DOE is that it can require requires a lot more time and effort than passively observing the process, particularly when there are a large number of variables.

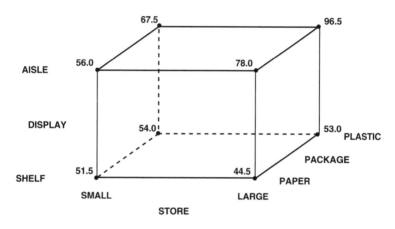

CubePlot (data means) for UNITS SOLD

FIGURE 7.7 Product display sales experiment.

Therefore, a common practice is to utilize multi-vari techniques from existing or easily collected data to identify the most probable drivers of variation and defects, and then to follow up with a designed experiment to verify and refine these conclusions. Often, multi-vari analysis is applied in the analyze phase, when BB teams are searching for root causes, and DOE is applied in the improve phase, when the teams need to determine specific actions to take to reduce variation and defects. It is our experience that DOE is the most underutilized Six Sigma tool in real economy applications.

Teams should carefully consider how DOE might be employed in their projects, and not assume that it won't apply solely because they are not in manufacturing. Hahn et al. (2000) discussed a Six Sigma project in credit card collections that utilized a DOE to produce almost $3 million savings annually. See Hoerl and Snee (2002) for more examples of DOE applications beyond the factory floor, such as in telemarketing and advertising.

Figure 7.1 shows that each of the tools discussed previously feeds into the control plan. The control plan is the key tool utilized in the control phase of DMAIC projects, and is also used in DFSS projects. Recall that the purpose of the control phase is to ensure that the improvements made in the improve phase are maintained over time. It is quite common in the business world to make significant improvements and then to see these improvements gradually slip away over time as management attention focuses elsewhere. The control plan outlines what variables the process owners need to monitor over time and what actions to take when these variables indicate a problem. Figure 7.8 shows a control plan developed for the process of responding to IT service requests. All the analyses done in earlier phases, using the tools discussed previously, help identify the key process variables and how they should be managed to maintain improvement. This is the critical information needed for the control plan.

Process: Date:
Purpose: Rev.:

| | | | | | | Check The Process | | Act/Fix Problem | |
Dept A	Dept B	Dept C		Output Measure	Input/Process Measures	Standard/Specification	Method For Sampling/Recording Data	Immediate Control/Fix	Process/System Improvement
Customer Requests Service	Customer Requests Service			Level Of Understanding		100% Of Customers With Full Understanding	Monthly Customer Survey Conducted By Measurements Group		Reviewed Monthly By Reg. SP Comm. And NPA BOM
				Level Of Satisfaction		90% Of Customers In Very Good And Excellent (SQMIS)	Monthly Customer Survey Conducted By Measurements Group SQMIS		Reviewed Monthly By Reg. SP Comm. And NPA BOM
	Issue PC Memo			Time Issuance		POS To Fax Transmittal On Receipt Within 15 Minutes	PC Samples 25 Fax Transmittals Per Day And Plots % Completed Within Standard By Day	Assign Individual To Handle All Fax Transmittals	• Reviewed Weekly By NPA SP Comm. • Reviewed Monthly By Reg. SP Comm, And NPA BOM.
				Quality Issuance		100% Of The PC Memos Are Accurate, Legible And Complete Requiring No Follow-Up With Individual PC Rep.	• PC Exception Reports— Track How Many Times Per Day Follow-Up Is Necessary With PC Rep By PCI. • Graph The Number Of Exceptions By Day And Tally Reasons By Week	• Train Individual Rep./Staff • Discuss/Review Suggestions At Scheduled PC Site Meetings	• Reviewed Weekly By NPA SP Comm. • Reviewed Monthly By Reg. SP Comm, And NPA BOM.
Issue BCRIS Order		Issue BCRIS Order		Timely (PCI Only) Issuance		100% Of The Fax Transmittals Are Input To BCRIS Within 45 Min. Upon Receipt	PCI Samples BCRIS Orders Per Day And Plots % Completed Within Standard By Day		• Measures Reviewed Weekly By NPA SP Comm. • Measures Reviewed Monthly By Reg. SP Comm, And NPA BOM.

FIGURE 7.8   Control plan for IT service requests.

Although control plans apply equally as well beyond the factory floor as on it, it is often the case that people working in real economy processes are not used to the disciplined and scientific approach required by a control plan. In manufacturing, on the other hand, engineers and operators are used to dealing with dangerous equipment and toxic chemicals that mandate the use of detailed procedures for handling such dangers. This is therefore more of a cultural issue than a technical issue, and we refer you to our discussion of how to address cultural issues in Chapter 2.

Statistical process control (SPC), the last tool shown in Figure 7.1, is frequently utilized in the control plan. SPC plots data over time against statistically determined action limits to detect when something noteworthy has occurred. In the control plan, the SPC plots, also known as *control charts*, are used as an early warning system to alert the process owners that a key variable is degrading, or in some cases improving. The process owners are then able to take prompt action to diagnose and correct root causes of the problem, hopefully prior to any change in process outputs noticeable by customers. By utilizing control charts based on statistically determined limits, the process owners don't fall into the trap of reacting to every routine movement of the process variables; they only react when there is scientific evidence that a true change occurred.

Figure 7.9 shows a control chart of the number of outgoing calls in an automotive loan collections office, as well as how it was utilized within the control plan (G. Powell, personal communication). During this project, the team made improvements to collections and determined that the number of outgoing calls was a key measure of process health. There was some concern that after the project was officially closed there would be a drop-off in outgoing calls, simply because management focus was taken elsewhere. As can be seen in this graph, a sudden drop-off did occur, but was quickly detected and addressed, returning the process to its improved state.

A key point of this discussion is that the overall toolkit in manufacturing and real economy projects is essentially the same, but the mix of tools typically applied does vary. Of course, there could be a further comparison between health care and finance projects, between e-commerce and marketing projects, and so on, which we will not take the time to discuss. Our experience is that differences between manufacturing and real economy projects are greater than between different application areas within the real economy.

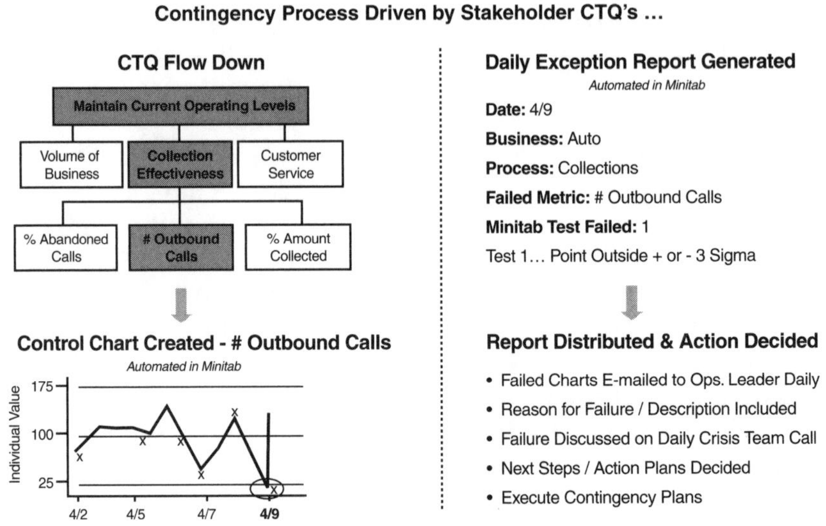
Contingency Process Driven by Stakeholder CTQ's ...
CTQ Flow Down
Maintain Current Operating Levels
Volume of Business
Collection Effectiveness
Customer Service
% Abandoned Calls
# Outbound Calls
% Amount Collected
Control Chart Created - # Outbound Calls
Automated in Minitab
Individual Value
175
100
25
4/2
4/5
4/7
4/9
Daily Exception Report Generated
Automated in Minitab
Date: 4/9
Business: Auto
Process: Collections
Failed Metric: # Outbound Calls
Minitab Test Failed: 1
Test 1... Point Outside + or - 3 Sigma
Report Distributed & Action Decided
• Failed Charts E-mailed to Ops. Leader Daily
• Reason for Failure / Description Included
• Failure Discussed on Daily Crisis Team Call
• Next Steps / Action Plans Decided
• Execute Contingency Plans

FIGURE 7.9 Control chart on number of outbound calls.

To summarize, in manufacturing applications we see greater use of the following:

- Continuous data GR&R studies
- DOE, particularly in response surface designs used for optimization
- Capability analysis for continuous data

In applications beyond the factory floor, we see greater use of the following:

- Evaluation of attribute measurement systems (e.g., accuracy)
- Process mapping
- Knowledge-based tools in general (because the desired data are often unavailable)
- Surveys (to gather data from people)

Some Additional Tools Particularly Useful Beyond the Factory Floor

Although the tools shown in Figure 7.1 form the core of those applied in real economy applications, many other tools are used. In particular, several tools have demonstrated broad applicability, perhaps broader applicability outside manufacturing than they have within manufacturing. We bring these tools to your attention without attempting to provide comprehensive instruction in their use. See the enclosed references for details. These additional tools are as follows:

- Quality function deployment (QFD)

- Surveys

- Monte Carlo simulation

- Discrete-event simulation

- Error-proofing

QFD (Breyfogle 2003) has been widely applied in product development, and more recently has proven useful in service development. QFD is a cross-functional, team-based methodology for taking vague or fuzzy customer needs and translating them into quantitative metrics (CTQs), and then deploying them to lower and lower levels of detail in requirements, all the way down to process control systems. QFD is a knowledge-based methodology that makes heavy use of matrices, and is particularly valuable in defining quantitative CTQs for Six Sigma projects beyond the factory floor.

Survey design and analysis is a diverse field that has been around for quite some time. However, because real economy applications are often heavily dependent on people, versus the online data acquisition systems in manufacturing, surveys often take a significant role in Six Sigma applications beyond the factory floor. They are often a major source of data in the measure and analyze phases of DMAIC projects. Although developing and evaluating surveys may sound trivial, it is well known that the wording of questions in surveys can significantly influence the results. In addition, the responses to surveys are typically discrete in nature (i.e.,

1 to 5 ratings), and hence the analysis of this data presents unique challenges. Hoerl and Snee (2002) discuss the use of surveys and provide additional references for further detail.

Monte Carlo is well known for its casinos, or games of chance, and Monte Carlo simulation shares some similarities. It basically means randomly drawing data from some assumed distributions, performing relevant calculations, repeating this process hundreds or thousands of times, and documenting the potential results. Consider an example. Suppose you want to roll up net income from three different P&Ls to calculate a corporate income. Each P&L estimates its income and provides the estimate to corporate. Traditionally, the finance organization would add up the three estimates and use this value as the estimated corporate income. However, after you understand Six Sigma, you realize that each of these three P&L estimates is subject to uncertainty and variation. You don't know exactly what their incomes will be, but you have estimates. Therefore, how far off from your estimated corporate income are you likely to be? Monte Carlo simulation helps you answer this question.

The basic idea is to document the uncertainty in each estimate, through estimating a statistical distribution, not just a "point" (single number) estimate. For example, instead of saying that P&L 1 estimates income of $200 million, you might suggest that the income of P&L 1 has a normal distribution with an average of $200 million and a standard deviation of $20 million. There are various ways to estimate this distribution, including analysis of historical data. If you have distributions for each of the three P&Ls, you can randomly select one value from each distribution, using the computer, and add them up. This would give you one plausible corporate income value. If you repeat this exercise 10,000 times, you will have an overall distribution of plausible corporate incomes. The income you actually experience is more likely to come from the middle of this distribution than from the tails. Such analyses provide more detailed and accurate information for financial forecasts.

Figure 7.10 shows a GE example of a simulated distribution for annual return on a new investment, with the 0% (break-even) point highlighted. This line reveals the likelihood of making money on the deal (91.1%), whereas the overall distribution gives management an idea of the range of potential results. This example uses the simulation application Crystal Ball, which is an Excel add-in. See Kalos and Whitlock (1986) for more information on the methodology of Monte Carlo simulation.

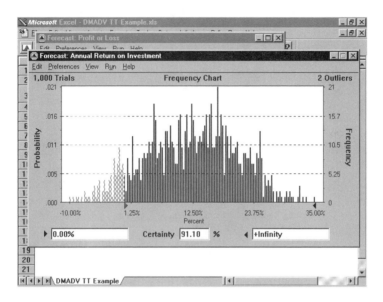

FIGURE 7.10   Example of Monte Carlo simulation output.

Discrete-event simulation is a similar concept, except that you are simulating discrete events, rather than simulating individual values to go into a formula. For example, you might want to simulate what happens when a loan application enters your business. Loan applications are the "discrete events" in this case. The rate of arriving loan applications and the time it takes to evaluate and approve each one are random variables. These variables will impact the backlogs or queues that develop in the process. Although it is difficult to develop analytical approaches to directly estimate the total cycle time of such processes—that is, it is difficult to develop an equation for cycle time—it is much easier to develop a flowchart of the process. You can then incorporate some Monte Carlo simulation into the flowchart, simulate how queues would develop, and understand their impact on cycle time. We show a GE example of discrete-event simulation for a small business loan application process in Figure 7.11, using the application Process Model.

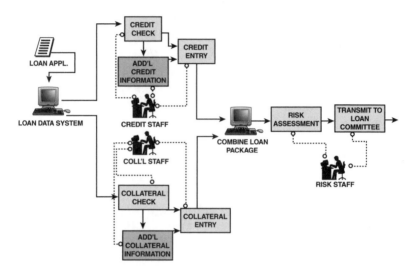

FIGURE 7.11   Discrete-event simulation model of small business loan application processing.

Note that application arrival rate is a random variable. What would happen if this rate were normally distributed with an average of 10,000 per day, with a standard deviation of 1,000? What if this arrival rate were exponentially distributed with an average of 5,000 per day? Using discrete-event simulation, you can simulate arrivals, and then track them through the system, moving items (loans in this case) through the flowchart based on various statistical distributions, such as time to perform a credit check. The key difference between discrete-event simulation and Monte Carlo simulation is that in discrete-event simulation you don't have an equation or formula; the flowchart is the formula. Rather than calculating outputs based on simulated inputs, it tracks discrete events as they move through the process through "brute force"—that is, keeping track of how long each item takes to flow through the process. See Law and Kelton (1991) for more information on discrete-event simulation.

Monte Carlo and discrete-event simulation are particularly valuable in design for Six Sigma projects because they enable you to simulate how a new process would perform without actually building it. This can save considerable time and money. Although the results are clearly dependent on your assumptions in the simulation, if the system fails to perform adequately even under optimistic assumptions, you can safely assume that this idea won't work and move on to others.

Error-proofing is a simple concept, although its actual application can be complicated. In essence, it just means making it difficult to make an error, or in some cases, it alerts people to the existence of an error prior to it being passed on in the process. For example, spell-checkers are a form of error-proofing; it is harder to make a spelling error when your computer is checking each word against a dictionary. Of course, someone can still type *own* when he or she meant *won*, but in general spell-checkers do prevent errors. Other examples include cars that beep when the ignition is turned off while the lights are on, computer systems that do not accept invalid entries, and irons that have automatic shutoff. See Breyfogle (2003) for additional information on this method.

Unique Technical Challenges Beyond the Factory Floor

This section addresses the two major challenges that are of a detailed technical nature in applications beyond the factory floor. In our experience, and the experience of many others, these are the technical issues that BBs struggle with the most in real economy applications. These are skewed (non-normal) data distributions, and the prevalence of discrete versus continuous data. These issues occur in manufacturing as well, but they occur more frequently outside manufacturing. We discuss the nature of these issues and present strategies for addressing them that are both theoretically valid and practically useful. Other issues encountered in the use of the Six Sigma tools beyond the factory floor are discussed in Snee (2003). We begin this discussion with the issue of normality.

Non-Normal Data Distributions

The normal distribution, also known as the *Gaussian distribution*, is the most fundamental continuous probability distribution in statistics. It is intended to represent the range of possible outcomes for a random variable, such as monthly sales, and the relative probability of any specific set of values occurring. Figure 7.12 shows an example of a normal probability distribution, in this case with an average of 100 and a standard deviation of 5. Of course, any other normal distribution with a different average or standard deviation would look identical; the only difference would be the scale at the bottom. Note that the distribution peaks at 100, indicating values in this region are more probable than those out in the tails (extremities) of the distribution.

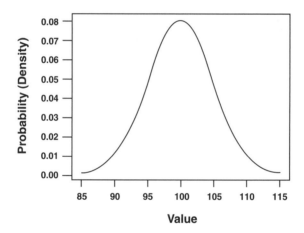

FIGURE 7.12   Normal distribution with average 100 and standard deviation 5.

This distribution is fundamental to statistics because many statistical techniques assume that data follow a normal distribution, and therefore the validity of these techniques is dependent on the truth of this assumption. Examples include standard regression analysis, *analysis of variance* (ANOVA), t-tests, and many confidence intervals. Some control charts also utilize the normal distribution in determining the limits on the charts. However, what if the data do not appear to follow a normal distribution?

Figure 7.13 shows data on the "goodwill," or the amount paid above the fair market value to acquire a company, for recent acquisitions of a large multinational company. Some amount of goodwill is almost always required to provide incentive for current owners to sell. These data certainly do not look like the distribution in Figure 7.12. These data would be called skewed to the right, because they are skewed (asymmetrical) and the height of the distribution tails off as you move to the right. This type of data is very common in real economy applications. In this case, the skewness occurs because it is virtually impossible to have negative goodwill; current owners are not going to sell en mass below fair market value. You can have extremely large values, but there can't be extremely low values, because zero acts as a natural barrier. This results in the skew to the right.

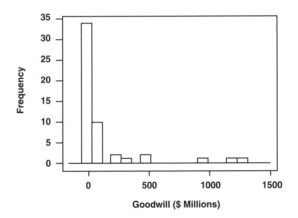

FIGURE 7.13   Histogram of goodwill.

Such data occur most often beyond the factory floor when you are analyzing cycle time, such as the time required to approve a patient's credit when being discharged from a hospital. When cycle time is your CTQ, you often have the same issue seen in Figure 7.13. You can observe very large cycle times, but you can't observe negative cycle times, often resulting in a right skew. Note that cycle time data is not *always* skewed, but tends to be when there is a significant amount of data close to zero. Non-normal data may occur in other ways as well, such as treating survey ratings on a 1 to 10 scale as a continuous variable. In this case, the data would be discrete (technically ordinal), because only ten unique values are possible and therefore the data could not follow the continuous normal distribution.

So if many statistical techniques assume a normal distribution, and if data in projects beyond the factory floor are frequently skewed, such as cycle time measurements, does this imply you can't use the standard statistical toolkit in these cases? This appears to be a logical assumption at first glance, and unfortunately has been taught by many Six Sigma providers and consultants. In reality, it is not true; we can apply our standard statistical toolkit, but must have deeper technical understanding to determine how to apply it. To explain how to do so, we will explain some finer points about the normal distribution and the normality assumption, and then discuss specifically how to analyze non-normal data.

The Truth About the Normal Distribution and the Normality Assumption

The most important truth to understand is that the normal distribution is a *conceptual model*; that is, it exists in theory, but has never occurred in the real world. Therefore, the real question to answer is not whether the data follow a normal distribution (they don't!), but rather whether the data appear to be *approximately* normal. This statement that the normal distribution has never occurred in practice may sound shocking initially, but is intuitively obvious after you examine the normal distribution closely.

For example, the theoretical normal distribution illustrated in Figure 7.12 goes from negative infinity to positive infinity—that is, it has no maximum or minimum value. Therefore, for real data to follow this distribution, the real data would have to be unbounded on both the high and low end. No real data do this. If time were the CTQ, for example, you cannot observe negative times; therefore time could not be exactly normally distributed. Similarly, if money (say dollars) were the CTQ, there is a finite amount of wealth on the planet; therefore dollars could never be exactly normally distributed.

Another reason why you never see exact normality in practice is the fact that continuous distributions have an infinite number of possible outcomes, by definition (to be mathematically precise, we should say "uncountably infinite"). This is illustrated in Figure 7.12 by the fact that the curve of the distribution is continuous; there are no gaps in it. The only way this could occur in practice is if you measured cycle time to an infinite number of decimal points. As soon as you round off the cycle time measurement, say to 2 decimal points, then many values are no longer possible (such as 50.12538762). This would result in gaps in the distribution, making it technically a discrete distribution (mathematicians would say "countably infinite"), again resulting in non-normality.

These are admittedly nit-picking arguments, but they do reveal why no real data will ever exactly follow the normal distribution, which is in reality a conceptual model. So if no real data are ever exactly normal, and if normality is an assumption of many statistical methods, how could these methods actually work in practice? The answer is that in practice you don't need exact normality; you only need approximate normality. The techniques continue to work well until you have significant departures from normality, as seen in Figure 7.13.

This important point is missed by many Six Sigma practitioners and consultants, who teach BBs to perform statistical hypothesis tests, testing whether data follow a normal distribution, prior to using formal statistical methods. Because you know the truth of this hypothesis ahead of time (no, the data are not normally distributed), a simpler and more logical approach is to plot the data, as in Figure 7.13, to see whether they are approximately normal. Another useful plot is the normal probability plot (Breyfogle 2003).

A second truth about the normality assumption is that the assumption does not generally apply to the original raw data, but rather to the residuals, or error terms, from models. For example, if you are trying to predict goodwill of acquisitions (y) based on the companies' total assets (x_1) and the years of amortization (x_2), a standard regression model you might use would be this:

$$y = b_0 + b_1 x_1 + b_2 x_2 + e,$$

where e represents the residual or prediction error (the difference between what the model predicts and what you actually observe), b_0 represents the constant term, and b_1 and b_2 are the slopes for the predictor variables x_1 and x_2, respectively. (See Hoerl and Snee 2002, p. 414 for a more detailed discussion of this case.) In such a model, the normality assumption is *not* for y, goodwill, but rather for e, the residual values!

Therefore, to evaluate the validity of the normality assumption in this case, you would not evaluate the normality of goodwill, but you would have to perform a regression analysis to calculate residuals and evaluate the normality of the residuals. Again, you would be looking for approximate normality rather than exact normality. It is true that extreme non-normality in the original data, goodwill in this case, is an indicator that the residuals are likely to be extremely non-normal. However, in many cases the original data are not approximately normal, but the residuals are. This is because the original data contain the effects of the x variables, total assets and amortization in this case. Therefore, performing a hypothesis test on the original goodwill data to test for normality, a practice that is unfortunately commonly taught, is both theoretically invalid and practically inappropriate.

A third important truth about the normal distribution and the normality assumption is the impact of the central limit theorem. This famous theorem states that whenever one calculates averages from random samples, these averages will tend to follow a normal distribution *regardless of the distribution of the original data*. In other words, even if goodwill is extremely skewed, by taking averages of five different acquisitions, and analyzing these averages, you will tend to observe an approximately normal distribution. Although this theorem is counterintuitive to most people, it is mathematically proven. Figure 7.14 illustrates how quickly sample averages begin to look like a normal distribution, even when the original data are extremely non-normal. This graph shows histograms of sample averages for sample size 1 (i.e., original data), 2, 5, and 10 for a very non-normal distribution, the exponential.

Histrograms of Sample Averages of Size 1, 2, 5, and 10 From an Exponential (λ=1) Distribution

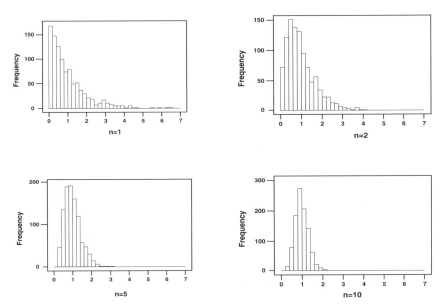

FIGURE 7.14   The central limit theorem.

The practical impact of this theorem is that when analyzing averages rather than individual values, as is often the case in Six Sigma, normality becomes much less of a concern. For example, standard t-tests and ANOVA are tests of averages. Therefore, as is well known in statistical circles (e.g., Box et al. 1978, 89–91), both the t-test and ANOVA are insensitive to the assumption of normality—that is, they continue to work well even when the original data are not normal. So again, the common practice of teaching BBs to test for normality prior to using a t-test or ANOVA makes little sense. Of course, there are times when the normality assumption is still important, such as for tests of variances (e.g., Bartlett's test).

Strategies For Handling Non-Normal Data

Skewed data, such as the goodwill data seen in Figure 7.13, occur frequently in applications beyond the factory floor. A number of valid approaches can be used to analyze such data in statistical analyses. The best approach for any given situation will depend on several factors unique to that problem. Therefore, the advice that follows should be viewed as a set of options rather than a "cookbook" to be followed religiously. The main options are as follows:

- Utilize transformations

- Do nothing

- Utilize techniques designed for the appropriate distribution

- Utilize non-parametric techniques

Transformations simply measure the variables of interest in alternative metrics, often for the purpose of achieving a closer approximation to the normal distribution. For example, you can measure temperature in degrees Fahrenheit, Celsius, or Kelvin. You can measure money in dollars, euros, or yen. Re-expressing temperature in Kelvin from Fahrenheit is an example of a transformation. There are other benefits of using transformations in statistics, but we focus on normality here. The field of transformations is a broad one, and you are referred to Hoerl and Snee (2002, Section 9.8) for a more detailed treatment of this topic.

When the transformation is a non-linear function, it has the ability to normalize skewed data to be approximately normal, at least in some cases. For example, in Figure 7.15 we show the logarithm of goodwill. The logarithm, or log, is a transformation that frequently arises in engineering and financial applications, among many others. Note that the log of goodwill looks much closer to a normal distribution. Again, we are only looking for approximate normality, and only for the model residuals, not for the original data. Common transformations used in Six Sigma projects include the log, the square root (especially for discrete counts), and the inverse, (that is, $1/y$), although there are certainly many other transformations.

After you have appropriately transformed the variables of interest, you can perform your statistical analysis without worrying about the effects of non-normality. Of course, there is no guarantee that an appropriate transformation can be found for each data set, and finding the best one often requires repeated attempts. A more formal methodology for finding appropriate transformations than trial and error is the Box-Cox (Box et al. 1978) approach.

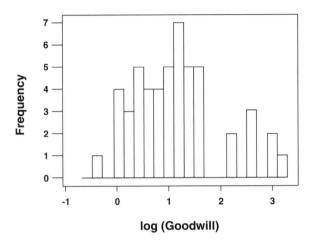

FIGURE 7.15   Histogram of logarithm of goodwill.

Often when sharing with others the results of analyses done in a transformed metric, particularly management, it is a good idea to show graphs of the data in original units of measurement, and then note the key conclusions of the analysis. For example, you might show a plot of goodwill versus total assets in original units, and note that statistical analysis verified a correlation between these two variables. The correlation analysis would likely have been done in transformed units. The reason for this approach is that managers often become confused when told that log of sales is related to the square root of advertising expenses. What is the log of sales, and how do I spend the square root of a dollar on advertising? Fortunately, you can mathematically convert equations developed in transformed units back to the original units, if needed.

A second method for analyzing non-normal data is to do nothing (that is, proceed as if the data were normally distributed). As we have seen, this approach is generally acceptable when any of three criteria are met:

- The data are approximately normal.

- The statistical method being used is based on averages.

- The statistical method being used is insensitive to the normality assumption.

With very large data sets, statistical normality tests will generally indicate that the data are not normally distributed. This is because no real data will be exactly normal, and because large sample sizes, say in the tens or even hundreds of thousands, provide enough statistical power to detect very minor deviations from an exact normal distribution. In many such cases, however, plots of the data reveal an approximate normal distribution, which is good enough for practical purposes. BBs can apply standard techniques in the vast majority of such situations.

If you are comparing averages, through such techniques as the t-test or ANOVA, the central limit theorem makes the assumption of normality far less important. Therefore, you rarely need to worry about normality with these methods, even with sample sizes as low as five per group. You can generally proceed with confidence using these tests, despite non-normal data distributions. It should be noted, however, that appropriate transformations might provide a more insightful analysis.

Also, many techniques that theoretically assume a normal distribution are known to be insensitive to this assumption. In other words, they continue to work well when the assumption is violated. In addition to the methods previously discussed that are based on analysis of averages, such as ANOVA and t-tests, estimation of the coefficients in regression analysis is another example of a technique insensitive to the normality assumption.

In some cases, you can determine the specific non-normal distribution from which the data appear to come. For example, some cycle time data tend to follow a Weibull distribution. Fortunately, there are statistical techniques specifically developed for handling Weibull distributed data, such as Weibull regression. Similarly, a regression methodology known as *generalized linear models* (GLM) enables users to appropriately analyze data from a wide family of distributions, including the exponential and even some discrete distributions.

A more general approach, particularly useful when you don't know what distribution the data are likely to come from, is to use so-called *non-parametric* methods. These methods don't assume a particular probability distribution, and are therefore appropriate over a wider variety of potential problems and data sets. For example, when comparing variances, the assumption of normality is an important issue, because you are not testing averages, hence the central limit theorem does not help you. Some tests for comparing variances, such as Bartlett's test (Box et al. 1978), assume that the data come from a normal distribution and are sensitive to this assumption.

In other words, this technique's performance tends to deteriorate for even minor departures from normality. However, there are alternative non-parametric techniques, such as Levene's test (Levene 1960, 278–292), that can be used to compare variances with non-normal data. Keep in mind, however, that in general non-parametric tests are not as powerful (that is, not as able to detect differences) as tests based on a specific distribution.

In summary, much of the data from applications beyond the factory floor are not normally distributed, or even approximately normal. However, although the assumption of normality can be an important issue in statistics, more often than not it isn't. Even when it is, BBs can utilize valid approaches to analyze these data. Therefore, lack of normality is a technical issue that merits consideration, but it is not a barrier to proper application of the Six Sigma approach.

What About Discrete Data?

Another technical issue that occurs frequently with real economy applications is discrete data. Often these data are some type of accuracy measurement, such as accuracy of a customer order, or perhaps a survey rating. This can cause concern on projects because, as with non-normal data, many of the standard statistical techniques assume continuous data. These standard techniques include regression analysis, ANOVA, t-tests, tests on variances, Xbar and R control charts, and standard capability analysis. BBs who have been trained on these techniques may become frustrated when accuracy is the CTQ of primary interest on their project, and they are not sure how to proceed with the resulting discrete data. For example, what should the BB do when his or her only data are 187 accurate orders and 23 inaccurate orders? Fortunately, there are valid approaches for analyzing such data, just as there are valid approaches for analyzing non-normal data.

There are three primary approaches to the analysis of discrete data commonly used in Six Sigma projects:

1. Apply statistical methods for discrete data

2. Analyze aggregate data using standard (continuous data) techniques

3. Do nothing (that is, use standard techniques on the original data)

Let's discuss each of these approaches in turn, including when it would make most sense to use. Just as there are statistical methods for non-normal data, there are statistical methods specifically designed for analyzing discrete data. When there are only two possible outcomes, such as accurate or inaccurate, the binomial distribution is often used. Such data are often referred to as *defectives data* because each item is either classified as defective or not defective. When counting the number of discrete defects or events in a single unit, such as the number of scratches in the finish of a car, the Poisson distribution is often used. Such data are often referred to as *defects data* because the number of defects for each item can be counted. See Hoerl and Snee (2002) or Breyfogle (2003) for more background on these and other discrete probability distributions.

Most statistical packages, such as Minitab or JMP, have appropriate methods, sometimes based on these alternative distributions that perform the same type of analysis as their continuous data counterparts. For example, when the CTQ is accuracy, logistic regression can be used in place of standard linear regression. Binary logistic regression predicts the probability of a defect (or inaccuracy) for any combination of explanatory (x) variables, and constrains these probabilities within the range of 0 to 1. When comparing multiple processes to see whether any are producing higher inaccuracy (defect) levels than others, BBs can use the Chi-square test in lieu of a t-test or ANOVA.

Minitab and JMP also provide specialized process capability analysis for binomial (defectives) or Poisson (defects) data, as well as control charts based on these distributions, versus the normal. Such charts include the p and np chart for binomial data, and the c and u chart for Poisson data. Wheeler and Chambers (1992) also suggest using individuals and moving range charts (X&MR) for discrete data that do not appear to follow the binomial or Poisson distributions. Here is a list of standard continuous data methods and their corresponding discrete method.

Objective	Continuous Data Method	Discrete Data Method
Compare two averages	t-test	Chi-square test
Compare several averages	ANOVA	Chi-square test
Compare variances	F, Bartlett's, or Levene's test	N/A
Predict response (y) values	Linear regression	Logistic regression
Quantify process capability	Capability analysis	Capability analysis*
Identify special causes	Xbar and R charts	np, p, c, and u charts

*Specialized capability analysis based on appropriate discrete distribution

Note that statisticians generally do not test variances for discrete data, because for the typical discrete distributions encountered in practice, such as the binomial and Poisson, the variance is just a function of the process average. Therefore, if BBs test for differences in the average, they are also testing for differences in variance, by default. More advanced methods for discrete data exist, such as so-called *categorical data analysis methods* (Agresti 1990). Admittedly, utilizing these discrete data methods adds to the complexity of real economy projects and to training requirements. Despite the additional effort required, this approach of using appropriate discrete data methods is generally the preferred approach.

The second option is to analyze aggregate data and then to use standard continuous data techniques. For example, in a designed experiment for accounts receivable, a BB might look at the percent of time that a particular approach to collections led to a payment being made in a given month. (An alternative approach is to look at amount of payment.) Perhaps members of the team collected on 100 accounts for each combination of the DOE. If the BB were to analyze percent of payments made on the 100 accounts for each combination of the DOE, the central limit theorem applies. (Yes, it even applies to discrete data!)

Therefore, it would be appropriate to analyze percent of payments—or as is often done for theoretical reasons, the square root of percent of payments (Hoerl and Snee 2002, 425)—as if it were a continuous metric. Similarly, it is known that the square root of a Poisson count tends to be approximately normal (Box et al. 1978, 144–145), with constant variance, allowing use of standard techniques with this transformation of defects data. As noted previously, Wheeler and Chambers (1992) recommend the use of individuals and moving range control charts with aggregated discrete data, such as percent inaccurate.

The third option mentioned above for discrete data is to do nothing and to proceed as if the data were continuous. This approach is appropriate in certain circumstances, but is clearly inappropriate in others, so a certain degree of experience and knowledge is required to apply it properly. One example of analyzing discrete data as if they were continuous is in surveys, where results are often given on a 1 to 5, or 1 to 10 scale. This approach can be a dangerous practice, however, because it assumes that the scale is equidistant—that is, that the difference between a 1 and a 2 is the same as between a 2 and a 3. This may not be the case, rendering even basic statistics such as the average, difficult to interpret. This is not an approach we recommend for general use, although we acknowledge that it is appropriate in some cases.

Lean Services?

Does Lean manufacturing have any place in improvement efforts beyond the factory floor? Absolutely! However, one needs to understand what Lean and Six Sigma are at their core to properly integrate them in an overall improvement system. Because Lean manufacturing involves manufacturing, it is by definition not applicable beyond manufacturing. However, some of the concepts in Lean manufacturing are generic and can be applied in services. We discussed the proper integration of Six Sigma and Lean manufacturing in Snee and Hoerl (2003), and hence for this discussion we restrict ourselves to issues specific to applications beyond the factory floor.

Several consulting firms and authors promote a hybrid approach to improvement, mixing equal parts of Six Sigma and Lean manufacturing. Although we certainly value the concepts Lean manufacturing brings to the party, we think that such approaches are typically based on trying to fit some Six Sigma tools into a Lean manufacturing approach. Conversely, we have found that Six Sigma provides a richer overall improvement methodology and framework, and we therefore think that fitting selected Lean manufacturing concepts into the Six Sigma methodology is a more fruitful approach.

Even staunch Lean proponents, such as George (2003, 46-47) acknowledge that Lean does not provide the required infrastructure needed to sustain improvement over the long haul. This is primarily due to the origins of Lean manufacturing. Lean began as a documentation of the Toyota production system (Monden 1983), which was the most advanced manufacturing system at that time. Because Lean was initially defined empirically by the practices of Toyota, it should be considered more as a collection of good operating principles rather than an improvement methodology. In addition, the generality of Six Sigma allows it to be applied to improving CTQs such as waste, non–value-added work, and cycle time, the traditional focus areas of Lean.

These Lean principles, which are certainly powerful and effective, include providing manufacturing lines of sight, logically designing work cells, outstanding housekeeping, single-piece flow (versus discrete batch processing), and several others. Although these principles do not provide a formal improvement methodology, they can provide improvement even beyond the factory floor. For example, outstanding housekeeping is just as important in a hospital as it is in a factory. Virtual "line of sight" can be obtained in financial services through workflow technology that allows real-time tracking of each invoice, loan application, or check in the system, analogous to an engineer being able to physically see from the beginning of a manufacturing line to the end.

In addition, some widely used tools, such as error-proofing and just-in-time inventory systems, have their roots in the Toyota production system, and could therefore be claimed by Lean. We believe that such effective tools should be adapted and used in the Six Sigma toolkit without taking the time to debate which improvement methodology deserves the "credit" for the tool.

Two specific places where the Lean manufacturing principles are particularly valuable in real economy applications are to make an assessment of current operations in the analyze phase of DMAIC and to guide design of new service processes in DFSS projects. For example, in the analyze phase of a DMAIC project in a hospital, a BB might want to audit the current process against relevant Lean principles to identify opportunities for improvement. How is the housekeeping? Are the work areas for nurses laid out in a logical fashion that avoids wasted time and effort? And so on. Similarly, when designing a new mortgage-approval process, Lean principles would suggest that the new system provide virtual "line of sight" to all mortgages at various stages of the overall process.

To conclude, we believe that those deploying Six Sigma in the real economy should utilize Lean principles and tools where appropriate. However, we are concerned that attempting to deploy both approaches fully in one initiative may double the work without doubling the benefit. Conversely, it might lead to half-hearted implementation of each effort. Often consultants and authors have primary loyalty to specific initiatives. Business leaders can't afford to do this; they need to pull out the meat from any initiative and leave the bones behind.

Summary

This book discusses Six Sigma beyond the factory floor at three levels: overall deployment, individual projects, and specific methods and tools. This chapter has addressed the unique challenges typically encountered when applying the individual methods and tools in the real economy. As in the other levels, tool application beyond the factory floor turns out to have more similarities with manufacturing than differences. Nevertheless, some unique issues occur more often outside manufacturing. These include the prevalence of discrete versus continuous data, skewed (non-normal) data distributions, and changes in the typical mix of tools used. Although each of these issues presents a challenge, a deeper understanding of the statistical methods involved provides insight to effectively address each issue. In particular, there is unfortunately a great deal of misinformation being taught about normality, and the normality assumption in statistics. We hope that we have helped to clear the air on this important issue.

References

Agresti, A. 1990. *Categorical data analysis.* New York: John Wiley and Sons.

Automotive Industry Action Group. 1995. *Measurement system analysis.* Suite 200, 26200 Lahser Road, Southfield, MI 48034.

Box, G. E. P., W. G. Hunter, and J. S. Hunter. 1978. *Statistics for experimenters.* New York: John Wiley and Sons.

Breyfogle, F. W. 2003. *Implementing Six Sigma*, second edition. New York: John Wiley and Sons.

George, M. L. 2003. *Lean Six Sigma for service.* New York: McGraw-Hill.

Hahn, G. J., N. Doganaksoy, and R. W. Hoerl. 2000. The evolution of Six Sigma. *Quality Engineering* 12 3:317–326.

Hoerl, R. W., and R. D. Snee. 2002. *Statistical thinking; improving business performance.* Pacific Grove, CA: Duxbury.

Kalos, M.H., and P.A. Whitlock. 1986. *Monte Carlo methods.* New York: John Wiley and Sons.

Koselka, R. 1996. The new mantra: MVT (multivariable testing). *Forbes* (11 March) 114–118.

Law, A. M., and D.W. Kelton. 1991. S*imulation modeling and analysis.* New York: McGraw-Hill.

Levene, H. 1960. *Contributions to probability and statistics.* Palo Alto, CA: Stanford University Press.

Monden, Y. 1983. *The Toyota production system*. Norcross, GA: Industrial and Management Engineering Press.

Snee, R. D. 2003. Eight essential tools. *Quality Progress* (December) 86–88.

Snee, R. D., and R.W. Hoerl. 2003. *Leading Six Sigma: a step-by-step guide based on experience with GE and other Six Sigma companies*. Upper Saddle River, NJ: FT Prentice Hall.

Wheeler, D., and D. Chambers. 1992. *Understanding statistical process control*, second edition. Knoxville, TN: SPC Press.

Wheeler, D. J., and R.W. Lyday. 1989. *Evaluating the measurement process*, second edition. Knoxville, TN: SPC Press.

Windsor, S. E. 2003. Attribute Gauge R&R. *Six Sigma Forum Magazine* (August) 23–28.

8

MAKING SIX SIGMA YOUR STRATEGIC SIGNATURE

"Where there is no vision, the people perish."
—Proverbs 29:18

Your Six Sigma initiative is now up and running. You are getting improvements in all areas of the company—all processes, all functions, suppliers, and customers. You have recognized that Six Sigma can be applied not only to ailing processes, but also to any sub-par process, enabling the company to drive continuous improvement across all its business processes. You have overcome some barriers, and Six Sigma is working. Now you are thinking about how you can sustain and grow your Six Sigma initiative. You want to get even more out of Six Sigma. The way to sustain and grow your Six Sigma initiative is to make Six Sigma part of, if not completely, your strategic signature. The same Six Sigma methodology that arose at Motorola almost 20 years ago flourished at AlliedSignal, achieved legendary status at GE under Jack Welch, and has moved quickly beyond manufacturing to administration, finance, business processes, new product development, and supplier performance. It has become, in effect, the strategic signature of organizations as diverse as 3M, Bank of America, DuPont, and W.R. Grace.

Making Six Sigma your strategic signature is the subject of this concluding chapter. This perspective also provides a useful summary of the key elements of Six Sigma. Following our definition of a strategic signature, we present and discuss six elements of making Six Sigma part of how you do your business. These elements together will take you a long way toward making Six Sigma your strategic signature.

The Strategic Signature

What is a strategic signature? Strategy has two components, one variable and one constant. The variable is the organization's specific market strategy. Whether the market strategy is to be a low-cost provider, to occupy a niche, to bundle goods with value-added services, or to enter new markets, its specifics are likely to change as market and industry conditions change. The constant in strategy is the organization's focus on continuous improvement. No matter the market strategy, its execution must continuously improve or the company will inevitably lose ground to superior competitors. GE's market strategies for its many businesses—from aircraft engines and power generation to financial services, medical imaging, television programming, and plastics—not only differ from each other, but also change as conditions change. The constant remains Six Sigma—GE's strategic signature. Similarly, as discussed in Chapter 3, Bank of America provides a variety of financial services that have and will continue to change over time. They are also working on adapting Six Sigma as their strategic signature to drive efficiency, quality, customer delight, and revenue generation.

Just as Picasso's signature on a painting, no matter the subject, is worth millions of dollars, Six Sigma's signature on a strategy can also mean exceptional financial performance, as the results demonstrate at the companies that have seriously adopted it. Our knowledge of the results obtained by several companies suggests that Six Sigma initiatives typically return 2% to 4% of sales to the bottom line in the second and third years for small companies, and 1% to 2% of sales in the second and third year for large companies. At GE, according to figures published by the company, Six Sigma returned $8 billion to the bottom line from 1999 to 2002 alone.

Bank of America, one of the world's largest financial institutions with a market capitalization of $116 billion at the end of 2003, started their Six Sigma initiative in 2001. Less than 3 years later, Six Sigma has become an integral part of the culture at Bank of America. To date Bank of America has more than 10,000 associates trained as *Black Belts* (BBs), *Green Belts* (GBs), in *design for Six Sigma* (DFSS), in Lean operations, and as Champions. Key improvements include the following:

- Reducing missing items on customer statements by 70%

- Reducing by 88% defects in reliability of automated and electronic channels: ATMs, telephone banking, and online banking

- Trimming response cycle times for certain account requests from 3 days to 10 minutes

- Increasing number of same-day payments by 22%

- Improving deposit processing by 35%

Six Sigma initiatives at Bank of America have made contributions totaling almost $2 billion in 2003 alone, with almost half of that in added revenue generation (Jones 2004). Best of all, customer delight at Bank of America has improved more than 25% in the past 3 years. This experience clearly demonstrates that the use of Six Sigma as a strategic signature is not restricted to manufacturing organizations. It can apply equally well to organizations in other sectors of the economy beyond the factory floor. Even at companies such as GE and 3M, however, making Six Sigma your strategic signature requires deployment across the organization, including the *real economy* functions, such as finance and human resources.

Much has been said about use of Six Sigma by large companies such as DuPont, Honeywell, and 3M. But Six Sigma can also benefit smaller companies. W.R. Grace, with $1.5 billion in sales, adopted Six Sigma and in the first 3 years achieved bottom-line results of $26 million, $50 million, and $41 million, respectively. Iomega, another approximately $1.5 billion company, achieved bottom-line results of $50 million, $75 million, and $148 million in the first 3 years of Six Sigma (English 2001). Even smaller companies—for example, in the $50–400 million sales range—have successfully implemented Six Sigma. Some smaller companies report that their limited resources make it difficult to pursue Six Sigma aggressively, but experience shows that strong leadership can overcome the limitations.

Such successes in large and small companies, manufacturing and real economy alike, have given Six Sigma brand recognition on Wall Street. This explains why many companies prominently mention their deployment of Six Sigma in their annual reports—DuPont put it on the cover of their 1999 report. There are other kinds of strategic signatures—total quality management, reengineering, acquisition and divestiture—but because they have either been largely subsumed by Six Sigma, or have failed to live up to their promise over the long term, they today have the aura of fading brands or the signatures of artists who have not stood the test of time.

New Ways of Thinking

Making Six Sigma your strategic signature requires some new ways of thinking about your organization, and about Six Sigma itself. As is well known, Six Sigma is a data-driven, process-focused methodology that drives improvement in all business processes. As organizations implement Six Sigma over time, they eventually begin to look for ways to make the approach part of how work is done on a regular basis. The result is an ever-broadening use of Six Sigma beyond process improvement. In time, Six Sigma becomes the organization's defining characteristic. It provides focus, reduces costs, grows revenues, empowers and develops people, enhances teamwork, provides a common corporate language and methodology—and separates the organization from the competition. However, instead of waiting for evolution to take its course, you can consciously move from simply improving processes to putting Six Sigma in place as a system of continuous improvement. To do so, you should:

- Use Six Sigma as a leadership development tool.
- Think of Six Sigma not just as a methodology, but also as an infrastructure.
- Use Six Sigma across all functions.
- Use Six Sigma to create a common corporate culture.
- Manage Six Sigma projects as a portfolio.
- Think improvement, not training.

By taking these steps you can make improvement part of how you run your organization, enabling all those in the organization to do *both* of their jobs: doing their work, and improving how they do their work. Although this approach has already been taken by real economy organizations (Bank of America, for example), it is perhaps an even greater competitive advantage here because of its relative uniqueness versus between manufacturing organizations.

Use Six Sigma as a Leadership Development Tool

Organizations are increasingly using Six Sigma as an effective leadership development tool. Companies such as GE, Honeywell, 3M, DuPont, and American Standard require Six Sigma BB and GB experience for managerial advancement. One could debate whether such experience should be mandatory, but by basing advancement on Six Sigma experience and results, top executives at these companies ensure that the principles of continuous improvement drive leaders at every level.

Jack Welch, after choosing Jeffrey Immelt to succeed him at GE, looked even further into the future. In the company's 2000 annual report, he observed: "It is a reasonable guess that the next CEO of this company, decades down the road, is probably a Six Sigma Black Belt or Master Black Belt somewhere in GE right now, or on the verge of being offered—as all our early-career (3 to 5 years) top 20% performers will be—a 2- to 3-year Black Belt assignment. The generic nature of a Black Belt assignment, in addition to its rigorous process discipline and relentless customer focus, makes Six Sigma the perfect training for growing twenty-first century GE leadership" (GE Annual Report 2000).

It is easy to see why Six Sigma is so effective in this function when we recall that a key role of the leader is to help an organization move from one paradigm to another paradigm. This requires employees to change the processes and procedures used to do their work, and Six Sigma provides precisely the right concepts, methods, and tools for doing so. Because of the uniqueness of such a culture beyond manufacturing, Six Sigma can have even greater lasting impact as a leadership development tool.

Not Only a Methodology, but Also an Infrastructure

Companies that make Six Sigma their strategic signature do not think of it as just one methodology among many for improving processes. Rather, they regard it as a broad organizational infrastructure comprising three components: a structured approach to problem solving, process design, and improvement; proven analytical techniques; and a human system.

As we have already seen, Six Sigma employs two proven approaches to problem solving and process improvement: DMAIC and DFSS. The DMAIC framework is used to improve existing processes and has five key phases: *define, measure, analyze, improve,* and *control.* Six Sigma BBs and GBs define the problem, measure the gap, analyze to find the root causes, identify, test and implement improvements, and put a control plan in place to sustain the gains. For generating and designing new processes, DFSS is used to achieve precedent-shattering, breakthrough improvements that cannot be achieved with existing processes.

It is noteworthy that many real economy organizations, such as banks and insurance companies, design and implement new products and services at a more rapid pace than most manufacturing organizations. Examples include new types of credit and debit cards, new bundled insurance policies (auto, home, personal excess liability), and new auto leasing programs.

Similarly, the analytical techniques that Six Sigma integrates into its approaches to problem solving are proven and widely recognized. Among the most prominent are the following:

- Process maps, cause-and-effect matrices, measurement system analysis, and process capability studies to understand the process, establish baseline process performance, and measure the performance gap

- Pareto charts, failure modes and effects analysis, and multivari studies to analyze processes and identify root causes

- Design of experiments to optimize processes and establish cause-and-effect relationships

- Control plans to hold the gains of the process improvements identified by the Six Sigma methodology

A unique characteristic of Six Sigma is that these tools are integrated with phases of DMAIC, and are linked and sequenced so that the output of a tool is the input of one or more other tools. This logical linking and sequencing of the tools makes them easier to learn and use effectively. Although we have found the tools to be most impactful when logically integrated, there are certainly many opportunities to utilize the tools individually, outside Six Sigma projects. By creating broad competency in the use of the tools through Six Sigma training, you will encourage use of individual tools on an as-needed basis as well.

For example, Roger Hoerl was with the GE *corporate audit staff* (CAS) during their primary deployment of Six Sigma. Although many of the CAS audits were not intended as Six Sigma projects during this time, Hoerl found that auditors began to use individual tools where appropriate. In one case a business manager told the leader of an audit that historical data indicated where the problem areas were—that is, the areas on which the audit should focus. Rather than accepting this input, as he had typically done in the past, the audit manager now asked to see the data, so that he could analyze it himself. An appropriate statistical analysis contradicted many of the business leader's assertions, resulting in a completely different focus for the audit, and subsequently a more value-adding audit.

The capstone of this infrastructure is the people, the Six Sigma leaders through whom projects are achieved: Champions, *Master Black Belts* (MBBs), BBs, and GBs. Six Sigma is most effective when this cadre of leaders work together as a team with each person knowing his or her role and the roles of all the other players (Snee 2003). Typically, a leadership team, often called the *Six Sigma Council*, selects a Champion from middle management to serve as the business and political leader of a project. As you have seen, Champions facilitate selection of projects, remove barriers to success, and review progress regularly. Champions choose from their organizations a number of BBs, each of whom directs an employee team charged with a specific improvement task. The BB leads the team, acts as project manager, and assigns work. MBBs, who usually have completed several BB projects, serve as technical leaders who enable the organization to integrate Six Sigma into its operations. GBs usually work on a portion of a BB project or lead a less-strategic project.

By establishing a cadre of Six Sigma leaders and adopting the analytical techniques and the DMAIC approach as your organization's general, all-purpose problem-solving tool, you can build the foundation of a continuous improvement culture across the organization. Although this is always a competitive advantage, its relative uniqueness in the real economy makes it an even greater competitive advantage here. Recall from Chapter 2 that organizations beyond the factory floor rarely benefit from a pervasive improvement culture, or the employ of many trained in the scientific method.

A vast Six Sigma how-to literature exists, and Six Sigma providers and trainers are plentiful. But the key to establishing Six Sigma in the larger strategic context depends on whether you think of it as merely a technique or—more productively—as an infrastructure that forms the backbone of your organization. Ideally, it should be an infrastructure that is as concrete, empirical, quantitative, and tangible as your IT architecture or your business-planning processes.

Use Six Sigma Across All Functions, Including Customers and Suppliers

All the work that organizations do is accomplished through processes. Indeed, organizations are made up of systems of interconnected processes. And because Six Sigma is fundamentally about improving processes, its application across all functions stamps an indelible signature on the organization as a whole. The deployment of Six Sigma across all functional areas within manufacturing organizations has been one of the themes of this book, along with its deployment to health care, financial organizations, and other sectors of the economy.

Typically, Six Sigma is applied first in operations. Although operations may mean manufacturing, it may also mean providing health care in a hospital, transporting goods in a transportation company, or serving food in a restaurant chain. Its use quickly expands to general business processes such as accounts receivable, accounts payable, and logistics. Then it may move into R&D, new product development, human resources, legal, and sales and marketing. As all of the processes in an organization become integrated in the Six Sigma initiative, attention also turns to inducing suppliers to use Six Sigma to improve the quality of the goods and services they supply. Finally, the organization introduces customers to the benefits of Six Sigma.

As teams on Six Sigma projects analyze processes, they often find that they must move upstream or downstream to identify root causes of problems and to implement improvements. Sales processes, for example, often depend on the timely execution of contracts by the legal department and approval by the risk department. Improving the process requires that all relevant functional areas collaborate to remove costly bottlenecks. More complex processes may involve the collaboration of even more functions. As Six Sigma spreads across the organization, functional barriers are reduced and eventually come down. This is another reason why deployment of Six Sigma beyond the factory floor is so critical to manufacturing organizations.

As companies mature in the use of Six Sigma, they find new and inventive ways to apply the methodology. One of the latest applications—"*at the customer, for the customer*" (ACFC), pioneered, once again, by GE—introduces customers to Six Sigma and helps them use the approach to improve their performance and their bottom lines. Typically, GE BBs conduct projects within the customer's organization solely for the benefit of the customer (that is, with no fee charged by GE). In some 1,500 Six Sigma projects, GE helped its aircraft engine customers improve their operating margins by a total of $230 million in 2000 alone, with an average improvement of $150,000 per project. During the same period, the company helped its medical systems customers, over the course of 1,000 projects, improve operating margins by $100 million (Welch 2001, 338).

DuPont, with its long history of helping customers improve processes, has also adopted the ACFC. Like many companies, DuPont initially used Six Sigma to increase its own productivity. By taking Six Sigma to customers, DuPont is not only benefiting customers, but also using the initiative to ensure customer loyalty and attract new customers to achieve growth.

You will quickly learn that the quality and the cost of the materials from suppliers have a big effect on the quality and cost of products and services that you produce (both average level and variability). It is not unusual for 40% to 60% of the final cost of a company's product to derive from the costs of materials purchased from suppliers. This can be true in real economy applications as well, such as the cost of money (interest rates), or the costs of inaccuracies in credit histories (variation) in commercial and consumer lending. Because you cannot overlook such a high cost, or the effects of variation in materials on the performance of processes, you may wonder how to get suppliers to use Six Sigma to improve their performance.

Companies have introduced suppliers to Six Sigma in a variety of ways. One way is to identify a few high-impact projects and form customer-supplier teams to complete the projects using Six Sigma. If the supplier doesn't have BBs available to work on the project, the customer supplies the Six Sigma expertise and any needed training. Tremendous progress is made when both the customer and the supplier have one or more BBs on the project team.

Another approach is for the company to make available supplier training programs that are partially funded by the customer, and that make available both Champion and BB training, at a minimum. An effective way to create such a program is to start with a few good projects of interest to both parties, and then use their success to expand the program. It is essential that the supplier's management be involved in the effort. An executive workshop is a good way to help build this involvement because it helps communicate what Six Sigma is and the benefits the supplier organization can expect to receive.

Use Six Sigma to Create a Common Corporate Culture

Just as Six Sigma can create a common language across functions, it can create a common language across cultures. Most Six Sigma companies that have significant global operations use Six Sigma as a means of creating a common corporate culture in highly cross-cultural organizations. From Japan, to India, to Europe, to South America, to North America, these companies use Six Sigma to create a culture that seeks continuous improvement, values data-based decision making, and assumes a process orientation to getting work done. These regions have many cultural differences, but in these companies everyone, regardless of national culture, speaks the language of Six Sigma to improve and manage processes and to solve problems.

It is difficult to place an economic value on the creation of a global corporate culture. However, organizations that have struggled to integrate global operations realize the financial impact that lack of a global culture causes. With a global business culture, it is not only easier to integrate operations, it is also much easier to move individuals from country to country and enable them to fit in and be productive.

Manage Six Sigma Projects As a Portfolio

Six Sigma is about improving processes by solving problems. As Joseph Juran, one of the pioneers of the improvement movement, put it, "All improvement takes place project by project and in no other way." What is a project? Again, Juran stated, "A project is a problem scheduled for solution."

As we have discussed in this book, problems typically fall into two categories: solution known and solution unknown. Solution-known projects are considered "just-do-it" projects, and are completed by a project manager. Solution-unknown projects require Six Sigma methodology, and they are completed by BBs or GBs.

To make improvement a routine managerial process, just like budgeting or any other managerial process, all improvement initiatives should be combined into an overall improvement system and managed as a portfolio. This portfolio management approach should be linked to the strategic needs and priorities of the organization (Snee and Rodebaugh 2002). As discussed in Chapter 6, the organization's improvement portfolio will generally include a mixture of projects in three main categories:

1. Solution-known projects, such as installing a new computer network. The solution to the problem has been defined. A project manager and necessary resources are assigned, and funds are allocated. The project plan is developed and followed to completion.

2. Six Sigma projects, where the problem has no known solution. A BB or GB is assigned to the project, and the Six Sigma methodology is used to find and implement the solution.

3. Other general improvement initiatives that are broader than an individual project, such as ISO 9000, digitization, or a new performance-management system.

The organization's annual improvement plan should be a blend of these three types of initiatives, and include projects related to such diverse areas as productivity improvement, cash generation, customer satisfaction, revenue growth, and organizational learning and improvement. Although manufacturing organizations can benefit from such formal management of the improvement process, this approach is certainly rare in hospitals, the media, banks, and legal offices, and will therefore provide a greater competitive advantage beyond the factory floor.

We also note that some organizations bring all three types of improvement efforts under the Six Sigma umbrella and use *Six Sigma* as the name for their overall improvement initiative. Some take it even further, recognizing that a subset of the Six Sigma tools can be used on almost all improvement projects and encouraging their use whenever possible. These tools include the following:

- Process maps

- Cause-and-effect matrices

- Failure modes and effects and analysis

- Control plans

- Control/trend charts of key project performance parameters

This type of thinking helps an organization make Six Sigma an integral part of how the organization runs its business on a daily basis.

Managing the portfolio of projects as a group generally provides greater benefits than managing each project in isolation. The reasons for these additional benefits are the ability to target strategic areas for improvement, avoid duplication of effort, leverage benefits in one area to others, and ensure project coverage across all areas of interest. Improvement project portfolios are typically managed at the corporate, business unit, facility (plant in manufacturing), function level, or at all levels, depending on the size of the organization. We recommend an improvement annual cycle, which is typical. The planning for a yearly cycle often begins in the fourth quarter, with the process and financial objectives determined and the projects selected that will help the organization deliver its strategic goals for the coming year.

The leadership team that developed the plan reviews quarterly the status of the improvement plan and progress toward objectives. Typical questions include the following:

- Is the plan on schedule?

- Are the results coming in as planned?

■ Have the assumptions underlying the plan changed (new competitors, economic upturn/downturn, shift in consumer demand)?

■ Are changes needed?

■ Should some projects be closed?

■ Should new projects be added to the plan?

These questions are asked in each of the four quarterly reviews done throughout the year. In addition, the fourth-quarter review includes planning for the following year.

Think Improvement, Not Training

If Six Sigma is good for leadership development, it is equally good for what might be called "followership" development: the training of rank-and-file employees. Here too it requires a shift in thinking. Despite the recession of the early 2000s, organizations continued to spend significant sums on employee training. Unfortunately, much of this training is focused on training per se, and not on helping the organization improve in a real and measurable way. Therefore, many organizations have little to show for their investment in training. That is one reason why management often doesn't support training. Training events may be cancelled to make room for other priorities, and training budgets are often the first to get cut when business takes a downturn.

An improvement, rather than training, mindset is needed, as shown in Table 8.1. A clear, measurable business benefit should be the goal of every training event. In other words, training should take place in the context of specific projects focused on improving process performance, in such a way that the bottom line is also improved. In other words, training is a "how" (how we achieve improvement) rather than a "what" (what we are trying to accomplish). Six Sigma, by utilizing the project-by-project approach to improvement and linking projects to business priorities, transforms training into improvement (Snee 2001a, 2001b).

TABLE 8.1   Improvement vs. Training Mindset

Training Mindset *Focused on training*	Improvement Mindset *Focused on improvement (train to build needed skills and knowledge)*
Train everyone	Train those who need it
Learn, then get results	Get results as we learn
Work on anything; results will follow	Focus on getting breakthrough bottom-line results, > $250K/project
Get everyone involved	Involve people as needed to support projects
Use large teams to involve more people	Keep teams small to get improvements quickly
Measure number of people trained	Measure bottom-line impact ($$) and number of people trained

Six Sigma training is designed to create the skills and knowledge that managers, Champions, BBs, and others need to implement the project-by-project approach to improvement. It is worth noting that Six Sigma training should pay for itself very quickly. BB projects should produce bottom-line results that are typically in the $175K to $250K range. This is true both on the manufacturing floor and beyond. The total cost of BB training is typically around $20K per BB. A single project usually more than pays for the training of the BB.

As noted elsewhere, we recommend in-depth training with management typically receiving 2 to 3 days, Champions 2 to 5 days, BBs 4 weeks, and GBs 2 weeks of training. Over time, more specialized training is added as the need arises during the deployment of Six Sigma. In financial services, for example, leadership may decide to add specialized courses in credit scoring. This field evaluates the credit worthiness of those applying for some type of credit, such as mortgages. In every instance, the training focuses on what participants need to do their jobs in the deployment of Six Sigma. The result is that the Six Sigma infrastructure, described above, begins to emerge: managers, Champions, BBs, and others can now use the Six Sigma approach to improve processes in such a way that bottom-line results are produced.

Focusing on improvement, and not training per se, requires a different way of thinking about the role and contribution of training in the organization. Training should be regarded as an opportunity to build the skills and knowledge needed to improve the performance of the organization in the future and to produce measurable results right now. To be sure, time is spent in all the training venues on understanding Six Sigma and its strengths, limitations, and benefits. However, the number-one agenda item is always the successful completion of projects that improve process performance and produce significant bottom-line results.

Putting a Stamp on the Organization

Success does not come overnight. Certainly, almost any process can be improved or streamlined, but you should be wary of claims that promise instant success with no significant investment of resources or effort. The most important key to success is the commitment and involvement of top leadership. Significantly, the people who have understood this most clearly—and put it into practice—are some of the best and the brightest CEOs of their generation. They know that chief executives have the greatest opportunity to put their stamp on an organization at the beginning of their tenure. Many of these leaders, having experienced firsthand the success of Six Sigma at GE or AlliedSignal, made Six Sigma virtually their first significant initiative when they became CEOs at other companies.

When W. James McNerney, Jr., formerly president of GE Aircraft Engines, assumed the leadership of 3M in 2001, he instituted four major initiatives—global sourcing, cost reduction, e-productivity, and faster commercialization of products. But overriding them all was a permanent, company-wide Six Sigma initiative. As a company spokesman told *Industry Week*, "Our other initiatives are shorter term, tied to our 3-year strategic plan, but Six Sigma is forever. It's the umbrella." Similarly, former AlliedSignal executives including Daniel P. Burnham at Raytheon, Paul Norris at W.R. Grace, and Fred Poses at American Standard instituted Six Sigma when they became chief executives.

With the commitment and involvement of top leadership to approach Six Sigma strategically—using it to develop leaders, creating an improvement infrastructure, crossing functions, creating a common culture, managing improvement as a portfolio of projects, and shifting from training to improvement—a company can expect to move more quickly toward reaping its long-term benefits. Typically (when Six Sigma is properly deployed), the first 12 to 18 months produce such useful results as bottom-line improvement and increased customer satisfaction. As a result, Six Sigma gains credibility and momentum, and the initial savings it creates can fund its future expansion.

After 2 or 3 years, during the phase of its expansion in the organization, the longer-term benefits begin to emerge. Cross-functional teamwork spreads. Leadership strength and depth increase as a result of Six Sigma experience. The culture of the organization begins to shift toward a scientific way of thinking about how to manage, including a greater focus on processes, data-based decisions, and the effects of variation on the decision-making process. People begin to work in a new way. In short, Six Sigma becomes the strategic signature—stamping everything the company does.

Summary

Six Sigma has much to offer in the way of direct financial benefits to those organizations that properly deploy it. However, even greater long-term benefits are available to those who are able to go beyond immediate financial benefits and make Six Sigma their strategic signature. This approach provides real economy organizations in particular with a long-term strategic advantage, because of the scarcity of competitors who have also made Six Sigma their strategic signature. Utilizing Six Sigma as a strategic signature does require a strong management commitment (you can only have one strategic signature) and a new way of thinking throughout the organization.

There are several key areas that require a new way of thinking, which will broaden and deepen your use of Six Sigma. Leaders should view Six Sigma holistically, for example: as a means of developing future leaders, creating value-adding corporate infrastructure, and integrating global cultures, in addition to being an effective improvement methodology. Further, leaders must drive Six Sigma across the entire organization—all functions and locations—and actively manage improvement projects as an integrated portfolio. Finally, leaders should view Six Sigma training as a means to an end—bottom-line improvement, rather than as an end in itself. All the leaders that we have seen apply these concepts have been extremely successful with Six Sigma; we are confident you will be as well. We wish you well in your Six Sigma journey and look forward to hearing about your experiences.

References

English, W. 2001. *Implementing Six Sigma: the Iomega story*. Presented at the Conference on Six Sigma in the Pharmaceutical Industry, Philadelphia (November 27-28).

Jones, M. H., Jr. 2004. Six Sigma… at a bank? *Six Sigma Forum Magazine* (February) 13-17.

Snee, R. D. 2001a. Focus on improvement, not training. *Quality Management Forum* (Spring) 7-8, 16.

Snee, R. D. 2001b. Make the view worth the climb: focus training on delivering better business results. *Quality Progress* (November) 58-61.

Snee, R. D. 2003. The Six Sigma sweep. *Quality Progress* (September) 76-78.

Snee, R. D., and W. F. Rodebaugh. 2002. Enhance your project selection process: every company should be able to manage its project portfolio and create an overall organizational improvement system. *Quality Progress* (September) 78-80.

Welch, Jack. 2001. *Jack: straight from the gut*. New York: Warner Books.

APPENDIX —————

ACFC—"At the customer, for the customer" projects

ANOVA—Analysis of variance

ASQ—American Society for Quality

BB—Black Belt

C&E—Cause and Effect

CAP—Change Acceleration Process

CEO—Chief Executive Officer

CHC—Commonwealth Heath Corporation

CTQ—Critical to quality metrics

DFSS—Design for Six Sigma

DMAIC—the Define, Measure, Analyze, Improve, Control project sequence

DMADV—the Define, Measure, Analyze, Design, Verify approach to DFSS

DOE—Design of experiments

FMEA—Failure modes and effects analysis

GAAP—Generally accepted accounting practices

GB—Green Belt (someone trained in Six Sigma, but applying it part time)

GE—General Electric Corporation

GR&R—Gauge Repeatability and Reproducibility (measurement system evaluation)

HR—Human Resources

ISO 9000—International Organization for Standards quality standard

IT—Information Technology

MBB—Master Black Belt

MSA—Measurement systems analysis

P&L—Profit and loss center

QFD—Quality function deployment

R&D—Research and Development

R&R—Reward and recognition

SIPOC—Process map identifying suppliers, inputs, process steps, outputs, and customers

SPC—Statistical process control

SOP—Standard operating procedure

TQM—Total quality management

INDEX

A

acronyms, list of, 313-314

analyze phase (DMADV framework)
corporate default prediction project case study, 161, 164
improvement system creation, 228

analyze phase (DMAIC framework)
improvement system creation, 230
litigation document management project case study, 177-178

pharmaceutical batch record review process case study, 185-187
project failure, 216-217

Arthur Andersen (corporate default prediction project case study), 157

attitude, as barrier to Six Sigma deployment, 36-38

audit system, as deployment plan element, 133-134

H

health care (deployment road map advice), 137-138

Hickie, David (Motorola Finance deployment case study), 87-88

hidden factory, 52

Hoerl, Roger
management reviews, 210
Six Sigma as infrastructure as well as methodology, 301

holistic view of Six Sigma, 4
and process management, 218, 221, 225
reasons for not deploying, 32-38

human element, differences between manufacturing and real economy, 46

human resources (HR), deployment road map advice, 141

I

improve phase (DMAIC framework). *See also* **process improvement**
improvement system creation, 230
litigation document management project case study, 178-179
pharmaceutical batch record review process case study, 187-188
project failure, 217-218

improvement, 194
what to expect from Six Sigma, 16

improvement culture, differences between manufacturing and real economy, 41-43

improvement mindset versus training mindset, 146, 308-310

improvement projects, 18-19. *See also* **process improvement**
failure, 213, 215, 218
and holistic view of Six Sigma, 218, 221, 225
success factors. *See* project success factors

improvement system. *See also* **process improvement**
creating, 225-227
DMADV framework, 227-229
DMAIC framework, 229-231

industrial revolution, 8

information technology (IT), deployment road map advice, 143-144

infrastructure, Six Sigma as, 300-302. *See also* **supportive infrastructure**

initiative launch phase (deployment road map), 115-116

inputs. *See* **process inputs**

insurance (deployment road map advice), 140

integration of initiative phase (deployment road map), 119-122

Iomega, financial results of Six Sigma implementation, 298

IT (information technology), deployment road map advice, 143-144

Leading Six Sigma

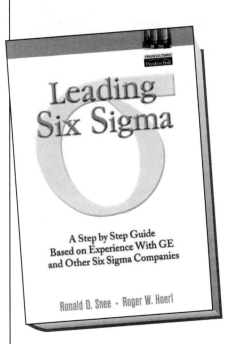

In *Leading Six Sigma*, two of the world's most experienced Six Sigma leaders offer a detailed, step-by-step strategy for leading Six Sigma initiatives in your company. Six Sigma consultant Dr. Ronald D. Snee and GE quality leader Dr. Roger W. Hoerl show how to deploy a Six Sigma plan that reflects your organization's unique needs and culture, while also leveraging key lessons learned by the world's most successful implementers. Snee and Hoerl share leadership techniques proven in companies both large and small, and in business functions ranging from R&D and manufacturing to finance. They also present a start-to-finish sample deployment plan encompassing strategy, goals, metrics, training, roles and responsibilities, reporting, rewards, and management review. Whether you're a CEO, line-of-business leader, or a project leader, *Leading Six Sigma* gives you the one thing other books on Six Sigma lack: a clear view from the top.

ISBN 0130084573, © 2003, 304 pp., $29.95

Six Sigma for Green Belts and Champions

Now, there's a comprehensive guide to Six Sigma for the "green belts" who manage Six Sigma, and "champions" who drive it at the executive level. Howard S. Gitlow and David M. Levine, present a complete executive framework for understanding quality and implementing Six Sigma. They systematically walk you through the five-step DMAIC implementation process, with detailed examples and real-world case studies. You'll learn how to make the business case for Six Sigma; manage Six Sigma statistics, even prepare for certification exams. Output from the Minitab statistical software package, widely used in Six Sigma© Management, is illustrated.

ISBN 013117262X, © 2005, 736 pp., $49.95